HAMLET ON STAGE

HAMLET ON STAGE

The Great Tradition

John A. Mills

Contributions in Drama and Theatre Studies, Number 15

GREENWOOD PRESS
Westport, Connecticut · London, England

Library of Congress Cataloging in Publication Data

Mills, John A., 1931–
    Hamlet on stage.

    (Contributions in drama and theatre studies, ISSN
0163-3821 ; no. 15)
    Bibliography: p.
    Includes index.
    1. Shakespeare, William, 1564–1616. Hamlet.
2. Shakespeare, William, 1564–1616—Characters—Hamlet.
3. Shakespeare, William, 1564–1616—Stage history.
4. Actors. I. Title. II. Series.
PR2807.M54   1985   822.3'3   84-22461
ISBN 0-313-24660-2 (lib. bdg.)

Library of Congress Catalog Card Number: 84-22461
ISBN: 0-313-24660-2
ISSN: 0163-3821

First published in 1985

Greenwood Press
A division of Congressional Information Service, Inc.
88 Post Road West
Westport, Connecticut 06881

Printed in the United States of America

10 9 8 7 6 5 4 3 2 1

For Joy, Kevin, and Jennifer

CONTENTS

ILLUSTRATIONS

PREFACE

The history of *Hamlet* on the stage is vast; to tell anything like the whole story would doubtless require several volumes. I therefore decided, early in my exploration of the historical materials, to deal only with portrayals of the play's central character, to write not a stage history of *Hamlet* but a stage history of Hamlet. Even that topic quickly proved unmanageable without further delimitation. At least a slim volume, I found, could be written solely on the several women and children who have acted the role of Hamlet. These exotic but peripheral figures having been excluded, other categories to be omitted came more or less readily to mind: foreign-language Hamlets, however well received; amateur Hamlets, however well-intentioned; and Hamlets by actors of "the second rank," however well connected (e.g., Charles Kean, H. B. Irving).

All this lopping off, some if it effected with considerable reluctance, left me with a study in the shape here presented, a study of Hamlet as impersonated by actors who collectively make up "the great tradition" of English-language acting of Shakespeare in general and of Hamlet in particular. In borrowing the notion of a "great tradition" from F. R. Leavis' study of the English novel, I run less risk of controversy than he did. The roster of the great Hamlets, prior to the twentieth century at any rate, is not much in dispute: Richard Burbage, Thomas Betterton, David Garrick, John Philip Kemble, Edmund Kean, William Charles Macready, Edwin Forrest, Edwin Booth, Henry Irving, Johnston Forbes-Robertson—one calls the roll with little fear of contradiction. Even among Hamlets of the first half of the present century, the preeminence of John Barrymore, John Gielgud and Laurence Olivier seems a settled matter. Devoting separate chapters to the Hamlet portrayals of each of these major figures, considered in chronological order, seemed the natural organization for a study of the main currents in Hamlet impersonation over the course of the play's long life. For the years since Olivier's Hamlet (1948) the selection of major figures was more hazardous, but I trust that I have made choices which, while certainly open to challenge, are not merely quixotic. Richard Burton's 1964 American Hamlet, directed by John Gielgud, was the focus of world attention (albeit partly for nonaesthetic reasons); moreover, electronically transmitted to movie theaters around the country, it was seen by more spectators than most of the major Hamlets of the past. That fame, coupled with the critical acclaim given Burton's earlier, London Hamlet (1953), justifies enrolling Burton among the commanding figures in the tradition and giving him a chapter to himself. Other than Burton, no contemporary actor has been so strongly associated with the role as to warrant attention equivalent to that given Garrick, Kemble, Kean and the others. Nicol Williamson (1969), having been seen in Britain and the United States on both stage and screen, comes closest, and I therefore devote most of my concluding chapter to his portrayal of Hamlet. Departing from the pattern adhered to throughout, I also briefly examine there the performances of three other actors: Peter O'Toole (1963) as a transitional figure, and David Warner (1965) and Albert Finney (1975) as actors who, together with Williamson, defined what I take to be the most distinctively contemporary style now in evidence and who thus did collectively for this age what actors in the great tradition had done individually for their own.

Although only my name appears on the title page, this study is the product of the labor of many hands. The numerous scholarly works from which I derived indispensable information I have named in the notes and bibliographical essay. Several individuals aided me not only through their published works but personally as well. Richard Hosley first suggested the project and put me in touch with Charles Shattuck, who thereafter gave me invaluable advice on a wide variety of topics. My colleague J. P. Wearing also gave me wise counsel and support at several critical junctures, as did my former teachers Hubert Heffner and Richard Moody. To all of them I tender my heartfelt thanks.

For satisfying, with unfaltering courtesy and efficiency, my often burdensome requests for access to original source material, I am deeply grateful to the directors and staffs of the following institutions: the Reading Room and North Library of the British Museum (now the British Library), London, and the Newspaper Library at Colindale in

North London; the Enthoven Collection at the Victoria and Albert Museum, London; the Ellen Terry Memorial Museum, Smallhythe, Kent; the Folger Shakespeare Library, Washington, D.C.; the Harvard Theatre Collection, Cambridge, Mass.; the Interlibrary Loan Department of the University of Arizona Library, Tucson, Arizona; the Joint University Libraries, Nashville, Tennessee; the New York Public Library; the Theatre Collection at Lincoln Center, New York City; the Shakespeare Centre Library at Stratford-upon-Avon; and the Walter Hampden–Edwin Booth Theatre Collection and Library, New York City.

I am grateful also to the Board of Trustees of the State University of New York, the Board of Regents of the University of Arizona, and the administrators of the Humanities Research Fund at the University of Arizona for financial support in a variety of forms. My greatest benefactor was the John Simon Guggenheim Memorial Foundation, whose award of a Fellowship made possible a year of essential research in Great Britain. I am honored to join the long line of scholars and artists whose work has been made possible by this most admirable of institutions.

NOTE

All *Hamlet* line numbers refer to *The Riverside Shakespeare*, ed. G. Blakemore Evans (Boston: Houghton Mifflin, 1974).

Promptbooks are referred to by the numbers (e.g. *HAM* 36) assigned them by Charles H. Shattuck in *The Shakespeare Promptbooks* (Urbana and London: University of Illinois Press, 1965).

About the Author

JOHN A. MILLS is Associate Professor of English at the University of Arizona. He is the author of *Language and Laughter: Comic Diction in the Plays of Bernard Shaw*. His published articles have appeared in *Shakespeare Quarterly, Theatre Survey, Shaw Review,* and *Quarterly Journal of Speech.* Mills has also acted in several Shakespearean plays and has directed numerous productions in the university and community theatre.

HAMLET ON STAGE

1

ENTER HAMLET

The first Hamlet,[1] the Hamlet of Richard Burbage (1567?–1619), eludes the historian as deftly as the Ghost eludes Horatio and the sentinels: " 'Tis heere. 'Tis heere. 'Tis gone."

References to the play in the years immediately following its composition (1600–1601)[2] do little more than tantalize. Like the Ghost, they will not speak, charge them how we may. Apprised of the fact that Dr. Gabriel Harvey scribbled a note about the play in the margin of his Chaucer, one turns to it eagerly, only to find the smug observation that "the wiser sort" could be expected to prefer *Hamlet, Prince of Denmark* to the same author's *Venus and Adonis*—a judgment derived, or so it would appear, from a reading of the play, not a viewing in the theater.[3] In alluding in 1604 to a "mad Hamlet [who] puts off his cloathes, his shirt he only weares," poet Anthony Scoloker at least seems to have his eye bent on the stage of the Globe, but when all is said and done he really tells us little more than what we might have surmised from Ophelia's description of the Prince's disordered dress.[4] Not until the death of Burbage, in 1619, do we get a piece of straightforward eyewitness reportage by a contemporary; one of the dead actor's eulogists recalled fondly that he had "oft . . . seen him leap into the grave," and though the author does not say he means Ophelia's grave, it seems more than likely, since "young Hamlet" is named among Burbage's roles just three lines earlier.[5] Beyond these snippets, all is supposition. As William Armstrong has observed, "How Burbage played Hamlet is almost as conjectural as what song the sirens sang."[6] He might have added that scholars are nevertheless drawn to such conjecture as irresistibly as ships were lured to rocks.

One ground for speculative reconstruction of that first performance might be the personality of Burbage himself. The actor is not the character, to be sure, and to argue from one to the other is a perilous undertaking. But the great likelihood that Shakespeare created Hamlet with Burbage's special qualities in mind may perhaps be allowed to prick us on.

Our earliest glimpse of the Globe's star performer comes from one of those transcripts of legal proceedings which have proved so valuable to students of the period. In 1590, when he was about nineteen years old, Burbage took a leading role in a real-life brawl at his father's playhouse, the Theatre. A recent court decision had awarded a share of that establishment's profits to the widow of one of the original investors; when, in company with three male supporters, she arrived before a performance one afternoon to collect her due, young Richard, according to the surviving depositions, "fell upon . . . [one] and beat him with a broom staff, calling him 'murdering knave,' [and] scornfully and disdainfully playing with [another's] nose, said that if he dealt in the matter, he would beat him also, and did challenge the field of him at that time."[7] In private life, it seems, Burbage was a man given to immediate, direct and forceful action. Dare we assume that he brought something of this quality into his characterization of Hamlet? There are other indications that he did.

Elizabethan actors most probably played a "line" of characters, a group of roles generally and loosely suited to the actor's own physiognomy, physique and temperament. Of the other three Shakespearean protagonists clearly assignable to Burbage—Othello, Lear, and Richard III—all are strong and able men, at home in the world of affairs and accustomed to forceful action.[8] E. E. Stoll has argued that a "hero . . . actuated by craven scruples and reflective cowardice would, in those rough-and-ready times, have found small favor on the tragic stage. Comedy, the comedy of humours, was the place for him."[9] Thus, whatever else it may have been, Burbage's Hamlet was probably very unlike the delicate, pot-bound flower so beloved of Goethe and the Romantics.

Other evidence points to a similar conclusion. According to James G. McManaway, the cuts for performance marked in the earliest Restoration promptbooks probably reflect Elizabethan playhouse practice as well. Since these omissions strip Hamlet of "most of the lines in which [he] reproaches himself," McManaway concludes that "a spectator who saw a performance of this . . . version would never question the valor of the Prince or suspect that he was tardy in driving to his revenge."[10]

Paul S. Conklin finds that early seventeenth-century allusions to the play, viewed collectively, point to a stage Hamlet who was "a straightforward avenger . . . primitive . . . direct . . . elemental . . . Kydian."[11] Other qualities of the Prince—his eloquence, his melancholy madness (viewed as comic, for the most part)—impressed themselves on early commentators, but it is essentially a Hamlet leaping to his revenge who is fondly recalled over and over again during the first decades of the play's existence.

In short, such faint markings in the dust as can still be discerned point to a Hamlet quite at odds with our typical modern conceptions. Certain textual hints about Burbage's physical appearance in the role add to that impression. Gertrude calls her son "fat," and though editors have warned us not to take the word literally, it may well be an accurate description of Burbage's condition; his only surviving portrait suggests a big man, tending to flabbiness, and like it or not it is probably what we must take to be Hamlet's first incarnation.[12]

No doubt we must also picture Hamlet as bearded ("Who . . . plucks off my beard and blows it in my face?" [II.ii.572–73]). Though the world has preferred its Hamlets clean-shaven through most of the play's history, the Elizabethan audience would have been baffled at the sight of a beardless Prince; every contemporary man-of-affairs wore face hair, and Shakespeare's actors must have followed the fashion in this as they did in matters of dress.

To these data may be added a final item of considerably greater substance. Of the few facts known about Burbage, none is more striking than the intense affection his contemporaries lavished on him. The eulogies addressed to him at his death seem to reveal much more than the conventional sense of loss at the passing of an admired artist; they suggest strongly that Burbage was an actor who infused each of his portrayals with immense personal charm. If this was in fact the case, that quality of magnetic attractiveness must have contributed heavily to the impact of his Hamlet characterization.

No less problematic than the question of Burbage's interpretation is the closely related question of his acting style. Was he "formal" or "natural"? Confronted with those alternatives, one is tempted to answer "neither." The naturalists seem always in danger of foisting a desperate anachronism upon us: Stanislavski in doublet and hose. The formalist creed, on the other hand, hovers on the brink of an exquisite aestheticism which we can scarcely imagine being palatable to the 'prentices and alewives jostling each other in the yard. The truth probably lies on some middle ground between these "fixed poles of formality and reality."[13] At any rate, the lengthy description of Burbage's acting, in the eulogy quoted earlier, points forcibly toward some such compromise. On the one hand we read:

> Oft have I seen him, leap into the Grave
> Suiting the person, which he seem'd to have
> Of a sad Lover, with so true an Eye
> That there I would have sworne, he meant to die,
> Oft have I seen him, play this part in jest,
> So lively, that Spectators, and the rest
> Of his sad Crew, whilst he but seem'd to bleed,
> Amazed, thought even then he died in deed,
> O let not me be checked, and I shall swear
> Even yet, it is a false report I hear,
> And think that he, that did so truly feign
> Is still but Dead in jest, to live again, . . . [14]

Alfred Harbage, in defending the formalist position, quotes these lines and declares their value "nugatory," on the ground that they tell us only *what* Burbage did, not how he did it—that is, whether formally or naturally.[15] Be that as it may, the lines do tell us unequivocally that Burbage achieved a credible representation of character in action, an illustration of life so powerful that it "convinced" not only the spectators but also the other actors on stage ("the rest / Of his sad Crew"). That is no trifling piece of information. At the very least it renders untenable the extreme formalist contention that what the Elizabethan audience saw and heard was little more than a "recited poem." Whatever his means may have been, Burbage's portrayal was, in aim and effect, natural.

But the eulogy also contains some words of comfort for the antinaturalists:

> How did his speech become him, and his pace,
> Suit with his speech, and every action grace
> Them both alike, whilst not a word did fall,
> Without just weight, to ballast it with all.
> Hadst thou but spoke to death, and used thy power

Of thy enchanting tongue, at that first hour
Of his assault, he had let fall his dart
And quite been charmed, by thy all charming art.

Though open to varying interpretations, this passage seems to point toward a palpable degree of artifice on the part of the actor—to a conscious display, in both voice and body, of histrionic skill served up for the delectation of the observers.

We thus get a picture of a style both natural and formal—a style capable of rendering a convincing representation of life ("so true an eye"), but life greatly heightened and idealized by qualities belonging purely to the stage ("power of . . . enchanting tongue"). It was, to put the matter another way, a preeminently theatricalist or presentational style of playing, one in which the actor made open confession of his identity *as* actor and then proceeded to enact "the pangs of despis'd love," or whatever, while inviting the audience to note and marvel at the skill with which he did so. The Globe actors, it must be supposed, no more confined themselves to the actual deportment of their characters' real-life counterparts than Shakespeare confined himself to the actual speech of living persons. Elizabethan acting must have abounded in prodigies of physical and vocal virtuosity, much as Elizabethan dramatic composition abounded in prodigies of lyricism and metaphoric complexity. But there was nothing in this to prevent the spectator from "believing" that a character had "dyed in deed" when he was "but Dead in jest."

In short, we shall probably not be much in error if we think of Burbage and his fellows as twentieth-century Shakespearean actors viewed through a distorting glass: magnified and quaintly altered, but not to such a degree as to be unrecognizable—not, that is, transformed into exotic beings out of, say, Japanese Noh.

As for stage business, nothing substantial has been preserved beyond the one possibility already noted—Hamlet's leap into the grave.[16] None of the staging cruxes which were to exercise the ingenuity of later producers can be solved with finality by citation of Elizabethan precedents. How, for example, the "counterfeit presentment of two brothers" (III.iv.54ff.) was managed on Shakespeare's stage remains an open question. An engraving in Nicholas Rowe's *Shakespeare*, published in 1709, shows portraits of both the dead and the living King on the wall of Gertrude's closet, but even if the engraving is a true reflection of established stage practice—it may be merely a fanciful illustration—there is no evidence that the procedure originated at the Globe.[17] On the contrary, the portraits, if they were used at all, are more likely to have been a Restoration innovation very much in keeping with the revolutionary shift to pictorial scenery which occurred in that period.

Two other possibilities have been suggested and widely employed since. Hamlet and Gertrude may each have worn miniatures, he of his father, she of Claudius, a practice given some warrant in the text by Hamlet's earlier reference to his father's "picture in little" (II.ii.366). Or the Prince may have asked Gertrude, and the audience, to see the two brothers in the "mind's eye," as he had earlier seen his father in his first conversation with Horatio (I.ii.185). Precisely what Burbage did we do not know.

The fencing match has also provoked much stage experimentation, as regards both the choice of weapons and the method of effecting the crucial exchange of Hamlet's blunted instrument for the fatal weapon of Laertes, "unbated and envenom'd too." On both points the Elizabethan evidence is conflicting and inconclusive. In the Second Quarto (Q2) daggers as well as "*Foiles*" are explicitly called for on the "*table prepared*," a stage direction which seems to point incontestably to combat with rapier and dagger. Curiously, however, Q2 makes no mention of any exchange and, indeed, seems to forbid it in having Laertes say, "The treacherous instrument is in *my* hand" (Sig. 01; emphasis added). The Folio reverses this state of affairs: it is silent on the matter of daggers, prints the direction "*In scuffling, they change rapiers*" and has Laertes say, "The treacherous instrument is in *thy* hand" (3777; 3797; emphasis added).

There may be a hint here of a change in stage practice between the earliest performances of the play and the printing of the Folio in 1623, a change reflecting a falling out of fashion of the rapier-and-dagger style of fence. According to J. Dover Wilson, "the vogue [for rapier and dagger] was a temporary one, and had passed away before the text of *Hamlet* was printed in 1623, so that it is not surprising to find no daggers mentioned in the Folio stage-direction." But Wilson is sure, on the strength of Q2, that "there can be no reasonable doubt that both [daggers and 'Foiles'] were used by Burbadge [*sic*] and his stage-opponent at the original performance."[18]

Whatever the particulars, of this we may be sure: the duel would have been managed with great care, since it had to satisfy an audience well schooled in swordplay and apt to be intolerant of anything slapdash or tawdry. Fencing matches, both as self-standing exhibitions and as climactic dramatic scenes, had been a staple of London entertainment since the early days of the public stage.[19]

Such are the scraps and shavings of the historical record. They seem to indicate that what the Elizabethan audience saw—what they were in large measure *given* by Burbage and his company—was an essentially orthodox revenge tragedy, a familiar form, as circumscribed by convention as the modern screen western, which it somewhat resembled in its climactic face-off and general carnage. In yard and galleries alike, Hamlet seems to have been perceived as a fairly conventional stage hero, a protagonist typical of the genre.

But we need not conclude that there was no one present capable of discerning the nuances, the fine shading, the inner depths of thought and character which our own age values so highly. Alfred Harbage declares that he can find no evidence that "the Elizabethans, individually or collectively, were vastly different from us" and wryly warns against too harsh an assessment of the taste of Shakespeare's contemporaries: "Of course, our instincts may still instruct us that no one out of a London shop could possibly have appreciated *Hamlet*—just as no one out of a Stratford shop could possibly have written it."[20] Anthony Scoloker, who as already noted probably saw the play at the Globe, wrote that his own work, "Daiphantus," should "come home to the vulgars element, like Friendly Shakespeare's tragedies, where the Commedian rides, when the Tragedian stands on tip-toe: Faith it should please all, like Prince Hamlet."[21] Perhaps the comment points to a full spectrum of appreciation among the first spectators, from the visceral to the cerebral.

Whatever the first audiences made of it, a new and uncommonly bright star had appeared in the firmament of dramatic art. As Harbage says, with the Globe premiere *Hamlet* "was launched on its career as the greatest theatrical attraction of all time."[22] It is that career which we are now to follow.

NOTES

1. That is to say, the first Shakespearean Hamlet; with the earlier version (c. 1589), believed to be the work of Thomas Kyd, I am not here concerned.

2. The date of the play's first performance cannot be precisely fixed, but as of 26 July 1602 it had been "latelie Acted," according to the Stationer's Register.

3. The *Shakspere Allusion-Book: A Collection of Allusions to Shakspere from 1591 to 1700*, ed. John Munro (London: Oxford University Press, 1932), 1:56. Harvey's note is undated and could have been made at any time between the book's publication in 1598 and his death in 1630; another inscription, however, referring to a work published in 1600, suggests that the Hamlet reference may also have been made after that date.

4. Anthony Scoloker, "Daiphantus, or the Passions of Love," in ibid., 1:133.

5. "A Funerall Ellegye on ye Death of the famous Actor Richard Burbedg," in ibid., 1:272.

6. William Armstrong, "Actors and Theatres," *Shakespeare Survey* 17 (1964): 191.

7. Quoted by Edwin Nungezer, *A Dictionary of Actors* (New Haven: Yale University Press, 1929), pp. 67–68.

8. On the authority for these attributions and on the subject of "lines," see T. W. Baldwin, *The Organization and Personnel of the Shakespearean Company* (Princeton, N.J.: Princeton University Press, 1927), p. 237 and passim. Bernard Beckerman (*Shakespeare at the Globe: 1599–1609* [New York: Macmillan, 1962], p. 162) has challenged the notion of "lines." I agree with him that Baldwin's use of them is much too rigid, but I see no objection to concluding that Shakespeare created characters tailored to Burbage's temperament in the very general sense I have suggested.

9. E. E. Stoll, *Hamlet: An Historical and Comparative Study*, University of Minnesota Studies in Language and Literature, No. 7 (Minneapolis: University of Minnesota Press, 1919), p. 27.

10. James G. McManaway, "The Two Earliest Prompt Books of *Hamlet*," *Papers of the Bibliographical Society of America* 43 (1949): 289–90.

11. Paul S. Conklin, *A History of Hamlet Criticism: 1601–1821* (1947; reprint, New York: Humanities Press, 1968), pp. 9, 10.

12. Nineteenth-century commentators suggested emendation to "faint" or "hot" (see *A New Variorum Edition of Shakespeare: Hamlet*, ed. Horace Howard Furness [1877; reprint, New York: American Scholar Publications, 1965], 1:446). The modern tendency has been to gloss it as "sweaty" (see, for example, *The Riverside Shakespeare*, ed. G. Blakemore Evans [Boston: Houghton Mifflin, 1974], p. 1184, n. 287).

13. Beckerman, *Shakespeare at the Globe*, p. 111. Beckerman provides an excellent summary of the protracted quarrel between formalists and naturalists and then offers his own view; he concludes that Elizabethan acting was "ritualistic" or "ceremonious," a style in which the actor, drawing freely on

establ¡sned conventions, sought to relate his character to a recognizable social group or type while at the same time employing "an artistry which imitated the ideal rather than the specific" (ibid., p. 153). In a more recent study of the question, Daniel Seltzer concludes that the style was a mixture of "small" and "large" effects ("The Actors and Staging," in *A New Companion to Shakespeare Studies*, ed. Kenneth Muir and S. Schoenbaum [Cambridge, Eng.: Cambridge University Press, 1971], pp. 35–54).

14. Quoted by Nungezer, *Dictionary of Actors*, pp. 74–75.

15. Alfred Harbage, "Elizabethan Acting," *PMLA* 54 (1939): 692.

16. The sole textual authority for the leap is in the First Quarto (Q1) (Sig. I1^v), though it seems to be corroborated by the anonymous elegy to Burbage. The Folio has "*Leaps in the grave*" (3444), apparently in reference to Laertes; Q2 has no stage directions, but Laertes' line "Now pile your dust upon the quick and dead" (Sig. M4^{a}v) would seem to require his presence in the grave.

17. Arthur Colby Sprague, *Shakespeare and the Actors* (Cambridge, Mass.: Harvard University Press, 1944), p. 162.

18. J. Dover Wilson, *What Happens in Hamlet* (1935; reprint, Cambridge, Eng.: Cambridge University Press, 1970), p. 280.

19. T. F. Ordish, *Early London Theatres* (London: E. Stock, 1894), p. 46.

20. Alfred Harbage, *Shakespeare's Audience* (New York: Columbia University Press, 1941), p. 157.

21. *Shakspere Allusion-Book*, 1:133.

22. Harbage, *Shakespeare's Audience*, p. 49.

2

THOMAS BETTERTON

On 31 September 1607 the captain of HMS *Dragon*, at anchor off "Serra Leona," made an entry in the ship's journal: "I envited Captain Hawkins to a ffishe dinner, and had Hamlet acted abord me: wch I p*er*mitt to keepe my people from idlenes and unlawfull games, or sleepe."[1]

In a few short decades such performances would themselves be considered "idlenes and unlawful games" and would be forbidden by the Puritan regime, but in the meantime the professional theater in London flourished. Richard Burbage died on 13 March 1619 and was immediately replaced in the roll of the King's Men by Joseph Taylor (1586–1652), who thus became the world's second Hamlet. He seems to have been a worthy successor, acting the role "incomparably well," keeping it regularly before the eyes of the public and court until the closing of the theaters in 1642.[2]

During the long cold night of Puritanism which followed, lovers of Hamlet had to be content with "a piece of him." The "incomparable Robert Cox" and his small company, "under pretence of rope-dancing, or the like," enacted vignettes from the old plays, among them the first part of the *Hamlet* graveyard scene, called for the purpose "The Gravemakers." Despite the considerable risk involved, "great was the confluence of the auditors."[3] But except for such fragmentary revivals the stage life of *Hamlet* ceased during the Interregnum. As a Restoration prologue was to recall, "They that would have no King would have no Play."[4] The return of the Prince of Denmark had to wait upon the return of England's king.

In fact, it had to wait a bit longer than other pre-Commonwealth favorites. Charles and his court came back from exile in late May 1660, and though theatrical production resumed almost immediately, *Hamlet* was not seen for more than a year. Samuel Pepys records what was apparently its earliest revival and perhaps reveals also the reason for delay: "Aug. 24, 1661: To the Opera, and there saw 'Hamlet, Prince of Denmark,' done with scenes very well."[5] The reference is to *changeable* scenery, only recently introduced on the London stage, and chances are that producer William Davenant had held up a presentation of the play until he was in possession of "the Opera," his new theater in Lincoln's Inn Fields, a tennis court expressly converted to accommodate the Italianate movable scenery which had become his abiding passion.[6] *Hamlet* was the first play by Shakespeare to be associated with this "epoch-marking" conversion to perspective scenes and very nearly the first play of any sort to be so mounted in England, having been preceded in this dubious honor only by *The Siege of Rhodes* and *The Wits*, two works by Davenant himself.[7]

In November 1661 Pepys also saw " 'Hamlett' very well done" without scenes, at Gibbon's Tennis Court, the other of the two houses whose managers now held, by royal patent, exclusive right to produce plays in London. This must have been the last production of the play in the old manner, since in the apportioning of plays which followed shortly after, *Hamlet* was given to The Duke's Men under Davenant and was thenceforward performed always in the continental style he had brought in.[8] John Evelyn also saw this last platform-stage production and reported that "now the old plays began to disgust this refined age," an opinion which may have been influenced by the "old-fashioned" style of the staging.[9]

In any case, Evelyn's harsh opinion was not the majority one, as regards either the old plays generally or *Hamlet* in particular. John Downes, speaking of Davenant's August production, declared, "No succeeding Tragedy for several Years got more Reputation, or Money to the Company than this."[10] The new stagecraft probably contributed in an important way to this success, but the chief cause lay elsewhere. Again Pepys is indispensable; after his restrained comment on the scenery, he concludes, "But above all, Betterton did the prince's part beyond imagination."[11]

Thomas Betterton (1635–1710) was then twenty-six years old and already a seasoned professional. For the next fifty years, as playwright, artistic director, business manager—but above all as actor—he would dominate the theater of his day as only a handful of men have been able to do since. He acted at least 132 roles, in new plays and old, tragedies as well as comedies. He was Lear and Falstaff, Alexander and Dorimant.[12] And he was Hamlet, "the best part," Pepys avowed, "that ever man acted."[13]

Betterton's portrayal probably owed a great deal to stage tradition; John Downes claimed that "Sir William [Davenant] (having seen Mr. Taylor of the Black-Fryars company act, who being instructed by the Author Mr. Shakspeur [*sic*]) taught Mr. Betterton in every particle of it; which by his exact performance of it, gain'd him esteem and reputation, superlative to all other plays."[14] This cannot have been strictly true—Shakespeare had been dead three years when Taylor took up the role—but the general tenor of the statement is credible enough: Shakespeare certainly instructed Burbage, and Taylor was undoubtedly familiar with Burbage's treatment of the role, either from having seen him or from being instructed in it by the senior members of the King's Men, or both; and Taylor might well have passed on his knowledge to Davenant, who "taught Mr. Betterton."

In any case, the desire to preserve established forms, to be "exact," as Downes says, in the imitation of models, was a characteristic of the age in the theatrical arts as in others. So strong was its hold that it was said Ben Jonson's plays could no longer be acted because with the demise of the older actors "their manner of action . . . is now lost [and] there are none now living who can rightly Humour those parts."[15] It was probably Burbage's "manner of action," that is to say, his business and physical deportment, which Davenant taught to Betterton and which Betterton duly transmitted to succeeding generations. The story is told of an old critic who, in the reign of George II, refused to see any great merit in the performance of a new Hamlet, declaring, "He did not upset the chair, sir [upon seeing the Ghost in Gertrude's closet]. Now Mr. Betterton always upset the chair."[16] It seems likely that Betterton did employ this curious bit of business; it is certainly depicted in the illustration in Nicholas Rowe's *Shakespeare* of 1709, and whatever the relation of that picture to actual stage practice, this is hardly the sort of detail a mere illustrator would be likely to invent.[17] If Downes is right about Betterton being taught "in every particular," the device may go back through Taylor to Burbage and the Globe. Betterton may also have been imitating earlier Hamlets in going about with his "stockings fouled, / Ungartered and down-gyvèd to his ankle," as in Ophelia's description (II.i.76–77); he is so depicted in the Rowe illustration.[18]

Concrete externals of this kind are the most readily transmissible

This must have been true of Betterton's style generally. Rowe himself—in a rare moment of fraternity between study and stage—found the actor's portrayal completely to his liking, and Rowe was a thoroughgoing neoclassicist, a man who could say of the death of Falstaff that "*tho*' it be extremely Natural, [it] is *yet* as diverting as any Part of his Life." [27] If unvarnished nature was scarcely to be tolerated even in comedy, we can be sure that it received little scope in the staging of one of the revered tragedies.

Still, neoclassicism was no monolith, and shaped by it as he undoubtedly was, Betterton was probably not one of its most religious adherents; *one* hand, as we have seen, is heretically above his eyes. He probably departed from strict orthodoxy also in his manner of delivery. There is considerable evidence that tragic actors of the day spoke in a sort of recitative, a technique of near-singing variously referred to as "canting" or "toning." [28] The practice is repeatedly alluded to not only in eighteenth-century stage histories but also in numerous contemporary dramatic parodies of the tragic manner. Gildon, however, again in his Betterton persona, pointedly deplores the practice, declaring that "there is no greater Opiate in Speaking, nothing so dull and heavy, and fit to lull us asleep, as a whole Discourse turning still on the same *Note* and *Tone*." [29] Colley Cibber too, for whom Betterton was "an Actor as Shakespeare was an Author, without Competitors," specifically condemns the practice, deploring "that dangerous Affectation of the Monotone, or solemn Sameness of Pronunciation." [30] It seems safe to say, then, that Betterton rejected the fashionable mode, leaving to lesser men the practice of intoning stage dialogue "as a country clerk does a psalm." Nevertheless, his delivery certainly had a musical dimension which represented some heightening of nature, a degree of artificiality corresponding to that found in gesture and movement. Cibber declares that Betterton's voice was as "strictly ty'd to Time and Tune" as that of a singer, with the result that his delivery of Tragic verse fully satisfied "my Judgement, my Ear, and my Imagination." [31]

Information on Betterton's interpretation of Hamlet, as opposed to the style of acting he employed in playing it, could be bounded in a nutshell, though it is happily more ample than in the case of his two predecessors. Some hint of interpretation is of course to be found in the style itself. The refinements imposed on bodily and vocal deportment by the neoclassical concern for decorum must inevitably have resulted in a refined and decorous Prince. If we look for a difference between Betterton's impersonation and Burbage's, it is probably to be found in this area. Betterton's Prince—we can assume with some confidence—was a gentleman, to a degree that Burbage's most probably was not.

If what we know of the acting style did not point us in this direction, the changes to be found in Betterton's acting text clearly would. Though *Hamlet* escaped the gross alterations visited on *Macbeth*, *Measure for Measure* and others during the Restoration, it was significantly altered for production, as can be readily seen in the so-called "Players Quartos," beginning with the Quarto of 1676. Partly in compliance with the requirement in his patent that he purge the old plays of "all prophaneise and scurrility," partly out of a sense of personal prudery, but chiefly in deference to neoclassical taste, Davenant made numerous excisions calculated to raise the general level of "refinement."[32]

Thus, in place of the racy "I do not set my life at a pin's fee" (I.iv.65) Betterton's audience was given the comparatively lame retort: "I do not value my life."[33] Similarly, Hamlet is allowed to call Claudius only a "smiling," not a "damned," villain (I.v.106) and to accuse him not of having "Popp'd in between th' election and my hopes" (V.ii.65) but of having more decorously "stept." Gone also is most of the discourse on "how a King may go a progress through the guts of a beggar" (IV.iii.19ff.).

Most of the cuts, however, have to do either with sexual explicitness or with lack of reverence in matters of religion. All references to the deity are summarily expunged (even "how like a god!"). Hamlet is also deprived of the lines "Then trip him, that his heels may kick at heaven, / And that his soul may be as damn'd and black / As hell whereto it goes" (III.iii.93–95). With the thoroughness of the true zealot, Davenant also seeks out and eliminates "Not shriving time allowed" (V.ii.47), Hamlet's similar damnation of Rosencrantz and Guildenstern.

Perhaps the most interesting of Davenant's textual tinkerings are in speeches containing sexual references; it is noteworthy that, though heavily laundered, such passages are not sanitized into mere priggishness. Thus, Betterton did not say "That's a fair thought to lie between maids' legs" (III.ii.119), but he did say, "Lady, shall I lie in your lap?'' and "Do you think I meant country matters?'' In the same scene, at 246ff., he was allowed to keep "I could interpret between you and your love, if I could see the puppets dallying,'' but Ophelia did not reply with "You are keen my Lord, you are keen''; Hamlet went right on, without the intervening cue, to the further indecency: "It would cost you a groaning to take off mine edge.'' Davenant seems to have used half-measures also at III.iv.91; Hamlet lost "honeying and making love / Over the nasty sty'' but kept "live in the rank sweat of an incestuous [*sic*] bed.'' Totally eradicated, however, was Hamlet's repartee with Rosencrantz and Guildenstern about the "privates,'' the "secret parts of Fortune'' (II.ii.233–35).

Thus robbed of much of his spice, Betterton's Hamlet must have been a comparatively bland protagonist. He could not quite be turned into one of those paragons of rectitude who served as heroes in the popular tragedy of the day—the age in which he was created had been too far gone in "barbarity'' to allow for that—but he could be scrubbed up and made presentable, and it was a Hamlet thus rehabilitated and reformed who elegantly trod the stage during the fifty years of Betterton's tenure in the role.

Other information about his interpretation comes primarily from the last years of that remarkable career. What may be styled the earliest extant review of a Hamlet performance concerns itself with Betterton's last appearance in the role, on 20 September 1709; in the *Tatler*, which had been founded only five months earlier, Mr. Greenhat reported to Isaac Bickerstaff:

Had you been to-night at the play-house, you had seen the force of action in perfection: your admired Mr. Betterton behaved himself so well, that, though now about seventy [he was 74], he acted youth; and by the prevalent power of proper manner, gesture, and voice, appeared through the whole drama a young man of great expectation, vivacity, and enterprize.

Hazelton Spencer saw in this notice "a striking endorsement of the historical critics' view of Hamlet as the *beau ideal* of active young-manhood, rather than a dream-sick weakling,'' and there seems little reason to reject that reading.[34] It is amply supported by the cuts made in the Davenant-Betterton acting version. As spoken by Betterton, the "O What a rogue and peasant slave'' soliloquy (II.ii.550ff.) was shorn of nearly every hint of irresolution and self-reproach. This Hamlet

compares himself unfavorably to the actor in the very general terms of
the opening lines—down through "Had he the motive, and that [*sic*]
for passion / That I have?" but he does not call himself a "dull and
muddy-mettled rascal" or "a coward" ready to suffer passively the
plucking of his beard or the tweaking of his nose. Gone also are "What
an ass am I" and "Must like a whore unpack my heart with
words, / And fall a-cursing, like a very drab. . . . " The worst he
will say of himself is that he may be "pigeon-livered, and lack gall,"
but that seeming self-rebuke, we should remember, is only conditional
on the very forcefully stated "or ere this / I should have fatted all the
region kites / With this slave's offal. . . . " From that line Betterton
went immediately to "Hum, I have heard / That guilty creatures . . .
" without flogging himself into action on "About my brains. . . . "
Having laid his plans, he finished the speech in the familiar way, passing over, however, the reference to "my weakness and my melancholy," which may be the most significant cut of all.

Another cardinal sign of "weakness and melancholy" in Hamlet's
character was also eliminated by the omission of IV.iv, in which Fortinbras appears with his army and Hamlet is provoked to self-recrimi-
nation in the "How all occasions do inform against me" soliloquy
(32ff.). Fortinbras' entrance in Act V was retained, but since he had
been neither seen nor mentioned prior to that, the play was effectively
stripped of the contrast between him and Hamlet.

Betterton also spoke not a word of Hamlet's advice to the players
(III.ii.1–45), and though the reason for that cut may simply have been
the inescapable necessity of shortening the playing time,[35] the result
was a Hamlet significantly diminished in sensitivity and intellectuality.
His stature in those departments was reduced at least another cubit by
an excision which a modern spectator would surely find the most re-
grettable omission of all; of Hamlet's philosophic musing (V.ii.219–
24) just before going off to the fateful duel, he spoke only the first
sentence, "Not a whit, we defy augury."

At first glance these alterations might seem to be precisely opposite
in kind to the group of expurgations and "corrections" noted earlier,
and in a sense that is the case; the role was cut, so to speak, both from
below and from above, but that is only to say that by working from
opposite directions Davenant arrived eventually at a desired midpoint
between the two. The result was a Hamlet cleansed of crudity, on the
one hand, and complexity on the other—in short, a Hamlet regular-

ized, a Hamlet with Romantic idiosyncrasy peeled off to reveal the Classical ideal. Small wonder that Mr. Greenhat saw in the performance an example of "virtue represented on stage with its proper ornaments," a spectacle which, he congratulated himself, had proved thoroughly edifying to the youthful cousin whom he had thoughtfully "carried" with him to the theater.

Others found Betterton's septuagenarian Prince somewhat less palatable than the *Tatler* correspondent. Anthony Aston said that "when he threw himself at *Ophelia's* Feet, he appear'd a little too grave for a young Student . . . and his *Repartees* seem'd rather as *Apothegms* from a *sage Philosopher*, than the *sporting Flashes* of a young Hamlet." Aston thought that for this reason Betterton should have resigned the role to a younger actor, but he admitted that such a replacement "might have Personated, though not have Acted, it better."[36] The point is of some interest because Betterton seems to have had inadequacies of "personation" to compensate for even as a young man. Contemporaries describe him as badly proportioned and inclined to corpulence, and the Kneller Studio portrait appears to bear the reports out.[37]

What he lacked in physical attractiveness Betterton more than made up for by the beauty of his performance. Cibber said that "every line that came from [him] was charming," whereas Robert Wilks (1665–1732), Betterton's successor, though he clearly excelled in looking the part, gave pain to the ear in "half of what he spoke."[38] Cibber also contrasts the two actors in their interpretations of the Prince's first meeting with the Ghost; Wilks reacted with a "straining Vociferation requisite to express Rage and Fury," while Betterton, much more appropriately:

open'd with a Pause of mute Amazement! then rising slowly, to a solemn, trembling Voice, he made the Ghost equally terrible to the Spectator, as to himself! and in the descriptive Part of the natural Emotions which the ghastly Vision gave him, the boldness of his Expostulation was still govern'd by Decency, manly, but not braving; his voice never rising into the seeming Outrage, or wild Defiance of what he naturally rever'd.[39]

Barton Booth, who played the Ghost to both Wilks and Betterton, confirms Cibber's account and in the process delivers what may stand as his contemporaries' estimation of Betterton's portrayal; upbraiding Wilks for having bullied "that which you ought to have revered," Booth declared, "When I acted the Ghost with Betterton, instead of my awing him, he terrified me. But divinity hung round that man!"[40]

NOTES

1. *Shakespeare's Centurie of Prayse*, ed. C. M. Ingleby, 2nd ed., The New Shakspere Society Publications, Series IV: Allusion Books, No. 2 (London: N. Trübner, 1879), p. 79.

2. [James Wright], *Historia Histrionica* (1699; reprint, New York: Garland Publishing, 1974), p. 4.

3. Francis Kirkman, "Preface," *The Wits, or Sport upon Sport*, ed. John James Elson, Cornell Studies in English, 18 (1672–73; reprint, Ithaca, N.Y.: Cornell University Press, 1932), p. 268.

4. Quoted in Leslie Hotson, *The Commonwealth and Restoration Stage* (Cambridge, Mass.: Harvard University Press, 1928), p. 208. The prologue was written by Davenant for a court performance of Ben Jonson's *The Silent Woman* on 19 November 1660.

5. *The Diary of Samuel Pepys*, ed. Henry B. Wheatley (London: G. Bell, 1924), 2:82.

6. Hazelton Spencer, *Shakespeare Improved* (Cambridge, Mass.: Harvard University Press, 1927), p. 183.

7. John Downes, *Roscius Anglicanus* (London: H. Playford, 1708), p. 20.

8. Robert W. Lowe, *Thomas Betterton* (1891; reprint, New York: B. Blom, 1971), pp. 75–76.

9. *Diary and Correspondence of John Evelyn*, ed. William Bray (London: G. Bell, 1898), 1:380.

10. Downes, *Roscius Anglicanus*, p. 21.

11. *Diary of Samuel Pepys* 2:82.

12. *The London Stage 1660–1800: Part 1, 1660–1700*, ed. William Van Lennep (Carbondale: Southern Illinois University Press, 1965), p. civ.

13. *Diary of Samuel Pepys*, 31 August 1668, 8:90.

14. Downes, *Roscius Anglicanus*, p. 21.

15. Wright, *Historia Histrionica*, p. 3.

16. Montague Summers, *The Restoration Theatre* (New York: Macmillan, 1934), p. 283.

17. According to Sprague, "The precise degree to which this famous picture represents the contemporary staging of the scene is doubtful. At certain points, the artist seems to have had in mind the practice of his own day; at others, he appears to have been merely 'illustrating,' without any great attempt at accuracy, the text before him" (Arthur Colby Sprague, *Shakespeare and the Actors* [Cambridge, Mass.: Harvard University Press, 1944], pp. 162–63).

18. In Q1676 Ophelia merely says "his stockings loose," and in the illustration the right stocking is shown at mid-calf rather than down at the ankle.

19. Thomas Davies, *Dramatic Miscellanies* (London: Author, 1783–84), 3:272.

20. Quoted in A. M. Nagler, *A Source Book in Theatrical History* (New York: Dover, 1952), p. 219.

21. Charles Gildon, *Life of Mr. Thomas Betterton* (London: R. Gosling, 1710), p. 70.

22. Anthony Aston, *A Brief Supplement to Colley Cibber, Esq., His Lives of the Late Famous Actors and Actresses* (London: Author, 1747), p. 5.

23. *The Tatler*, No. 167, Thursday, 4 May 1710.

24. Gildon, *Life of Mr. Thomas Betterton*, p. 67.

25. Ibid., pp. 76–77.

26. A more pronounced concern for bodily decorum is revealed in such passages as the following: "The Mouth must never be writh'd, nor the Lips bit nor lick'd, which are all ungenteel and unmannerly actions . . . " (ibid., p. 72). "[A] Shrug of the Shoulders . . . seems more adapted to Comedy than Tragedy, where all should be great and solemn . . . " (ibid., p. 73).

27. Nicholas Rowe, *The Works of Mr. William Shakespear* (1709; reprint, New York: AMS Press, 1967), 1:xviii. Emphasis added.

28. For a variety of views on this topic, see Arthur Colby Sprague, "Did Betterton Chant?" *Theatre Notebook* 1 (1946): 54–55, and letters of response to that article, in *Theatre Notebook* 1 (1947): 75, 99–100, 115–16. See also John Harold Wilson, "Rant, Cant, and Tone on the Restoration Stage," *Studies in Philology* 52 (1955): 592–98.

29. Gildon, *Life of Thomas Betterton*, p. 104.

30. Colley Cibber, *An Apology for the Life of Mr. Colley Cibber, Comedian*, ed. B. R. S. Fone (1740; reprint, Ann Arbor: University of Michigan Press, 1968), pp. 59–60, 61.

31. Ibid., p. 66.

32. Spencer, *Shakespeare Improved*, pp. 183–84.

33. This and the other cuts referred to here are to be found, designated by quotation marks, in *The Tragedy of Hamlet Prince of Denmark: As it is now Acted at his Highness the Duke of York's Theatre* (1676; reprint, London: Cornmarket Press, 1969).

34. Spencer, *Shakespeare Improved*, p. 9. Arthur Colby Sprague, in his excellent account of Betterton's Hamlet (*Shakespearian Players and Performances* [Cambridge, Mass.: Harvard University Press, 1953]), disagrees with Spencer, arguing, "Mr. Greenhat is insisting that an old actor had succeeded splendidly in a young part, not explaining to us how he had interpreted it" (p. 9).

35. Since 1900 the play has frequently been performed in its entirety, but

prior to that the text was always pared down substantially. Besides those already mentioned, Davenant made the following excisions: I.i.72–125 (on the quarrel with Norway); I.ii.17–41 (on the quarrel with Norway); 95–106, 110–16 (Claudius on Hamlet's mourning); I.iii.11–16, 22–28, 31–46 (Laertes' advice to Ophelia, including "your chaste treasure open . . ."); 56–81 (Polonius' advice to Laertes); 117–31 (Polonius' instructions to Ophelia); I.iv.17–38 (on Danish drunkenness); 40–51 (Hamlet's first words to the Ghost); II.i.1–71 (Polonius and Reynaldo); II.ii.40–84 (the return of the Ambassadors); 336–63 (on the "aery of children, little eyases"); 444–64 (Hamlet's "rugged Pyrrhus" recitation); 475–82, 494–98, 511–18 (the First Player's recitation); III.ii.60–62, 67–71 (Hamlet's compliment to Horatio); 23 lines between Player King and Queen; 275–84 (Hamlet's "cry of players" speech and the "O Damon dear" verse); 293–95 ("For if the King like not the comedy"); III.iii.11–23 (Rosencrantz on "the cess of majesty"); III.iv.151–55 ("compost on the weeds"); 162–70 ("refrain tonight"); 182–85 ("a pair of reechy kisses"); 189–96 ("unpeg the basket on the house's top); 202–10 ("my two school-fellows"); IV.iii.21–31 ("Your worm is your only emperor"); 58–68 ("Do it, England"); IV.v.52–55, 62–63 (bawdy lines in Ophelia's song); IV.vii.21–24, 75–76, 78–81, 111–23, 149–54 (Claudius conspiring with Laertes); 170–71 ("That liberal shepherds give a grosser name"); 176–77 ("awhile they bore her up"); V.ii.7–8, 20–23, 42–43, 60–63 (on Hamlet's shipboard activities). Most of these cuts were adopted, with variations, by subsequent producers. For a thorough study of the subject, see Claris Glick, "*Hamlet* in the English Theater—Acting Texts from Betterton (1676) to Olivier (1963)," *Shakespeare Quarterly* 20 (1969): 17–35.

36. Aston, *Brief Supplement*, p. 5.

37. For detailed descriptions, see ibid., pp. 3–4, and Cibber, *Apology*, p. 69. For the Kneller Studio portrait, see the frontispiece of Philip H. Highfill, Jr., Kalman A. Burnim and Edward A. Langhans, *A Biographical Dictionary of Actors . . . 1660–1800* (Carbondale: Southern Illinois University Press, 1973), vol. 2. The original is in the National Portrait Gallery in Washington, D.C.

38. Cibber, *Apology*, p. 315.

39. Ibid., p. 60.

40. Davies, *Dramatic Misccellanies*, 3:32.

3

DAVID GARRICK

"Nature and Nature's laws lay hid in night," wrote Alexander Pope; "God said, Let Newton be! and all was light!" What Sir Isaac Newton did for physics, David Garrick (1717–1779), in large measure, did for acting, and the nature and impact of his Hamlet must be assessed in that context.

It is also true that in broad outline Garrick's impersonation differed little from Thomas Betterton's; it was an essentially strong-willed, active Hamlet, a Hamlet consciously and energetically in pursuit of revenge. Like Betterton before him, Garrick omitted in performance those sections of the text which suggest vacillation and irresolution, inaction and passivity. In the soliloquy at II.ii.550ff. (which, incidentally, became in Garrick's text "O what a *wretch* and peasant slave am I"), he settled on his scheme for catching the king's conscience without first excoriating himself for cowardice and delay.[1] He also omitted altogether "How all occasions do inform against me" (IV.iv.32ff.), with its charge of "some craven scruple of thinking too precisely on the event" and its invidious comparison of Hamlet with the forceful Fortinbras. Unspoken also was the philosophic resignation of "There's a special providence in the fall of a sparrow" (V.ii.219ff.).

Such was the text Garrick played during most of his long career in the role, from 1742 to 1776.[2] In December 1772 he brought before the public a new version of the play containing radical alterations which he had long contemplated, alterations which bore heavily on the character of the protagonist. Garrick directed his editorial energies chiefly to the events of the play following the closet scene, having resolved, as he wrote to a friend, that he "would not leave the stage till I had rescued that noble play from all the rubbish of the fifth act."[3] He constructed a new final act, composed in large part of materials found in Act IV of conventional texts; room was made for those scenes by massive excisions of the original Act V material.[4] The result was a denouement which ran as follows: In scene one of the new Act V, Claudius sends Hamlet into England, accompanied by Rosencrantz and Guildenstern. In scene two they encounter the Norwegian force (which remains offstage) and the usual colloquy follows about the "patch of ground" they go to fight for, except that the Norwegian Captain's lines are given to Guildenstern. This done, Hamlet bids his escort "go a little before" and, left alone, begins the soliloquy "How all occasions do inform against me"—not heard in the theater, as we have seen, for more than a hundred years. But Garrick did not restore it in order to restore indecision and self-reproach to the character. Quite the contrary. He delivered the speech as Shakespeare wrote it, down to the last three lines, but then introduced an emendation, audacious in itself, and the harbinger of audacious things to come. Instead of saying, "O from this time forth, / My thoughts be bloody, or be nothing worth" (IV.iv.65–66), he said, "O from this time forth, / My thoughts be bloody all!—the hour is come—I'll fly my keepers—sweep to my revenge."

Events now proceed apace. Horatio, the Queen and a Gentleman enter, to be joined briefly by the distracted Ophelia and then by the King. Laertes bursts in, hot for revenge, is soon mollified by Claudius, and at Ophelia's reappearance turns his attention to his sister in her last distress. Upon her exit, Laertes curses the author of her pain in lines he ordinarily speaks from the grave, slightly interpolated and joined with lines properly found in his second interview with Claudius (IV.vii):

> O, treble woe
> Fall ten times treble on that cursed head.
> Let me but see him Heav'n
> Whose wicked deed thy most ingenious sense
> Deprived thee of! Twould warm the very sickness in my heart
> That I should live and tell him to his teeth,
> "Thus didst thou!"
>
> [V.i.246–49; IV.vii.55–57]

On this cue, Hamlet enters, shouting the lines with which he usually confronts Laertes in the grave: "What is he, whose grief / Bears such an emphasis?" (V.i.254–55). They quarrel, Claudius attempts to part them and Hamlet stabs him, shouting "Here, thou incestuous, mur-

d'rous, damnèd Dane / There's for thy treachery, lust and usurpation!''
The Queen runs off, crying, "Save me from my son," and is soon
reported mad. Hamlet impales himself on Laertes' sword and shortly
expires, declaring, "I can no more / Nor have I more to ask but mercy
Heav'n." Horatio ends the play.

Between Hamlet's vow, "I'll fly my keepers—sweep to my revenge," and his execution of Claudius a scant 215 lines have elapsed;
from his entrance in the final scene to the execution of his father's
murderer, a mere 31 lines. There has been no voyage to England, no
miraculous escape and return, no conspiracy by Claudius and Laertes,
no repartee or rumination in the graveyard, no leisurely recounting of
his adventures on shipboard, no banter with Osric, no reflection on the
workings of providence. In consequence, there has been no delay and
no passivity. It is unlikely that a more decisive, active avenger has
ever been presented to view.

This was Garrick's Hamlet only during the last four years of his career of course, but it tells us much about the general shape of his characterization during the long career which preceded it. It is safe to assume that the actor who rewrote the play along such lines must always
have had such a conception of the character and must have played it
that way, to the extent that the "unimproved" text allowed.

Garrick also followed Betterton in presenting a Hamlet cleansed of
impiety and sexual indelicacy, although the texts they used were not
precisely identical in these respects. Thus, though he omitted most of
the oaths, Garrick did allow his Hamlet to say "How like a god" in
the "paragon of animals" speech (II.ii.293ff.). On the other hand, he
exceeded his Restoration forebear in squeamishness in having the Prince
say to Ophelia only "Lady, shall I lie in your lap?" omitting the accompanying "Do you think I meant country matters?" (III.ii.112ff.),
which points up and underscores the lewdness of the first line. Elsewhere he followed, with only trifling differences, the long-established
practice of purging Hamlet's discourse of everything that smacked of
coarseness and impropriety.

But conform as he did to orthodox eighteenth-century notions of the
basic makeup of the character—as concerns both heroic resolution and
princely refinement—Garrick clearly brought to bear also gifts and
powers which made his impersonation a unique work of art of the highest
excellence.

As always in the theater, his physical person formed a cardinal ingredient in his characterization. In this respect, Garrick was neither the most favored nor the least favored among the Hamlets of the ages. On the debit side, he had the misfortune of being "the smallest man that ever attempted the character of a king or hero."[5] On occasion the handicap could be devastating; on Garrick's first entrance as Othello, his archrival, James Quin (1693–1776), a celebrated wit, remarked for all to hear, "There is the boy, but where is the teakettle?"—a mischievous reference to the fashion in great houses for employing a little black boy in Moorish dress to fetch in the tea (*Theatrical Monitor*, 24 October 1767). From time to time Garrick seems to have resorted to elevator shoes to correct the deficiency.[6] For most spectators, though, Garrick made up in grace what he lacked in height. He was perfectly proportioned and moved with the elegant coordination of an athlete. George III complained that he was "a great fidget; he never could stand still," but the royal opinion, in this as in other matters, was decidedly atypical.[7] Most found in Garrick's frequent employment of expressive movement an artful and pleasing substitute for dignity of stature. At other times, Garrick made his audience forget about his size by the compelling excellence of his rendering of emotion; as Robert Lloyd wrote, "The feeling sense all other want supplies / I rate no actor's merit from his size."[8]

Garrick was not much better provided for in voice than in body, but here too he made the most of his niggardly allotment. Other actors had greater range, power and melodiousness but used their gifts with less authority and finesse. Garrick could be heard and understood in every corner of the house, even "in the gentle whispers of murmuring love."[9] Superb technique diverted attention from natural deficiency.

Only in the third part of his physical equipment—the physiognomy—did Garrick find an artistic tool perfectly suited to his purposes. Arthur Murphy tells a story about a deaf-mute who was seen to take great pleasure in Garrick's performances; asked how he was able to follow the action, he replied, "Garrick's face was a language."[10] Especially eloquent were his eyes, said to have a piercing quality powerful enough to "penetrate a deal board."[11] This is high praise, to be sure, but taken all together Garrick's physical endowments must be reckoned as modest, at best—a fact which makes all the more impressive the preeminence he achieved, in the art of acting generally and in the role of Hamlet in particular.

As already suggested, the prime cause of that preeminence lay in Garrick's masterful exhibition of a radically new style of acting. His contemporaries called it "natural." In large measure they used the term to distinguish Garrick's style from the mode employed by James Quin, reigning star of the London stage at the time of Garrick's debut. In the *Rosciad* (1761), Charles Churchill sketched Quin with his usual deftness:

> Happy in art, he chiefly had pretence
> To keep up numbers, yet not forfeit sense;
> No actor ever greater heights could reach
> In all the labour'd artifice of speech.[12]

This "labour'd artifice," this "pretence to keep up numbers" (i.e., meter), Garrick shunned. As he later said, "when at first setting out in the business of an actor, I endeavour'd to shake off the fetters of numbers, and have been accus'd of neglecting the harmony of the ver-isification, from a too close regard to the passion, and the meaning of the author."[13]

Garrick had been anticipated somewhat in this reform by Charles Macklin (c. 1700–1797); William Cooke, Macklin's biographer, de-scribes that actor's method of teaching the new style in terms which may be applied to Garrick:

The principal part of his method seemed to be in restraining [his pupils] from those artificial habits of speaking which are too generally preconceived to be-long to the stage. Putting them thus in a course of nature, they felt the effects of her powers: and instead of that *titum tum* manner of speaking which was the predominant mistake of the old school, those who were capable of attend-ing to his advice, spoke the language of the character they represented, as little mixed with art as stage performance will admit of.[14]

The innovation did not win universal approval; those who did not fancy it thought it *too* "little mixed with art." This camp Fielding gently mocked in *Tom Jones*, in the much-quoted incident in which Partridge accompanies Tom to see Garrick play Hamlet; asked afterward which actor he thought the best, Partridge goes against the opinion of the town and says he likes the star less than the actor playing Claudius: "The king for my money; he speaks all his words distinctly, half as loud again as the other. Anybody may see he is an actor." Garrick's naturalism in the Ghost scene is simply lost on Partridge: " 'He the best player!' cries he, with a contemptuous sneer, 'Why I could act as well as he myself. I am sure, if I had seen a ghost, I should have looked in the very same manner, and done just as he did.' " [15] Johnson seems to have held a similar opinion. He told Mrs. Siddons that any one of Garrick's own scene-shifters was a better "declaimer" than Garrick himself. [16]

But for the most part even those who found Garrick's new style of delivery lacking in artistry felt themselves amply compensated for the loss: "He is not so good a reciter as Quin," runs a contemporary criticism, "but a better player." [17] Indeed, the avoidance of studied appeals to the ear seemed to be a positive virtue and itself a necessary condition of the most effective appeal to the emotions; this seems to be the gist of Hannah More's enraptured report to her family after seeing Garrick play Hamlet in 1774:

> So naturally . . . do the ideas of the poet seem to mix with his own, that he seemed himself to be engaged in a succession of affecting situations, *not giving utterance to a speech*, but to the instantaneous expression of his feelings, delivered in the most affecting tones of voice, and with gestures that belong only to nature. It was a fiction as delightful as fancy, and as touching as truth. [18]

In interpreting all this we must be careful to ask, "How natural—in the eighteenth century—was natural?" The safest answer, and the only one that can be put forward with any confidence, is that Garrick's style seemed natural *by comparison* with the extremely formal, artificial style practiced by most of his contemporaries. But there are tantalizing hints here and there that he may have been natural in a stricter, more absolute sense, that he may have been literally "like life." When, as Macbeth, he said to the First Murderer, "There's blood upon thy face," the actor playing opposite him heard such truth in the line that he blurted out, "Is there, by god?" thinking, as he later confessed, that he had broken a blood vessel. [19]

In another anecdote, although the observer is not fooled in this way into mistaking art for life, the story suggests that Garrick's naturalness was not merely "of the stage"; William Cooke saw him demonstrate to a young actor, in his study, the proper playing of Macbeth:

> When he came to the dagger scene, I observed his face instantly assume a mixture of horror, perplexity, and guilt, which I thought it impossible for hu-

man nature to *affect*; . . . I then saw the amazing effect of his art, in which, like a great original in painting, the nearer it was viewed, the more the delicate and master touches of the pencil were discernible.[20]

But whatever the degree of correspondence between Garrick's natural style and observable life, there was more to it than mere avoidance of "*titum tum*." Garrick also put a great distance between himself and most other actors of his day in his ability to immerse himself totally in whatever character he took in hand. Hannah More marveled at this rare ability: "A few nights before [seeing *Hamlet*] I saw him in 'Abel Drugger' and had I not seen him in both, I should have thought it as possible for Milton to have written 'Hudibras,' and Butler 'Paradise Lost,' as for one man to have played 'Hamlet' and 'Drugger' with such excellence."[21] Thomas Newton, a clergyman, writing to Garrick a few months after his debut, also remarked that, whereas other actors remained the same from role to role, Garrick completely transformed himself. Newton had seen him in four roles, including Richard III and Lear, and declared that he "never saw four actors more different from one another than you are from yourself."[22]

To this concern for sharp differentiation of characters, Garrick added an unusual emphasis on completeness in individual portrayals, taking pains to remain consistently in character from the beginning of a performance to the end. Thomas Davies was impressed that Garrick threw himself wholeheartedly into even the short scenes in *King John*, unlike other actors, who simply walked through them, saving themselves for the big, applause-catching moments. In Davies' view, Garrick's thoroughness was strong proof of his preeminence.[23]

All this testimony about Garrick's habits of working points toward a single important conclusion: to a degree probably never before seen in the English theater, Garrick made the revelation of character—in all its subjectivity, complexity and individuality—the single most important component in theatrical and dramatic art. Whereas Betterton, shaped for the most part by a Neoclassic aesthetic, had treated the character of Hamlet simply as one element in the overall design of the work, a design whose organizing principle was action, or plot, Garrick operated within a newly emerging Romantic aesthetic, according to which the all-important factor, the cardinal principle of artistic cohesion, was the moment-to-moment psychological response of the protagonist to his fluid situation.[24] To Garrick's depiction of those responses we now turn.

He wore the dress of his day, knee-breeches, waistcoat and suit coat of French cut, and accordingly declared, " 'Tis not alone my *mourning suit*, dear Mother," in place of "inky cloak" (I.ii.77). He played the speech tearfully, with "a kind of feminine sorrow," more bereaved by the loss of his father than stung by his mother's faithlessness (*St. James's Chronicle*, 20–22 February 1772). A nearly incapacitating grief also permeated his delivery of the first soliloquy (I.ii.129ff.), according to Georg Christoph Lichtenberg, a visitor from Germany in 1775:

Garrick is completely overcome by tears of grief. . . . The last of the words, "So excellent a King," is utterly lost; one catches it only from the movement of the mouth, which quivers and shuts tight immediately afterwards, so as to restrain the all too distinct expression of grief on the lips, which could easily tremble with unmanly emotion.[25]

Only near the end was a note of "righteous anger" sounded, and then only momentarily. Garrick was greatly aided in thus playing the speech very nearly as pure threnody by the elimination of most of the invective Shakespeare had included in it; like others before him, he did not compare Claudius to a satyr or his mother to "a beast that wants discourse of reason," nor did he hiss out his disgust at the wicked speed with which the two of them had posted to incestuous sheets.

His all-absorbing love for his lost father Garrick underscored again at the end of the scene; instead of saying "I will watch tonight; Perchance, 'twill walk again" in the matter-of-fact way to which the spectators had been long accustomed, Garrick "electrified" them by rushing "exultingly forward" and putting into the line all of Hamlet's vibrant hope for a speedy reunion with the beloved father whose loss he still so deeply mourns.[26]

Reference to Hamlet's love for his father in these accounts of Garrick's first scene suggest that he made it a distinctive feature of his characterization. Hannah More declares that it was nothing less than the cornerstone: "Hamlet experiences the conflict of many passions and affections, but filial love ever takes the lead; *that* is the great point from which [Garrick] sets out, and to which he returns; the others are all contingent and subordinate to it."[27] Nowhere does Hamlet have more opportunity to show the depth of his bereavement than in his encounters with his father's spirit, and the vast amount of contemporary commentary which those scenes—the first in particular—occasioned also lends support to the conclusion that Garrick laid primary stress on that aspect of the Prince's character. In the version of the play Garrick used, the audience had not long to wait to see further evidence of the hope and paternal love revealed at the end of I.ii. In the intervening scene of Laertes' leave-taking, his brotherly advice to Ophelia (I.iii.10ff.) was severely truncated and his father's "few precepts" (I.iii.58ff.) were eliminated altogether.

In the platform scene itself, the action was further speeded along by omission of Hamlet's animadversions on Danish drunkenness and his reflections on "some vicious mole of nature" (I.iv.17–38), so that the Ghost entered promptly on "more honored in the breach than in the observance." Garrick made this instant of encounter one of the most stunning moments in his entire portrayal; for the duration of his long career—and for decades thereafter—the scene would be cited over and over as one of the most sublime achievements of the actor's art. Lichtenberg's description conveys with arresting precision Garrick's power in the scene:

Hamlet has folded his arms under his cloak and pulled his hat down over his eyes; it is a cold night and just twelve o'clock; the theatre is darkened, and the whole audience of some thousands are as quiet, and their faces as motionless, as though they were painted on the walls of the theatre; even from the farthest end of the playhouse one could hear a pin drop. Suddenly, as Hamlet moves towards the back of the stage slightly to the left and turns his back on the audience, Horatio starts, and saying: "Look, my lord, it comes," points to the right, where the ghost has already appeared and stands motionless, before any one is aware of him. At these words Garrick turns sharply and at the same moment staggers back two or three paces with his knees giving way under him; his hat falls to the ground and both his arms, especially the left, are stretched out nearly to their full length, with the hands as high as his head, the right arm more bent and the hand lower, and the fingers apart; his mouth is open; thus he stands rooted to the spot, with legs apart, but no loss of dignity, supported by his friends, who are better acquainted with the apparition and fear lest he should collapse. His whole demeanour is so expressive of terror that it made my flesh creep even before he began to speak. The almost terror-struck silence of the audience, which preceded this appearance and filled one with a sense of insecurity, probably did much to enhance this effect. At last he speaks, not at the beginning, but at the end of a breath, with a trembling voice: "Angels and ministers of grace defend us!" words which supply

David Garrick. The Ghost Scene (I.iv). Engraving by J. McArdell, from the painting by Benjamin Wilson, 1754. Harvard Theatre Collection.

anything this scene may lack and make it one of the greatest and most terrible which will ever be played on any stage.[28]

What is most impressive in this account is "the almost terror-struck silence of the audience"; this was 1775, the *thirty-second* year of Garrick's portrayal, and a sizable portion of those present must have seen him perform it many times before. That Garrick could still hold them—an audience not much given to respectful attention under the best of circumstances—shows the full magnitude of his mastery.

The staggering start and long, terror-charged pause which so enthralled Garrick's audiences sound transparently stagey now, and indeed had begun to seem so to some of Garrick's contemporaries in the last years of his portrayal. Johnson was characteristically contemptuous; when Boswell asked, "Would you not, sir, start as Mr. Garrick does, if you saw a ghost?" Johnson replied, "I hope not. If I did, I should frighten the ghost."[29] Churchill also reports a negative response in some quarters but declares that, for him, "Each start is nature, and each pause is thought."[30] This was certainly the more widely held opinion. Garrick's ability to convey in an instant, through pantomimic action, a powerful impression of a specific mental state accorded well with the prevailing views on the workings of human psychology and satisfied perfectly the aesthetic sensibilities in which such views were grounded.[31]

To the start and the pause Garrick seems to have added another effect, derived perhaps from the great Betterton; Murphy says that during the "interval of suspense" before he spoke, "the audience saw him growing paler and paler."[32] When he at last broke the silence, Garrick addressed his father at much greater length than Betterton, who had omitted twelve lines following "Angels and ministers of grace defend us" (I.iv.40–51). Garrick used those lines—including "I'll call thee Hamlet, King, Father, Royal Dane"—to bring his terror gradually under control, overlaying that emotion with a marked feeling of "filial awe." His response to the Ghost's invitation to follow was "vehemently resolute" and his carriage as he moved off "awful and tremendous."[33] His throwing off of his friends' efforts to restrain him (I.iv.80ff.) afforded Garrick another opportunity for one of those lightning-swift changes of emotion in which the eighteenth-century audience so delighted; in a flash he went from "extreme passion to reverential awe,'' marking the change in ''eyes, feature, attitude, and voice.''[34]

One witness to a late performance of the scene claimed that Garrick's Hamlet ''bravely followed the spectre whilst his hair stood on end with horror,''[35] and Frederic Reynolds records a chance meeting with a barber, one Perkins, who claimed to have fashioned for Garrick's use in the scene a wig cunningly contrived to make ''each individual hair on his head stand upright''; Reynolds declares himself skeptical, preferring to assign Garrick's power in the scene to causes less mechanical:

Whether this story was related by the facetious perruquier, to puff himself, or to hoax me, I will not pretend to decide; but this I can say with truth, that though I did not see Garrick's hair rise perpendicularly, *mine* did, when he broke from Horatio and Marcellus, with anger flashing from ''his two balls of fire,'' (as his eyes were rightly called).[36]

Lichtenberg says only that the actor's hair was ''disordered'' (perhaps from his hat being knocked off), and no doubt we should leave it at that.

Garrick's audience did not hear ''Something's rotten in the state of Denmark'' (I.iv.89); instead the scene ended with Hamlet following the Ghost offstage, a ''strong'' ending which no doubt regularly produced the desired effect. At the performance Lichtenberg attended, the audience began applauding loudly at the Ghost's exit and continued until Hamlet was also out of sight.[37] Garrick exited with his sword pointed protectively against the wraith and sheathed it only on hearing the reassuring line ''I am thy father's spirit'' (I.v.9). A spectator wrote to say that the business had been used by every Hamlet he had ever seen and always struck him as ridiculous, since, as Marcellus says, the Ghost is ''as the air invulnerable,'' but Garrick retained it throughout his career.[38]

From the Ghost's lengthy account of his brother's murderous treachery, Garrick took for his own the line ''O, horrible, O, horrible, most horrible!'' (I.v.80) and was followed in that emendation by a great many actors and not a few editors.[39] Little other commentary on the scene has come down. The Bell text has Hamlet writing, on ''My tables—meet it is I should [*sic*] set it down / That one may smile, and smile and be a villain!'' (I.v.107–8). Lichtenberg took strong exception to

Garrick's playing the second line "with an expression and tone of petty mockery, almost as if he wished to describe a man who smiled perpetually and yet was a villain." But he was "gratified and charmed," upon witnessing a subsequent performance, "to hear him declaim the same words in a manner entirely in accord with my own sentiments, namely, in the purposeful tone of one bent on immediate action."[40] Lichtenberg concludes that the first reading he heard was the result of "deliberate experiment" (but why not the second?), and we thus discover the great actor, in the winter of his artistic life, still trying out new effects.

Following the usual concessions to decorum, Garrick's Hamlet did not call his father's spirit "boy" or "truepenny" or "old mole" or locate him in the "cellarage" (I.v.150ff.), but he retained the scene's other "wild and whirling words" (actually, "*windy* words" in his text) and probably began at that point to lay the groundwork for putting on an antic disposition. Certainly he made feigned madness an important part of his characterization; Hannah More refers to it in analyzing his portrayal, and Frederick Pilon, with Garrick clearly in mind, says that "at the conclusion of the first act, Hamlet . . . assumes the mask of insanity, to conceal his intentions, and lull the suspicions of the King his uncle."[41]

Ophelia's description of the Prince's distraction, in the next scene, omitted the reference to his "stockings fouled, / Ungartered and down-gyved to his ankle" (II.i.75–76), but Garrick and other Hamlets of the day seem nevertheless to have arranged their dress in at least partial conformity with it; a writer for the *Connoisseur* complained of the practice in terms which suggest that it had become a rigid convention: "They [actors] are afraid we should lose sight of Hamlet's pretended madness, if the black stocking, discovering the white one underneath, was not rolled half-way down the leg."[42]

We catch only a fleeting glimpse of Garrick's first encounter with the players—he delivered the line " 'The mobled queen?' " as if in doubt about its meaning[43]—but we know much about his playing of the soliloquy (II.ii.550–605) which that encounter prompts. Although he omitted the lacerating phrases of self-accusation (from "dull and muddy-mettled rascal" through "Zounds, I should take it"), Garrick evidently delivered the speech with withering intensity, so much so that Pilon felt constrained to speak of it defensively: "Rant consists in the misapplication, not in the great exertion of the voice. For in the impassioned part of his speech, every word Mr. Garrick utters, seems to rush from the burning mint of sensibility; which proves, that the loudest extent of voice will not offend, when the heart replies to it in sympathy."[44] Garrick's tone was not all rage, of course. Here again he showed his genius for sharp transitions. After "kindless villain" he went from hatred of the murderer to grief for the murderer's victim, from the desire for vengeance to the filial piety which inspires it.[45]

An act break and musical interlude followed at that point in Garrick's production, so the audience had to wait a bit before seeing the great actor perform the "To be or not to be" soliloquy (III.i.55–89). They must have waited with keen anticipation, for it is clear that the speech had by this time come into full possession of that unique glory which still surrounds it. Most of the audience knew it as well as the Lord's Prayer, according to Lichtenberg, and listened to it almost as though it *were* the sacred invocation, for "In this land, Shakespeare is not only famous, but holy." Lichtenberg also gives a meticulously observed verbal portrait of Garrick's appearance and conduct at this crucial moment (hair and clothing in disarray, countenance deeply contemplative, chin resting on right hand) but unfortunately turns to other matters instead of describing Garrick's interpretation of the speech.[46] Unlike the two earlier soliloquies, "To be or not to be" was spoken almost precisely as Shakespeare wrote it, the only evidence of an "improving" hand being a change from "native hue" to "healthful face."

Polonius apparently gave Ophelia no book to read on—the line referring to it is cut—so she must have occupied herself with orisons of her own composition until the moment when Hamlet turned his attention to her. He began with "gentleness and delicacy," according to Pilon, having forgotten momentarily his assumed role of madman; recollecting himself, he turned quickly to a frenzied tone.[47] Murphy and Davies also reveal that Garrick made pretended mental derangement, of a spectacular sort, his dominant action in the scene.[48] But it was apparently not all bedlamite frenzy and wild starting, at least not for the more discerning viewers. Thomas Wilkes could detect "real tenderness for Ophelia" shining through Hamlet's "ineffectual endeavors to hide it,"[49] and Richard Cumberland reported that Garrick's delivery of "To a nunnery" somehow "tempered the unmanly insult" and "operated as a softener to the asperity and coarseness of the poet."[50]

Garrick apparently used Hamlet's speech to the players (III.ii.1–45), spoken in its entirety, to chide his rivals and colleagues. He treated the speech as a lecture on his own style of acting and delivered it *con amore*, not in the manner of a princely amateur but as "a stage-manager and consummate master of the art."[51]

In the play scene, Garrick reclined at Ophelia's feet—as Betterton and others had before him—and there toyed with Ophelia's fan in such a way as to mask his close scrutiny of Claudius.[52] He demonstrated Hamlet's excitement upon becoming convinced of Claudius' guilt on the line "For some must watch while some must sleep" (III.ii.273) by producing a white handkerchief and twirling it around "with vehemence" as he paced up and down.[53]

Garrick answered his mother's summons much more expeditiously than previous Hamlets had because he expunged all of the "Now might I do it pat" speech (III.iii.73–96)—instituting a practice that would be followed until late in the nineteenth century.[54] Garrick was doubtless prompted to this action by the fact that many of his contemporaries found the speech keenly offensive. Garrick had included it when he first appeared in the role in Dublin in August 1742 and had been promptly chastised by a correspondent who described the speech as "abominable . . . a terrible blot and stain to [Hamlet's] character."[55] In later years, Francis Gentleman and Thomas Davies also denounced the passage, combining moral censure with aesthetic objections to the effect that it is "unnecessary" and "highly improbable."[56] Clearly, eighteenth-century spectators were unwilling to accept a Hamlet capable of plotting the death of his enemy's very soul; they demanded and got a Prince cleansed of the foul taint of blasphemy. Claudius was thus left, for the time being, to pray in solitude.

By way of further refinement of the text and of the character, Garrick also spoke fewer daggers to his mother than Shakespeare wrote for him; he did not, for instance, accuse her of being "Stew'd in corruption, honeying and making love / Over the nasty sty" (III.iv.93–94) or refer to his father's successor on the throne as "the bloat king" (III.iv.182). In tone, he seems to have struck a good balance between reverence and reproof, preserving "a proper air of filial affection amidst the most bitter reproaches."[57] Other actors were said to excel him in this scene in "the delicacy of address to a lady," but except for that he was reckoned "most perfect."[58]

For the stinging comparison between Gertrude's past and present husbands (III.iv.53–71), Garrick employed miniature portraits, following what Davies claimed had been "the constant practice of the stage, ever since the Restoration."[59] As already noted, the illustration of the scene in Nicholas Rowe's *Shakespeare* of 1709 suggests that wall portraits may have been in use during at least part of that period, but whatever the date of the introduction of miniatures, they have usually been the preferred articles from Garrick's time to the present.

For most of Garrick's audience the high point of the scene was the return of the Ghost; as Hugh Kelly contemptuously noted, spectators sat unmoved through Hamlet's upbraiding of his mother, every line of which "a plaudit should commend," but energetically signaled their approval of Garrick's reaction to the Spirit's reappearance:

> Then the loud paeans—then the claps begin—
> And pit, box, gallery, eagerly contend
> Exalted strife! who loudest shall commend
> The frantic ha! the Bedlamite—"look there—"
> The start—the heave—the stagger—and the stare![60]

To all this Garrick added—but only occasionally—the old knocking-over-the-chair business inherited from Betterton and since rendered failsafe by the creation of a specially rigged chair. Davies considered the maneuver merely "a poor stage-trick" and wished it reformed altogether.[61] Apparently he found adherents, because the business seems to have been abandoned after Garrick's time. Garrick added further to the impact of the Ghost's entrance by making it the occasion for another of his much-admired quicksilver transitions, from "looking after the apparition with wildness of terror [to] viewing his mother with pathetic concern."[62] The scene ended with the couplet "I must be cruel only to be kind; / Thus bad begins, and worse remains behind" (III.iv.179), the ensuing talk about "reechy kisses" and about the nature of Hamlet's madness being omitted, along with the characterization of Rosencrantz and Guildenstern as "adders fang'd" and the reference to the "engiber / Hoist with his own petar" (III.iv.180–217). The excision of this final speech also meant that Garrick did not announce his intention to "lug the guts into the neighbor room," but he apparently retained the actual business of "tugging in" the body, even though audiences were inclined to snigger over it.[63]

Other concessions to decorum were, however, duly made in following scenes. Instead of instructing Claudius on how "a King may go a progress through the guts of a beggar" (IV.iii.21–31), Garrick's Hamlet confined his ruminations on mortality to the mere mention of ''a certain convocation of politic worms'' feasting on the dead Polonius.

Hamlet was seen next in the graveyard, his encounter with the Norwegian powers (IV.iv) being omitted as usual. Of Garrick's tone and manner in the scene little notice has come down. A close student of the play who saw him during his first London season in the role found him much too solemn in his questioning of the Clown; having given the actor his opinion, he was rewarded, upon a return visit to the theater, to find that Garrick was now ''something easier with Goodman delver.''[64]

Events moved briskly forward to the catastrophe after the funeral scene. Garrick told Horatio nothing of his adventure-filled journey to England (V.ii.4–80), spoke less than was set down for him in his rallying of Osric, and ended the episode by speaking, as Betterton had done, only the first line of the great speech: ''Not a whit, we defy augury'' (V.ii.219). In making his apology to Laertes, he spoke less than Betterton had, omitting the following lines:

> Was't Hamlet wrong'd Laertes? Never Hamlet;
> If Hamlet from himself be ta'en away,
> And when he's not himself, does wrong Laertes,
> Then Hamlet does it not, Hamlet denies it.
> Who does it then? His madness. If't be so,
> Hamlet is of the faction that is wrong'd,
> His madness is poor Hamlet's enemy.
>
> [V.ii.233–39]

Johnson wrote of this speech: ''I wish Hamlet had made some other defence; it is unsuitable to the character of a brave or a good man to shelter himself in falsehood.''[65] It was no doubt some such sentiment which prompted excision; like other eighteenth-century Hamlets, Garrick used only the lines immediately preceding and following those just quoted, retaining the ''falsehood'' but in severely truncated form:

> What I have done
> That might your nature, honour, and exception
> Roughly awake, I here proclaim was madness.
> . . . .
> Let my disclaiming from a purposed evil

Free me so far in your most generous thoughts. . . .

[V.ii.230–33; 241–42]

The effect was to remove yet another disquieting ''blemish'' from the Prince's character.

Johnson also disliked the exchange of weapons in the heat of the duel, dismissing it as ''rather an expedient of necessity than a stroke of art.'' Though the business certainly seems clumsy enough in the reading, modern productions have made it an exciting and wholly credible part of the action. The fact that Garrick's staging of it failed to alter Johnson's opinion suggests that it may have been handled crudely on the Drury Lane stage, perhaps as nothing more than a mere accident.[66]

The play ended almost immediately after Hamlet's dying words. Fortinbras having been banished from the scene since early in the century, there remained no further business than for Horatio to speak a five-line coda, part of it lines Shakespeare wrote for him, part of it tin-eared interpolation and the rest lines cannibalized from Fortinbras:

> There crack'd the cordage of a noble heart.
> Good night, sweet Prince;
> And choirs of angels sing thee to thy rest.
> Take up the bodies; such a sight as this,
> Becomes the field, but here shews much amiss.

Such is the record—a surprisingly ample one, considering the distance which separates us from the performance. One misses in it, as usual, the kind of brilliantly illuminating description that would cause all the shards to fly magically back together again in the full beauty of their original form. Hannah More comes about as close as might reasonably be hoped for in providing what we seek and may therefore justly be given the last word:

One thing I must particularly remark, that, whether in the simulation of madness, in the sinkings of despair, in the familiarity of friendship, in the whirlwind of passion, or in the meltings of tenderness, he never once forgot he was a prince; and in every variety of situation, and transition of feeling, you discovered the highest polish of fine breeding and courtly manners.[67]

NOTES

1. The acting text used by Garrick through most of his career was essentially that found in *Bell's Edition of Shakespeare's Plays* [ed. Francis Gentleman], Vol. 3 (1774; reprint, London: Cornmarket Press, 1969). It corresponds in most respects to William Davenant's text; some exceptions: Garrick keeps I.i.112–25 (Horatio on the assassination of Julius Caesar), omits the dumbshow, and cuts IV.v.76–96 (Claudius' "O Gertrude, Gertrude, / When sorrows come . . . "). Other significant changes in Hamlet's lines are described later in this chapter. For an account of the evolution of Garrick's acting text, see G. W. Stone, "Garrick's Long Lost Alteration of Hamlet," *PMLA* 49 (1934): 895–96.

2. Garrick made his first London appearance in the role at Drury Lane on 16 November 1742, having acted it for the first time in Dublin during the preceding summer. His farewell appearance as Hamlet was on 30 May 1776.

3. David Garrick to William Young, 10 January 1773, quoted in Stone, "Garrick's Alteration," p. 893.

4. For the complete text of Garrick's altered Act V, see Stone, "Garrick's Alteration," pp. 906–21. To the earlier acts of the play, Garrick restored most of the material omitted in the standard acting text; for details, see George Winchester Stone, Jr., and George M. Kahrl, *David Garrick: A Critical Biography* (Carbondale: Southern Illinois University Press, 1979), p. 273.

5. John Hill, *The Actor: A Treatise on the Art of Playing* (1750; reprint, New York: B. Blom, 1971), p. 68.

6. Hill, writing in 1750 (ibid., p. 66), says, "He now leaves off the cork soals [*sic*] which us'd to give him half an inch in height," but John Taylor reports seeing him wear them as Hamlet in the last year of his career (*Personal Reminiscences by O'Keeffe, Kelly and Taylor*, ed. Richard Henry Stoddard (New York: Scribner, Armstrong, 1875), p. 273.

7. *The Reminiscences of Sarah Kemble Siddons, 1773–1785*, ed. William Van Lennep (Cambridge, Mass.: Harvard University Press, 1942), p. 13.

8. "The Actor," in *The Poetical Works of Robert Lloyd* (1774; reprint, Farnborough, Eng.: Gregg International Publishers, 1969), 1:13.

9. *The Life of Mr. James Quin, Comedian* (1766; reprint, London: Reader, 1887), p. 37.

10. Arthur Murphy, *The Life of David Garrick* (Dublin: Wogan Burnett, 1801), p. 371.

11. William Oxberry, *Oxberry's Dramatic Biography* (London: G. Virtue, 1825–27), 5:175.

12. "The Rosciad," in *The Poetical Works of Charles Churchill*, ed. Douglas Grant (Oxford: Clarendon Press, 1956), ll. 947–50, p. 30.

13. *The Letters of David Garrick*, ed. David M. Little and George M. Kahrl (Cambridge, Mass.: Harvard University Press, 1963), 1:92–93.

14. William Cooke, *Memoirs of Charles Macklin, Comedian*, 2nd ed. (London: J. Asperne, 1806), p. 149.

15. Henry Fielding, *The History of Tom Jones* (London: Folio Society, 1973), p. 599.

16. James Boswell, *Boswell's Life of Johnson*, ed. G. Birbeck Hill, rev. ed. by L. F. Powell (Oxford: Oxford University Press, 1934), 4:243. For a similar remark, to Boswell, see ibid., 3:184.

17. *The Museum*, 28 February 1747, 25:442; cited by Bertram Joseph, *The Tragic Actor* (New York: Theatre Arts Books, 1959), p. 93.

18. *The Letters of Hannah More*, ed. R. Brimley Johnson (London: John Lane, 1925), p. 47. Emphasis added.

19. *Personal Reminiscences by O'Keeffe, Kelly and Taylor*, p. 273.

20. William Cooke, *Memoirs of Samuel Foote* (London: Richard Phillips, 1805), 2:209.

21. More, *Letters*, p. 48.

22. Cited by John Forster, *Life and Times of Oliver Goldsmith*, 2nd ed. (London: n.p., 1854), 1:376.

23. Thomas Davies, *Dramatic Miscellanies* (London: Author, 1783–84), 1:102–3.

24. For a full discussion of this subject, see Joseph W. Donohue, Jr., "Garrick and Subjective Character," in *Dramatic Character in the English Romantic Age* (Princeton, N.J.: Princeton University Press, 1970), pp. 222–23 and passim. For a discussion of Garrick's contribution to the eighteenth-century shift in critical focus from the Neoclassical to the Romantic, see G. W. Stone, "David Garrick's Significance in the History of Shakespearean Criticism," *PMLA* 65 (1950): 183–97.

25. *Lichtenberg's Visits to England, as Described in His Letters and Diaries*, ed. and trans. Margaret Mare and W. H. Quarrell (Oxford: Clarendon Press, 1938), pp. 15–16.

26. Frederic Reynolds, *The Life and Times of Frederic Reynolds* (London: H. Colburn, 1826), p. 89.

27. More, *Letters*, p. 47. Davies reports a nearly identical impression; see Thomas Davies, *Memoirs of the Life of David Garrick* (London: Longman, Hurst, Rees & Orme, 1808), 1:64.

28. *Lichtenberg's Visits*, pp. 9–10.

29. Boswell, *Life*, 5:38.

30. Churchill, "The Rosciad," in *Poetical Works*, l. 1054, p. 33.

31. See George Taylor, " 'The Just Delineation of the Passions': Theories of Acting in the Age of Garrick," in *Essays on the Eighteenth-Century Stage*,

ed. Kenneth Richards and Peter Thomson (London: Methuen, 1972), pp. 51–72.

32. Murphy, *Life of Garrick*, p. 231.

33. Davies, *Memoirs*, 1:63.

34. [Francis Gentleman], *The Dramatic Censor; or, Critical Companion* (London: J. Bell, 1770), 1:56.

35. Friedrich Justinian Freiherr von Gunderode, *Beschreibung einer Reise aus Deutschland durch einen Theil von Frankreich, England und Holland* (Breslau, 1783), cited in John Alexander Kelly, *German Visitors to English Theatres in the Eighteenth Century* (Princeton, N.J.: Princeton University Press, 1936), p. 61.

36. Reynolds, *Life and Times*, pp. 88–89.

37. *Lichtenberg's Visits*, p. 11.

38. *The Private Correspondence of David Garrick*, ed. James Boaden (London: H. Colburn & R. Bentley, 1831–32), 1:13.

39. *A New Variorum Edition of Shakespeare: Hamlet*, ed. Horace Howard Furness (1877; reprint, New York: American Scholar Publications, 1965), 1:104, n. 80.

40. *Lichtenberg's Visits*, p. 31.

41. [Frederick Pilon], *An Essay on the Character of Hamlet as Performed by Mr. Henderson*, 2nd ed. (London: W. Flexney, [1777], p. 13.

42. *Connoisseur*, 19 September 1754, p. 203, cited by J. Joklavich, "Hamlet in Shammy Shoes," *Shakespeare Quarterly* 3 (1952): 217.

43. James Boaden, *Memoirs of the Life of John Philip Kemble* (1825; reprint, New York: B. Blom, 1969), 1:100.

44. Pilon, *Essay on the Character of Hamlet*, p. 16.

45. Davies, *Dramatic Miscellanies*, 3:68–69.

46. *Lichtenberg's Visits*, p. 16.

47. Pilon, *Essay on the Character of Hamlet*, p. 18.

48. Murphy, *Life of Garrick*, p. 31; Davies, *Dramatic Miscellanies*, 3:79.

49. Thomas Wilkes, *A General View of the Stage* (London: J. Coote, 1759), p. 250.

50. Richard Cumberland, "Theatrical Retrospections," in *Oxberry's Dramatic Biography*, 4:228.

51. Murphy, *Life of Garrick*, p. 31; Davies, *Dramatic Miscellanies*, 3:88–89.

52. The fan business apparently originated with Betterton's successor, Robert Wilks (1665–1732); see Arthur Colby Sprague, *Shakespeare and the Actors* (Cambridge, Mass.: Harvard University Press, 1944), p. 157. For an account of Garrick's staging of this and other scenes, see Kalman A. Burnim's reconstruction in *David Garrick: Director* (Pittsburgh: University of Pittsburgh Press, 1961), pp. 164–66.

53. Davies, *Dramatic Miscellanies*, 3:93.

54. Garrick restored it in his alteration of 1772; see Stone, "Garrick's Alteration," p. 903. It was subsequently cut by Kemble, Kean, Macready, Irving and others; see Claris Glick, "*Hamlet* in the English Theater—Acting Texts from Betterton (1676) to Olivier (1963)," *Shakespeare Quarterly* 20 (1969): 25.

55. *Private Correspondence of Garrick* 1:14.

56. See *Bell's Edition*, 3:53 n.; Davies, *Dramatic Miscellanies*, 3:101.

57. Wilkes, *General View*, p. 250.

58. Davies, *Dramatic Miscellanies*, 3:115.

59. Ibid., 3:106.

60. Hugh Kelly, "Prologue to the Romance of an Hour," in *The Town and Country Magazine or Universal Repository*, December 1774, p. 665.

61. Davies, *Dramatic Miscellanies*, 3:108.

62. Gentleman, *Dramatic Censor*, 1:56.

63. See Sprague, *Shakespeare and the Actors*, p. 169.

64. *Private Correspondence of Garrick*, 1:11, 21.

65. Quoted in *New Variorum Edition*, 1:440, n. 213.

66. Bernard Grebanier makes this point in his *The Heart of Hamlet* (New York: Crowell, 1960), p. 242.

67. More, *Letters*, p. 46.

4

JOHN PHILIP KEMBLE

When David Garrick played Hamlet for the last time, on 30 May 1776, John Philip Kemble (1757–1823), aged nineteen, was still an impecunious provincial stroller.[1] His bid to occupy Garrick's vacated London throne lay seven years off.

In the meantime, John Henderson (1747–1785) held sway. Though himself a provincial actor at the time of Garrick's retirement (he was known as the "Bath Roscius"), Henderson quickly captured the esteem of the capital upon first appearing there in the early summer of 1777.[2] His Hamlet, modeled on Garrick's, opened at the Haymarket on 26 June; according to one reporter, it drew from the audience "the most loud and repeated applause probably ever given in a theatre to any actor, Mr. Garrick excepted."[3] In 1782, a year before Kemble's arrival on the London scene, the London *Daily Advertiser* called Hamlet Henderson's best tragic role and rated his performance in it superior to that of any living actor, although he was "a long way behind Garrick" (2 November).

Henderson was obviously the man of the hour, and in choosing Hamlet for his London debut, Kemble offered him something like a direct challenge. His first appearance in the role, at Drury Lane (Henderson was now at Covent Garden) on 30 September 1783, thus set the critics immediately to work recalculating the order of merit. The London *Public Advertiser* found that the place assigned Kemble's Hamlet "ought to be in the highest class, often equal to David Garrick's, and never . . . inferior to Henderson" (1 October 1783). A London *Morning Chronicle* correspondent was willing to go much further: "The *general* result was to me, that Mr. Kemble was the first actor of the part (Garrick not in the least excepted) I had ever seen" (4 October 1783). But most found it difficult to say whether the newcomer had excelled Henderson, let alone rivaled the great predecessor of them both. The writer for the *St. James's Chronicle* divided the laurels:

> To speak of him [Kemble] by comparison—he does not deliver so much from the heart, and to it, as Mr. Henderson; he does not so truly impersonate the character, but his colouring is fashioned with more grace, and his delineations are more articulate and critical. In level speaking, he is superior to every one; in passion, Mr. Henderson and others are superior to him. (2 October)

Things might have gone on in that way, with Kemble easily matching but by no means eclipsing the older, more established Henderson, had not fate taken a hand. In November 1785, firmly established in the first rank of his profession and at the height of his powers, Henderson died, the apparent victim of food poisoning. Kemble was left without a peer (save his sister) on the English stage. Until the appearance of Edmund Kean, nearly thirty years later, he would have no serious rival in the role of Hamlet.

That is to say, no serious *living* rival; for Garrick, short of stature though he was, cast a very long shadow in death, and it fell on Kemble just as it had on Henderson. As Walter Scott remarked many years later, "Kemble in representing [Hamlet] was to encounter at once the shade of the murthered King of Denmark, and, in the mind's eye of the audience, that of the lost Garrick."[4] In Kemble's third season an admiring reviewer complained that even to suggest that the newcomer "treads close upon [Garrick's] heels [would] by some be considered as the hyperbolical raptures of eulogy" (London *Morning Chronicle*, 25 November 1785).

Such is the lot of any young artist seeking to win favor with a public still under the spell of a genius only recently departed. But in Kemble's case the problem was exacerbated by the fact that his whole approach to the art of acting seemed nothing less than a repudiation of all that Garrick had stood for. Kemble seemed to turn the artistic clock all the way back to James Quin; Nature, crowned Queen by Garrick, was once again banished from the stage. It was an act of aesthetic conservatism that would make Kemble a highly controversial artist throughout his career.

Something of this emerges from the commentary already quoted. Other reviews of his debut performance drive the point home. He was repeatedly faulted for resorting to "stage trick" and for having "taken wonderful pains to overmaster Nature.''[5] Two years later the London *Morning Chronicle* claimed that he had now rid himself of ''affectation and pedantry,'' but that was by no means a widely held view, either in that year or at any point in Kemble's long career. As late as 1802, reviewing the Hamlet debut of George Frederick Cooke (1756–1812), the *St. James's Chronicle* could write: ''As to Mr. Cook's [sic] Hamlet, we have no opinion to give. If Mr. Kemble and Mr. Cook were to open Schools for Recitation, we might compare their pretentions—but neither of them *perform* Hamlet, if it was performed by Garrick'' (25–28 September 1802).

Leigh Hunt also thought Kemble ''rather a teacher of elocution than an actor, and not a good teacher on that account.''[6] In his *Critical Essays*, published in 1807, he could manage only a backhanded compliment:

He does not present one the idea of a man who grasps with the force of genius, but of one who overcomes by the toil of attention. He never rises and sinks as in the enthusiasm of the moment; his ascension though grand is careful, and when he sinks it is with preparation and dignity. There are actors who may occasionally please more, but not one who is paid a more universal or profound attention.[7]

Another close student of the stage, John Galt, also granted Kemble's formal style only a grudging admiration; of his performance in *Hamlet* he wrote: ''It was a great effort of a great artist, but I could never discern aught in it save the rehearsal of an endeavour.''[8]

That such descriptions of Kemble's style were accurate enough—whatever the justice of their disapproving tone—is clear from the fact that the actor himself spoke of his art in distinctly similar terms. To a friend of James Boswell's he reported—with pride, one supposes—that ''he always endeavoured to restrain any impulse which might interfere with his previous study of his part.''[9] How totally unswerving his commitment to that principle was is clear from a remark by Mrs. Siddons. ''My brother John,'' she told a friend, ''in his most impetuous bursts is always careful to avoid any discomposure of his dress or deportment; but in the whirlwind of passion I lose all thought of such matters.''[10] Leigh Hunt no doubt had precisely this distinction in mind when he declared flatly that Kemble ''was no more to be compared to his sister than stone is to flesh and blood.''[11]

But the studied style had its fervent admirers—enough of them to maintain Kemble as London's leading tragic actor for over a quarter of a century. These were the believers in the supremacy of Art over Nature. Their aesthetic creed was articulated by Sir Joshua Reynolds in his highly influential lectures to the Royal Academy. Art of the higher kind was to have no "immediate intercourse with particular nature." Excellence consisted in "an agreement of the parts among themselves, that one uniform whole may be produced." [12] An anonymous contributor to a volume honoring Kemble's retirement looked back with pleasure at the actor's steadfast adherence to those principles:

Nature may be copied too closely, and she will then disgust. . . . The truth is, that the advocates for natural representation, forget what Mr. Kemble always bore in mind, that it is the best part of Nature only, which should be faithfully given; that stooping to represent the common defects of common life, either in person or action, degrades the character and the art, and only makes that too palpable, which even in reality had better be concealed. [13]

Such was the taste of the orthodox, and Kemble's playing of Hamlet was expressly designed to appeal to it. He fixed on melancholy as the essence of the character and sought to give a generalized and idealized portrait of that single trait. [14] Sadness hung like a visible color over everything he said and did. Levity, anger, tenderness, intellectual pleasure—all were subordinated, suppressed, subsumed. For William Hazlitt, a leader of the opposing school, the approach was wrongheaded and the result was dull rigidity: "Mr. Kemble unavoidably fails in this character from a want of ease and variety. The character of Hamlet is made up of undulating lines; it has the yielding flexibility of 'a wave o' the sea.' Mr. Kemble plays it like a man in armour, with a determined inveteracy of purpose, in one undeviating straight line." [15]

Kemble's mournfulness was as lofty as it was everlasting. He was a stunningly handsome man, in the patrician, not to say Olympian, mold. He looked less a creature of common clay than a figure chiseled in marble, a statue by Michaelangelo miraculously "animated and inspired." [16] On the stage, he molded his gestures and movement in a manner harmonious with the sculptured beauty of his physical form and was thought by some to have left fleshly nature too far behind in the process. "The general error of his manner is stiffness," said the *London Magazine* in November 1783. "He neither walks the stage,

John Philip Kemble. The Graveyard Scene (V.i). Engraving by H. Dawe, from the painting by T. Lawrence, 1801. Harvard Theatre Collection.

nor turns his head, or moves his body with ease; his attitudes are graceful, but he is perpetually in one or another. This may please the *groundlings*, but must ever offend the lover of natural acting.''

In the management of his voice, Kemble also conveyed an impression of preternatural stateliness, of imperturbable gravity. Neither strong nor tunable, his voice was best suited to "the soft notes of the pathetic,'' to "the liquid and insinuating [tones] of sorrow,'' and Kemble held it to that narrow range, seldom venturing into the great and terrible passions which required an energy he did not possess.[17] He was, moreover, afflicted with chronic asthma, which "necessitated a prolonged and laborious indraught of his breath, and obliged him for the sake of distinctness to adopt an elaborate mode of utterance, enunciating every letter in every word.''[18] The result was a style of speaking so slow and langourous that it prompted even those who otherwise admired his portrayal to complain of a tendency to "drawl and whine.''[19]

Husbandry of the lungs seems also to have dictated a resort to frequent and lengthy pauses, although Kemble's general commitment to gravity was a major factor as well. Mrs. Crawford, an actress at Drury Lane in the 1780s, recalled later that "the Kemble school was so full of *paw* and *pause*, that, at first, the performers, thinking their new competitors had either lost their cues, or forgotten their parts, used frequently to prompt them.''[20] In response to criticism, Kemble worked to curtail the number and duration of his silences and by the beginning of his third season in the role had taken twenty-five minutes off his playing time merely by doing so. Many thought there was room for greater tightening still. Richard Sheridan archly proposed to his star performer that attendance might be increased if music were played during his pauses.

Kemble's seemingly interminable pauses provided grist for the mills of his detractors, but this habit had heavy competition in that respect from another of the actor's elocutionary idiosyncrasies, his pronunciation. Leigh Hunt, never at a loss for a *mot* when it came to pillorying the great tragedian, called attention to the grossness of Kemble's phonetic aberrations by pretending to dismiss them as trifling: "I could mispronounce much better than he,'' said Hunt, "when I was a mere infant.''[21]

So conspicuous a part of Kemble's stage speaking was his fondness for esoteric pronunciation that critics were kept busy compiling lists of his latest infractions. "What should be thrown away,'' said a writer for the London *World* in 1788, "is some overcurious, super-service-able finesse in verbal pronunciation—as *appetit*, for appetite—rhap-*so*dy, with the middle syllable made too much of, and two or three more" (1 October 1788). Over the years, abuses of this kind came to number considerably in excess of "two or three more," as we will see when we come to consider in sequence Kemble's handling of individual speeches.

These wrenchings of standard English phonemes were a result of Kemble's characteristically donnish approach to his art, a tendency so pronounced that a supporter could without irony label him a performer "more deeply scientific, more learned, and more laborious in his profession, than is probably to be found in the annals of the British theatre."[22] Another, much more substantial fruit of Kemble's scholarly labors was his wide employment of "new readings," a term that seems to have been coined expressly to describe Kemble's shockingly novel interpretations of lines whose "meaning," it was widely supposed, had been forever fixed by stage usage.[23] Although at first generally condemned for thus departing from tradition, Kemble eventually won acceptance, in principle, for the actor's right to go his own way, even though his own exercise of the right in particular instances was not always admired.

In addition to changing hallowed interpretations of many lines, Kemble also went against custom by substituting genuine Shakespearean language for many of the playhouse emendations which had accumulated over the preceding century. Thus, for example, Hamlet was given back his "inky cloak" and allowed to speak of the "native hue" rather than the "healthful face" of resolution, Horatio heard "whirling" not "windy" words, and Hamlet's cracking heart was at last relieved of its spurious "cordage."[24] On the larger textual questions of cutting and arranging, Kemble showed himself considerably more orthodox. Garrick's radical alteration enjoyed a brief vogue after its author's retirement, but in April 1780 John Bannister (1760–1836) restored the traditional eighteenth-century text at Drury Lane; when Kemble joined the company three years later he followed suit.

There is something surprising in this. As we have seen, the Hamlet of this text was essentially a vigorous man of action, whereas Kemble's Prince was universally perceived as a man so weighed down with melancholy and so fastidiously formal that he seemed scarcely capable of crossing a room without first taking thought as to the efficacy and propriety of the act. Apparently we must conclude that Kemble in some measure acted "against" his text, conveying an image of the character more through the awesome quietism of his manner than by word or deed. In addition, however, he did make certain modest cuts of his own in the text to bring it more into harmony with the unearthly aloofness in which he sought to clothe the character. But these are best noted as we follow Kemble's step-by-step movement through the play.

At one of his early performances, if not at his debut, Kemble created a startling effect upon his first entrance by appearing in a costume radically different from the modern black velvet court dress regularly worn by stage Hamlets since the time of Thomas Betterton.[25] Kemble wore instead a "period" costume, composed of elements fashionable in Tudor and Caroline times. A recent writer on the subject has described it as "an Old English fantasy of somewhat Romantic inspiration: doublet, Baldric, trunk-hose, tights, and a lace collar falling open in proto-Byronic disarray."[26] Oddly, Kemble wore with this comparatively casual attire accessories more appropriate to court dress: the Order of the Elephant and the Order of the Garter. It was no doubt these innovations in costuming that led Kemble to restore "inky cloak" for "mourning suit" while at the same time cutting "customary suits of solemn black," the latter phrase—he must have thought—having been too long associated in the popular imagination with the customary stage dress.

The first soliloquy (I.ii.129–59), as Kemble spoke it, was an excellent example of his textual reforms. He said "self-slaughter" not "self-murder," brought back the wonderfully expressive "flat," which Garrick had unaccountably let drop, and even had the temerity to say "might not beteem," which as far back as William Davenant had yielded place to "permitted not." He was also the first since Davenant altered the text for stage use to speak the lines "that was to this Hyperion to a satyr" and "Heaven and earth! Must I remember." But despite all these gains in authenticity, some of Shakespeare's language was still deemed unsuitable for modern ears; no audience since Shakespeare's own had heard "A beast that wants discourse of reason / Would have mourned longer" (150–51) or "O most wicked speed: to post / With such dexterity to incestuous sheets" (156–57); Kemble preserved that tradition. His delivery of the soliloquy had all the earmarks of his characteristic style: it was addressed directly to the house, he "linger[ed] for some seconds on the 'oh!' with a strongly tremulous cadence,''[27] and the whole was "given with that scientific union of elocution and thought, which marks the finished labours of this actor" (London *Times*, 13 September 1796). It is curious that he was chided in an early review for saying "un*weed*ed" instead of following custom in putting the accent on the first syllable;[28] it appears that on this point it was Kemble's predecessors who were given to excessive nicety in the underscoring of meanings.

In the dialogue following the soliloquy, however, Kemble revealed himself as a nonpareil in the pursuit of fine points. With the entrance of Horatio and the sentinels, new readings began to follow close on one another's heels in a dazzling display of erudition. To Horatio's deferential salutation, "Your poor servant ever," Kemble replied, "Sir, my good friend; I'll change *that* name with you" (I.ii.162–63), instead of "*change* that name." An instant later he answered Marcellus' greeting "My good lord!" with "I am very glad to see you," but made a new point by delivering the next three words, "Good even, sir," to Bernardo.[29] New also was his sarcastic tone on "We'll teach you to drink deep ere you depart" (I.ii.175), delivered "as if glancing at the manners of the King 'draining his draughts of Rhenish down' '' (London *Public Advertiser*, 7 October 1783).

To these innovations—all introduced at his debut performance—he later added another, suggested by John Taylor, whose account of the incident vividly illustrates Kemble's scholarly cast of mind. Advised by Taylor that the line "Thrift, thrift, Horatio . . . . " (I.ii.180) should be given not angrily, the traditional reading, but as "ironical praise," Kemble "immediately took down a Polyglot Dictionary, and examined the derivation and accepted meaning of the word thrift in all the languages, and finding that it was always given a commendatory sense, he thanked me, and always after gave the passage in the manner I had suggested.[30]

His restoration of "dearest foe" for "direst foe," in the same speech, occasioned comment; one critic thought that, though "justified by the best copies," it was done "on principles too remote for a popular audience" (London *Public Advertiser*, 7 October 1783). But the change in this scene which triggered the largest explosion of discussion came in Hamlet's close questioning of his informants. The line "Did you not speak to it?" (I.ii.214) Kemble addressed exclusively to Horatio, and he emphasized "you" so as to separate him from the others. The

London *Public Advertiser* reported that the new reading was "received with approbation," but an anonymous author, writing six years later, declared that "the question . . . hath occasioned as great dispute in the dramatic, as Mr. Fox's India Bill . . . hath in the political world."[31] The same writer went on to offer an elaborate defense of the reading, arguing that as a friend of Hamlet, Horatio had naturally known the dead King better than Marcellus and Bernardo—mere soldiers in his service—and was therefore much more likely to be able to communicate with the King's perturbed spirit. Whether that was Kemble's own reasoning is not known, but it is likely. James Boaden says that Kemble once asked Johnson's opinion and was told: "To be sure, sir,—YOU should be strongly marked. I told Garrick so, long since, but Davy never could see it."[32]

Intellectually piquant as all these fresh morsels of interpretation doubtless were, they did not in themselves make up the full store of Kemble's appeal in the scene. One critic, H. Martin, was deeply impressed by the way he played "My father—methinks I see my father" and the lines immediately following (184–212): "The low tone of affection, the fixed eye of a visionary, the tremor and sinking of the voice, carried it to every heart. His perplexity when the tale of Horatio and Marcellus began—his fixed mute attention—not a finger moved—I doubt if he breathed even—I am sure I did not, for fear of disturbing him."[33] Boaden was moved by his tearful rendering of "He was a man, take him for all in all," preferring it to the customary tone of "stoical firmness."[34]

Kemble began the Ghost scene by pacing anxiously backward and forward.[35] This was new, and natural, but it was soon followed by something old and artificial. Kemble reproduced Garrick's terrified start on seeing the Ghost, except that he stood alone instead of being supported by his friends. As had been the case even in Garrick's day, there were those who found this maneuver painfully stagey and longed to see it abandoned. In his review of a Kemble performance in 1797, the critic for the London *Courier and Evening Gazette* devoted nearly a third of his space to the topic, pointing out the absurdity of the "elegant attitude" so carefully constructed by Kemble and every other Hamlet he had seen and recommending instead that Hamlet "remain transfixed, and, as it were, petrified with astonishment and horror" (6 October 1797). But despite such criticism, Garrick's start proved to be one of the most durable traditions of acting the role and was still being deplored by reviewers nearly a century later.

Kemble introduced more textual restorations and new readings in the scene: "I do not set my life at a pin's fee" (I.iv.65) finally replaced Davenant's anemic emendation "I do not value my life." Immediately following, Kemble said, "And for my soul, what CAN it do to *that*?" Boaden explained and praised the change: "Garrick here, with great quickness, said, 'What can it do to THAT?' There is, I think, more impression in Kemble's manner of putting it. In Garrick it was a truism asserted; in Kemble not merely asserted, but enjoyed."[36]

In the ensuing struggle with his companions, Kemble cut "By heaven, I'll make a ghost of him that lets me" (I.iv.85)—probably with a view to downplaying the choleric side of Hamlet's character; in Kemble's conception it was a rather fainthearted Hamlet who followed the Ghost:

The beckoning of the spirit called on him for decision—it was MADE, but not without a struggle. He shook off the restraint desperately; but at liberty, he did not march on with a bravado, as if to say, *You* fear a Ghost—*I* do not— see, I follow it.—No, he felt a nameless horror; but the dear shape it wore took off the worse sensations that any other form would have excited. *Step by step*, slow, trembling, yet eager, he followed; and when he uttered, *I'll go no further!* it was because he could not proceed—his limbs were all nervous—he had hardly power to give voice even to that sentence.[37]

Kemble illustrated the absence of bravado at this moment by making a different use of his sword than Garrick and others had done; instead of pointing toward the phantom, as if in warning that the bearer stood ready to defend himself vigorously, Kemble "retained it in his right hand, but turned his left toward the spirit, and drooped the weapon after him. . . . To retain it unconsciously, showed how completely he was absorbed by the dreadful mystery he was exploring."[38]

Kemble was censured for "making use of too much action" in this scene, but one defender, while admitting that such criticism was reasonable, argued that "his countenance is so highly expressive of that proper indignation against the murder of his father that we are inclined to make some allowance."[39] One new piece of action in particular set the critics to wagging their fingers. On "Remember thee?" (I.v.95), as the Ghost descended to the cellarage, Kemble threw himself down on one knee. The London *Public Advertiser* (7 October 1783) dismissed the business as obvious claptrap, but Boaden later defended it on the ground that "it suitably marked the filial reverence of Hamlet, and the solemnity of the engagement he had contracted."[40] Martin, though he did not credit the kneeling specifically, also found a ritual solemnity in Kemble's vow to remember, such that "all who heard it must have felt it was registered in Heaven."[41]

Kemble eliminated the reference to Hamlet's "tables" (I.v.107–9), thereby establishing a precedent which was followed through most of the nineteenth century. On "Yes, by Saint Patrick, but there is, Horatio, / And much offence too" (I.v.136–37), Kemble seemed about to confide in Horatio, but broke off abruptly "upon the pressing forward of Marcellus to partake the communication"; he thus made a sharp distinction between a trusted intimate and a mere retainer. "Strange to tell it," said the London *Public Advertiser*, "this distinction, which as the players call it, *tells* most forcibly, Garrick overlooked!" (7 October 1783).

Kemble did not give ocular proof of Hamlet's diseased wit by letting his hosiery droop; he no doubt considered the business too undignified. He did, however, allow his hair, which he wore powdered, to "flow disheveled in front and over the shoulders in the scenes of feigned distraction."[42] In the first of these scenes, where he is boarded by Polonius (II.ii.171ff.), Kemble punctuated his reading of the "satirical rogue's" slanderous remarks on old age by tearing the leaf from the book; "Why, we know not" the *Public Advertiser* superciliously remarked (7 October 1783).

He greeted Rosencrantz and Guildenstern with an air of gaiety,[43] or as much of that quality as he was capable of projecting; it was not his forte. Scott wrote, "Mirth, when he exhibited it, never exceeded a species of gaiety chastened with gravity."[44] His innate gravity also dictated great restraint in the depiction of Hamlet's simulated transformation. One critic found Kemble so lacking in the requisite "wildness" in this scene with the courtiers that he could not "help feeling some degree of fear lest those gentlemen should discover the madness of their young Prince to be merely assumed."[45] But Kemble's godlike self-possession could also be a powerful positive force; Martin confessed that he "could have almost worshipped him" for the dignity and refinement of tone with which he rebuked the two spies on "though by your smiling you seem to say so" (II.ii.310).[46]

There were more new readings in the scene. Garrick's Hamlet may have had to wonder what "mobled queen" (II.ii.502) meant. Kemble's, characteristically, *knew*; he spoke the line in simple sympathy for the lady thus described. He said "O Jephthah, judge of Israel, what a treasure *hadst* thou!" (404) and "What's Hecuba to him, or he to Hecuba / That he should *weep* for her?" (559–60) and was chided for not following John Henderson, who accented "thou" and "her" respectively (London *Public Advertiser*, 7 October 1783).

Kemble also indulged his taste for exotic pronunciation. "Beard" in "Com'st thou to beard me in Denmark?" (423–24) became "berd." "Caviare" and "general" (437), it was said, were "syllabicated in a style and tune so perfectly *French*, and consequently so exceedingly remote from the genius of English melody, as to jar upon [the] ears with discord."[47] At the performance Ludwig Tieck attended in 1817, Kemble won "a general burst of applause throughout the house" for the natural way in which he corrected Hamlet's faulty memory on " 'Tis not so, it begins with Pyrrhus" (451), but Tieck considered the reading a rare flower in the desert of Kemble's usual style of delivery: "Indeed, when one has been listening for a length of time to a slow, measured, wailing rhythm, regularly interrupted by considerable pauses, and by a succession of highly pitched inflections, one is quite taken by surprise on hearing once more the tones of nature, and the manner of everyday conversation."[48]

Kemble cut the first thirty-seven lines of the "rogue and peasant slave" soliloquy, taking it up only at "I have heard / That guilty creatures sitting at a play . . . " (II.ii.588). In this he much outdid his predecessors, who regularly retained Hamlet's comparison of himself with the player, cutting only five and a half lines, beginning "Remorseless, treacherous, lecherous. . . . "It is impossible to say what prompted Kemble's radical editing, but it may well have been a desire to conserve his strength; this is Hamlet's longest speech in the play, and it is followed almost immediately by the "To be or not to be" soliloquy and the strenuous scene with Ophelia. The part of the soliloquy Kemble did speak seems to have provoked little comment, save for one complaint about "ranting and stamping the foot"[49] on "I'll have grounds / More relative than this" (II.ii.603–4). On the concluding line, Kemble employed a "double sweep," a bit of formalist acting in which the hand is drawn across the body from the opposite shoulder, thrust straight up into the air and then carried back down and across to its original position.[50]

"To be or not to be . . . " (III.i.55–87) Kemble spoke without alteration but with many characteristic touches in delivery. He was praised for the "long sostenuto" with which he gave "Perchance to dre—a—m" (London *Public Advertiser*, 7 October 1783). The London *Morning Chronicle* (30 September 1783) scolded him for putting the emphasis on "pause" instead of on "must" in "must give us pause," but surely the actor was right and the critic wrong in this instance. On the other hand, the critic no doubt did well to find fault with Kemble for reading "with a bare bodkin?" with his voice "raised, as in an immediate interrogation." There was also a typical fillip of pedantry: "Sicklied" was pronounced with three syllables. As for the overall tone of the soliloquy, the *Chronicle* reviewer thought that "something of more depth of thought, reflection, rumination, . . . seemed wanted" but concluded that he had never seen any player "more touching and pathetic" (4 October 1783). Another observer accused Kemble of uttering the great soliloquy "with a solemn declamatory accent, like a sermon on a Fast-day" and of reducing Hamlet to "a dull discourser on a stale general moral, a grim debater on the pro and con of suicide" (London *Examiner*, 20 March 1814) but this harsh judgment was delivered by a reviewer in the course of praising Kean's playing of the same speech and should no doubt be weighed accordingly.

The same writer, on the same occasion, described with barely contained rage Kemble's playing of the nunnery scene:

Then in what manner did he treat the gentle Ophelia? What threatening of fists, what ferocity of voice, what stamping of feet, what clattering of doors? Had there been one spark of chivalry left among us, the pit and boxes would have sprung on the stage, and dashed to the earth the insolent intruder, who could so insult a lovely and harmless woman. But, alas, the fashionable in the boxes who hate their wives, and the honest simpletons in the pit who are afraid of theirs, seemed to rejoice at this triumph over the daughter of Polonius, as if it had avenged their own particular wrongs.

Shrill as this account evidently is, it describes Kemble's basic approach to the scene accurately enough; as Thomas Holcroft noticed, in 1805, "to persecute, nay to bully, Ophelia" was the established stage practice.[51] As we have seen, Garrick made of the scene a sort of palimpsest, with Hamlet's erased love dimly visible beneath the wild frenzy of his manner. A few thought they perceived a similar layering of emotion in Kemble's portrayal. A reviewer in 1799 praised "the suppressed attachment to Ophelia" (London *Morning Chronicle*, 20 September 1799). But it was probably not a strongly marked feature of this interpretation; Leigh Hunt, speaking of Kemble's acting generally, declared flatly: "Of the passion of love he can express nothing; the reason is obvious; love from its dependent nature must always . . . betray an expression of tender feebleness, and such an expression is unknown to Mr. Kemble's countenance."[52] The scene also contained a new reading; on "You jig and amble, and you lisp" (III.i.144) Kemble pronounced the last word "lithp." Even Boaden thought it "a refinement below him."

At his debut performance Kemble omitted Hamlet's instructions to the players (III.ii.1–45), but he restored the lines the next night, having been instructed by the London *Morning Herald* that they were "well worth his retaining, as the speeches are by no means derogatory to his merits" (1 October 1783). He spoke them regularly thereafter but might have been better advised not to; a critic writing in 1807 found that Hamlet's remarks on the art of acting *were* derogatory to Kemble's merits:

The [instructions to the players] did *not* flow "trippingly on the tongue"; and [were] far from being free from the customary defects of theatrical recitation. It had several false emphases—"I had as lieve [*sic*] the *town* crier spoke my lines"—"any thing so overdone *is from* the purpose of playing"—"have so strutted *and* bellowed," etc.—(we are not sure whether this last was not a purposed imitation of one of the customary defects of a rival actor).[53]

One feature of Kemble's studied and laborious style of delivery was an "occasional long whining inflection upon unimportant syllables." Thus in Hamlet's moving tribute to Horatio (given in full) Kemble said, "Thou art ee'enn as just a man" (III.ii.54).[54] But he won much praise for saying, in the same speech, "heart *of* heart," instead of following Garrick's reading, "heart of *heart*."[55]

Kemble seems to have restored, on his opening night, Hamlet's lubricious dialogue with Ophelia, beginning "I mean, my head upon your lap?" (III.ii.114), but abandoned it immediately thereafter. The London *Chronicle* correspondent, in the course of listing changes between Kemble's first and second appearances, exclaimed, "Oh, how glad I am to see that they have now left out that shocking indecency, when Hamlet talks to Ophelia about country matters!" (4 October 1783). From the same source we learn that Kemble tried "lolling on Ophelia's lap" at his first appearance but reverted, on the next night, to the customary practice of stretching out at her feet. Once installed there, he followed another custom as well: "He took her fan, and gallanted it with such easy grace; but soon he turned it to use—speaking to her, his eyes were scrutinising the dark soul of his uncle—behind its sticks he sometimes artfully shaded his observation.[56] John Finlay supplies further details of Kemble's playing at this crucial juncture: "Whenever the eye of the king would fall on Hamlet in any of the questions which he put to him, the face of Hamlet was always towards Ophelia, and he answered the questions as to the name and plot of the play carelessly, as if they were interrupting his situation, and as if he took no interest in the play farther than he had casually seen it."[57]

Boaden too thought that Kemble gave Claudius the argument of the play "in the finest manner possible . . . beyond all praise" and the London *Public Advertiser* (7 October 1783) called it "consummate art." These two critics disagreed, however, on Kemble's new reading of "Come, the croaking raven doth bellow for revenge" (III.ii.254), the latter contending that it should be given in Garrick's way, "as a kind of Anthropophaginian rant to the murderer," the former convinced that Kemble was correct in making it "a reflection of Hamlet applicable to his own case."[58]

Although it was apparently unremarkable in his early appearances, Kemble in time made Hamlet's exultation over the exposed guilt of Claudius (III.ii.271ff.) one of the most powerful moments of his performance. According to an account in the *True Briton* (25 October 1796), "that passage that seemed to make the chief impression on the audience . . . was the exclamation that followed the proof of the King's guilt. . . . It is difficult to describe the kind of *agonized triumph* that Kemble expressed on this occasion. It electrified the audience, who seemed to think they could harly applaud him enough." Martin, writing in 1802, also felt the galvanic force of the scene: "When the king rose and departed, [Kemble] absolutely electrified me with the passion of his conviction!—he threw himself into Horatio's arms with a desperation, an agony, a groan that tore his very heart. For my part, I felt as if his sorrow was my own."[59]

The scene drew to a close with further evidence of Kemble's textual tinkering. In the episode with the recorder (III.ii.350–56) he made another of those nice discriminations between characters that seemed to fascinate him. Having twice invited the hapless Guildenstern to "play upon this pipe," he made his third request to Rosencrantz, pointing the line "I do beseech *you*" and executing a "stately march" across the stage to him for that purpose, the following line, "I know no touch of it, my lord," having been transferred from Guildenstern to his school fellow. Boaden thought it "a poor thing, and indeed chilling what was to follow: too formal, in a word, for the condition of Hamlet's mind."[60] But the closing moments also saw a restoration: "Backed like a weasel" instead of the long accepted "Black."

Kemble followed custom in expunging Hamlet's "horrid hent" meditation over the kneeling Claudius (III.iii.73–96) and was no doubt fully in tune with the sentiments of the time in doing so. Hazlitt's desperate strategy of calling the speech "a refinement in malice, which is in truth only an excuse for [Hamlet's] own want of resolution,"[61] suggests that even those who possessed the highest degree of literary sophistication were still having trouble with Hamlet's hellish sentiments here.

Having cut the soliloquy, Kemble went his predecessors one better and also cut the incident which prompts it—Claudius' soliloquy and bootless attempt to pray (III.iii.36–72). Kemble thus went directly to Gertrude's closet, his offstage movement being covered only by the speeches in which Claudius declares his resolve to send Hamlet to England (III.iii.1–8), and Polonius reveals his fatal scheme to spy from behind the arras (III.iii.27–35).

Kemble made his first point in the closet scene with the dispatching of the busy counselor; he gave "Nay, I know not, is it the King?" (III.iv.26) with a "smile of exultation," an innovation which, it was claimed, Johnson had "sanctioned by his approbation" (London *Morning Chronicle*, 19 November 1785). One observer thought it more a grin than a smile and considered it more suitable to "the soul of Nero than to the pigeon-liver'd frame" of Hamlet (London *Public Advertiser*, 7 October 1783), but "the universal plaudits of the audience were not to be resisted" (*St. James's Chronicle*, 2 October 1783).

Kemble took from his pocket two miniatures for use in the "counterfeit presentment of two brothers" speech (III.iv.53ff.) and pointed his detestation of one and worship of the other by "flinging away, in the extremity of his indignation, the King's picture" and "pressing his father's portrait to his lips."[62] The business won great favor, though the *London Magazine* found him guilty of "*the most ridiculous grimaces . . .* when turning his eyes towards his uncle's picture" (November 1783).

The Ghost seems to have cut a ludicrous figure on occasion and to have made Hamlet himself look foolish; Tieck reported in 1817: "The Ghost with great complacency enters by one door, totters across the stage, and, not looking particularly either at Hamlet or the Queen, goes off through the opposite door, which closes behind him, while Hamlet, inaptly enough, hurries after him, and is only kept back by the door slamming in his face."[63] It may be that Kemble's part in this near-buffoonery was the result of declining powers; at any rate, Martin, who saw a performance some fifteen years earlier, paints a strikingly different picture: "I cannot describe what I felt when he said, 'He is gone, even now, out at the portal,' and threw himself passionately, yet fondly forward [on the floor?], as if to catch and detain the form so revered, so lamented."[64]

Kemble played the remainder of the scene, a mere twenty-seven lines in his version, with two new touches. Tate Wilkinson disliked one, admired the other: "When I see Mr. Kemble kneel to his mother . . . and *kiss her hand* (or *neck*, if he can reach it) with all the enthusiasm of filial love and duty, my idea of propriety is somewhat staggered, though the acting is super excellent, when in a short page he refuses to accept any token of love or filial affection from his parent."[65] Boaden took a different view of the kneeling, arguing that it was a natural posture for an affectionate son seeking to awaken his mother's finer feelings, but he joined Wilkinson in admiring Kemble's rejection of a proffered blessing from Gertrude, a point the actor made by saying," And when you are desirous to *be* blessed, I'll blessing *beg* of you," rather than the standard (used by Henderson) "And when you are desirous to be *blest*, I'll blessing beg of *you*." Boaden interpreted Kemble's reading as an example of Hamlet's "amiable self-delusion."[66] The overall impact of the scene must have been decidedly favorable. Thomas Davies, who saw Kemble's performance when his *Dramatic Miscellanies* was already in press and could therefore add only a brief account of it, singled out the closet scene for special emphasis: "In the impassioned scene, between Hamlet and his Mother, . . . Kemble's emphasis and action, however different from those of all former Hamlets we have seen, bore the genuine marks of solid judgement and exquisite taste. I never saw an audience more deeply affected, or more generously grateful to the actor who had so highly raised their passions."[67]

In his verbal sparring with Claudius in the scene where he is sent into England (IV.iii), Kemble scored a point with another delicately marked emphasis, this one borrowed from Henderson. He said: "Man and wife is *one* flesh" (IV.iii.52). The London *Public Advertiser* admiringly declared the reading "quite syllogistical" and asked, "How came it to escape Garrick?" (7 October 1783).

Boaden reports that "in the grave scene [Kemble] never entirely satisfied himself: he was too studiously graceful; and, under his difficulties, seemingly too much at ease." Boaden thought he lacked pathos on the line "What, the fair Ophelia!" (V.i.243) and so instructed him in Henderson's reading of it, whereupon "he readily came into the manner of his predecessor."[68]

Kemble made the fencing scene (V.ii.226ff.) the occasion for a display of elegant princely condescension and was sharply reprimanded for his pains. The London *Morning Chronicle* thought there was altogether too much "form and ceremony between Hamlet and Laertes" and pointed out that "the Prince is certainly to conduct himself with courteousness but he is not to play the part of a dancing-master" (1 October 1783). Thus schooled and chastised, Kemble used fewer bows on his second appearance, but a returning spectator found him still too obsequious and accused him of mistaking "servility" for "civility" (London *Morning Chronicle*, 4 October 1783). There was criticism too of the cool, graceful, unimpassioned manner in which Kemble made his early passes and parries in the duel, but his defenders pointed out that, prior to the revelation of Laertes' treachery, such deportment is precisely right for a man of breeding engaged in the gentlemanly art of fence.[69]

At the performance Tieck saw in June 1817, Kemble thrust the poisoned chalice to the King's mouth on "Here, thou incestuous, murderous, damned Dane" (V.ii.324). The business was new to Tieck, but he judged it "the right thing."[70] Kemble had evidently introduced it only recently; certainly it was not used prior to 1804.[71]

Kemble displeased some with his manner of dying. The *St. James's Chronicle* said it was "too much in the straining, stiffening, floundering style of theatrical expiration" (2 October 1783). This is a surprising observation in that it makes Kemble's death throes sound uncharacteristically naturalistic. There is a hint of natural acting also in the London *Public Advertiser*'s praise of "the snatching, elevated tone" Kemble employed on "this fell sergeant, death" (7 October 1783).

Kemble played Hamlet for the last time on 16 June 1817 and retired from the stage a week later with a performance of *Coriolanus*. He was sixty years old. Hazlitt memorialized the event for the London *Times* and reported that Kemble

played the part as well as he ever did—with as much freshness and vigour. There was no abatement of spirit and energy—none of grace and dignity. It is mere cant to say that Mr. Kemble has quite fallen off of late—that he is not what he was: he may have fallen off in the opinion of some jealous admirers because he is no longer in exclusive possession of the stage: but in himself he has not fallen off a jot.[72]

There was probably some sacrifice of truth to graciousness in Hazlitt's assessment of Kemble's powers, but he was surely correct in part in claiming that Kemble only *seemed* to be falling off because he no longer stood alone at the summit. No new Coriolanus had emerged to challenge Kemble's preeminence in that role, but a new Hamlet, as different from Kemble's as Kemble's was from Garrick's, had been exciting the town for three seasons. This was Edmund Kean. In his concluding assessment of what Kemble's acting had and had not been, Hazlitt seems to have had the contrasting image of Kean clearly in mind, and his valedictory for the retiring master may thus serve as introduction to his successor:

We think the distinguishing excellence of [Kemble's] acting may be summed up in one word—*intensity*; in seizing upon one feeling or idea, in insisting upon it, in never letting it go, and in working it up with a certain graceful consistency, and conscious grandeur of conception, to a very high degree of pathos or sublimity. If he had not the unexpected bursts of nature and genius, he had all the regularity of art; if he did not display the tumult of conflict of opposite passions in the soul, he gave the deepest and most permanent interest to the uninterrupted progress of individual feeling; and in embodying a high ideal of certain characters . . . he was the most excellent actor of his times.[73]

NOTES

1. See Herschel Baker, *John Philip Kemble: The Actor in His Theatre* (Cambridge, Mass.: Harvard University Press, 1942), p. 28. Kemble was born on 1 February 1757; he died on 26 February 1823.

2. Joseph Knight, "John Henderson," *Dictionary of National Biography* (1885–1890; reprint, Oxford: Oxford University Press, 1921–22).

3. *General Evening Post*, 28 June 1777. Similar comparisons with Garrick appeared in the London *Morning Post* (27 June 1777) and the *St. James's Chronicle* (1 July 1777). With the opening of the regular winter season Henderson appeared again as Hamlet at Drury Lane and was again very highly praised; see the London *Morning Post* (1 October 1777).

4. Walter Scott, review of James Boaden's *Memoirs of the Life of John Philip Kemble*, *Quarterly Review* 34 (1826): 211.

5. *The London Magazine*, quoted in *Oxberry's Dramatic Biography* (London: G. Virtue, 1825–27) 2:173–74; London *Morning Herald*, 1 October 1783; London *Morning Post*, 1 and 3 October 1783.

6. Leigh Hunt, *Autobiography* (1850), quoted in *Dramatic Essays [by] Leigh Hunt*, ed. William Archer and Robert W. Lowe (London: W. Scott, 1894), p. xxiii.

7. Quoted in *Dramatic Essays*, p. 11.

8. John Galt, *The Lives of the Players* (London: H. Colburn and R. Bentley, 1831), p. 311.

9. *Boswell's Life of Johnson*, ed. G. Birbeck Hill, rev. ed. by L. F. Powell (Oxford: Oxford University Press, 1934), 4:244.

10. Quoted by William Charles Macready, *Reminiscences, Diaries and Letters*, ed. Sir Frederick Pollock (London: Trübner, 1875), p. 112.

11. Hunt, *Autobiography*, quoted in *Dramatic Essays*, 1:xxiii.

12. Joshua Reynolds, "Discourse XIII," in *Discourses on Art*, ed. Robert R. Wark (San Marino, Calif.; Stanford University Press, 1959), pp. 234–35. The "discourse" was delivered on 11 December 1786.

13. *An Authentic Narrative of Mr. Kemble's Retirement from the Stage* (London: J. Miller, 1817), p. xxvi.

14. Ludwig Tieck is quoted to this effect by Theodore Martin in "An Eyewitness of John Kemble," *The Nineteenth Century* 7 (1880): 284; Tieck's remarks were originally published in *Dramaturgische Blätter* (1826). For a similar view, see Galt, *Lives of the Players*, p. 313.

15. William Hazlitt, "Characters of Shakespeare's Plays" (1817), in *The*

Complete Works of William Hazlitt, ed. P. P. Howe (London: J. M. Dent, 1930), 4:237.

16. John Adolphus, *Memoirs of John Bannister, Comedian* (London: R. Bentley, 1839), 2:243–44.

17. *The European Magazine and London Review*, October 1783, p. 309; London *Morning Post*, 2 October 1783.

18. Macready, *Reminiscences*, p. 112.

19. *London Magazine*, quoted in Oxberry, *Okberry's Dramatic Biography*, 2:174.

20. Quoted in Frederic Reynolds, *The Life and Times of Frederic Reynolds* (London: H. Colburn, 1826), p. 150.

21. Hunt, *Dramatic Essays*, 11.

22. Oxberry, *Oxberry's Dramatic Biography*, 4:229.

23. Boaden, *Memoirs*, 1:93.

24. Kemble published seven slightly different acting versions of the play, in 1796, 1797, 1800, 1804, 1808, 1811, and 1814. In discussing Kemble's alterations, I refer throughout to the edition of 1800, reprinted in 1971.

25. Boaden (*Memoirs*, 1:104) claimed that Kemble did not abandon the traditional costume until sometime after his debut, but that claim has been disputed by Raymond Mander and Joseph Mitchenson ("Hamlet Costumes: A Correction," *Shakespeare Survey* 11 [1958]: 124). More recently, Raymond J. Pentzell has adduced evidence in support of Boaden's view ("Kemble's Hamlet Costume," *Theatre Survey* 13 [1972]: 84).

26. Pentzell, "Kemble's Hamlet Costume," pp. 82–83.

27. Tieck, "Eye-witness," p. 284.

28. Boaden, *Memoirs*, 1:94.

29. Ibid., 1:94, 95.

30. *Personal Reminiscences by O'Keeffe, Kelly and Taylor*, ed. Richard Henry Stoddard (New York: Scribner, Armstrong, 1875), p. 226.

31. *A Short Criticism of the Performance of Hamlet by John Philip Kemble* (London: n.p., 1789), p. 8.

32. Boaden, *Memoirs*, 1:97.

33. [H. Martin], *Remarks on John Kemble's Performance of Hamlet and Richard III* (London: G. & J. Robinson, 1802), p. 4.

34. Boaden, *Memoirs*, 1:96.

35. Promptbook (*HAM*, 11) in the Shakespeare Centre Library, marked by Kemble and used by him at Covent Garden during the last ten years of his career, 1807–1817. Most of the Kemble notations for Hamlet refer to routine movements; the promptbook is also marked in various hands for actors who followed Kemble in the period 1817–1837.

36. Boaden, *Memoirs*, 1:97.

37. Martin, *Remarks*, p. 5.

38. Boaden, *Memoirs*, 1:98.

39. *Short Criticism*, p. 14.

40. Boaden, *Memoirs*, 1:98.

41. Martin, *Remarks*, p. 5.

42. Boaden, *Memoirs*, 1:104.

43. Ibid., 1:99.

44. Scott, *Quarterly Review* 34 (1826): 212.

45. *Short Criticism*, p. 11.

46. Martin, *Remarks*, p. 6.

47. Unidentified clipping, dated 1807, in the Enthoven Collection, Victoria and Albert Museum (hereafter "Enthoven clipping").

48. Tieck, "Eye-witness," pp. 284–85.

49. Enthoven clipping.

50. Gilbert Austin, *Chironomia; or, A Treatise on Rhetorical Delivery* (1806), p. 343; cited in Arthur Colby Sprague, *Shakespeare and the Actors* (Cambridge, Mass.: Harvard University Press, 1944), p. 149.

51. Thomas Holcroft, "Art of Acting," in *The Theatrical Recorder* (1805; reprint, New York: B. Franklin, 1968), 2:412.

52. Hunt, *Dramatic Essays*, p. 4.

53. Enthoven clipping.

54. Ibid.

55. Boaden, *Memoirs*, 1:101.

56. Martin, *Remarks*, p. 7.

57. John Finlay, *Miscellanies* (Dublin: n.p., 1835), p. 226. The play was performed on a raised stage up center, with Gertrude and Claudius seated down left and Hamlet at Ophelia's feet down right, directly opposite Claudius. See *Hamlet* in *John Philip Kemble Promptbooks*, ed. Charles H. Shattuck (Charlottsville: University Press of Virginia, 1974), vol. 2, illus. opposite p. 44.

58. Boaden, *Memoirs*, 1:102.

59. Martin, *Remarks*, p. 7.

60. Boaden, *Memoirs*, 1:102. The recorder itself Kemble obtained, following established practice, "by stepping behind the scenes to fetch it for the occasion" (London *Morning Chronicle*, 30 September 1783).

61. Hazlitt, "Characters," p. 234.

62. *Short Criticism*, p. 17.

63. Tieck, "Eye-witness," p. 294.

64. Martin, *Remarks*, p. 7.

65. Tate Wilkinson, *The Wandering Patentee* (York: Author, 1795), 2:6.

66. Boaden, *Memoirs*, 1:103.

67. Thomas Davies, *Dramatic Miscellanies* (London: Author, 1783–84), 3:151.

68. Boaden, *Memoirs*, 1:104.

69. *Short Criticism*, pp. 19–20; Davies, *Dramatic Miscellanies*, 3:151.

70. Tieck, "Eye-witness," p. 285.

71. A stage direction in the 1804 promptbook, given *after* "Follow my mother," reads: "Francisco advances with the Goblet to Hor.'s L.H." Other directions make it clear that Francisco has had the goblet since it was returned to him by Gertrude and is coming forward with it now so Horatio can seize it on "Never believ't" (*Kemble Promptbooks*, 2:81–83).

72. London *Times*, 25 June 1817. The article is unsigned but is clearly Hazlitt's; it repeats verbatim the "man in armour" description of Kemble's Hamlet.

73. Ibid. Earlier in the article, Hazlitt contrasts the two actors by name, with specific reference to Hamlet.

5

EDMUND KEAN

In *Sense and Sensibility*, published just three years before Edmund Kean's London debut in 1814,[1] Jane Austen gave one of her characters a speech which nicely differentiated two opposed schools of contemporary taste; speaking to Marianne Dashwood, the novel's exemplar of the emerging Romantic sensibility, Edward Ferrars defends his allegiance to a different mode of aesthetic response: "I like a fine prospect, but not on picturesque principles. I do not like crooked, twisted, blasted trees. I admire them much more if they are tall, straight and flourishing."

The contrast between Edmund Kean (1787–1833) and John Philip Kemble, and the opposition of their respective admirers, was very much of this kind. Described as "not only diminutive but insignificant"[2]— he was five feet four inches tall—Kean's appearance in the role so long identified with the majestic Kemble caused many an observer to deplore the passing of formal beauty from the tragic stage. Even so staunch a partisan as William Hazlitt admitted that Kean's appearance tended to "*vulgarize*, or diminish our idea of the characters he plays."[3] But even though there were still enough adherents of the Kemble religion around to keep up a steady harassing fire of criticism, the day of Kean, the day of the "picturesque," of nature "crooked, twisted and blasted," had irrevocably come, and the Romantic poets and critics flocked to his banner, ensuring his triumph.

Leigh Hunt, writing some years after the event but recapitulating opinions expressed at the time, put Kean's rise to stardom in the clearest historical perspective: "Garrick's nature displaced Quin's formalism: and in precisely the same way did Kean displace Kemble. . . . It was as sure a thing as Nature against Art, or tears against cheeks of stone."[4]

The triumph of nature over art. Such were the terms in which Kean's ascendancy was repeatedly celebrated. "The shrine thou worshippest is Nature's self," [5] wrote Byron in tribute. Even Fanny Kemble, who might have been expected to prefer the style of her illustrious uncle, praised Kean's elevation of nature over art in a telling metaphor: "If he was irregular and unartist-like in his performance, so is Niagara compared with the waterworks of Versailles." [6] Not content with encomium, Hunt offered a precise analysis of what was involved in Kean's aesthetic revolution:

The distinction between Kean and Kemble may be briefly stated to be this: that Kemble knew there was a difference between tragedy and common life, but did not know in what it consisted, except in *manner*, which he consequently carried to excess, losing sight of the passion. Kean knew the real thing, which is the height of the *passion*, manner following it as a matter of course, *and grace being developed from it in proportion to the truth of the sensation*, as the flower issues from the entireness of the plant, or from all that is necessary to produce it. Kemble began with the flower, and he made it accordingly. He had no notion of so inelegant a thing as a root, or as the common earth, or of all the precious elements that make a heart and a life in the plant, and crown their success with beauty. [7]

As Hunt rightly observed, Kean's enshrinement of nature sent the artistic pendulum swinging back to David Garrick, a fact which Mrs. Garrick underscored by proclaiming Kean her husband's rightful heir— earnestly longed for, one supposes, during the long "usurpation" of Kemble. [8] Kean resembled Garrick not only in his pursuit of nature but also in particular techniques employed to that end. Like Garrick, who "endeavour'd to shake off the fetters of numbers," Kean ignored the ordered cadence of blank verse in favor of a style designed to express with the greatest immediacy the intellectual or emotional content of the line. Indications are that he went much further in that direction than his eighteenth-century counterpart; Samuel Taylor Coleridge wrote, "To destroy all sense of Metre is the avowed aim of Mr. Kean, no less than his constant practice." [9]

The two actors were also remarkably similar in their use of the visual aspects of the art. Both tended to "bustle about" a great deal on the stage—possibly as a means of compensating for their lack of imposing height. [10] Kean also followed Garrick in depending heavily on the riveting expressiveness of his eyes; James Hackett described them as "black, large, brilliant, and penetrating, and remarkable for the shortness of their upper lid, which discovered a clearly-defined line of white above the ball, rendering their effect when fixed upon an object very searching.''[11] ''An eye like an orb of light'' was Fanny Kemble's description.[12]

As with Garrick, the eyes were merely the most arresting feature of a marvelously plastic physiognomy, on which Kean was able to register with unerring precision a rich variety of moods and attitudes. Hazlitt made this delicately modulated play of features the very keystone of Kean's acting and declared that those spectators seated so far from the stage as to be unable to discern it were not seeing Kean's art at all and might just as well have stayed home. In abrupt and lengthy pauses Kean worked up in his face the passion to be expressed vocally, and for those who could not see the expression the pauses could seem only arbitrary and ''unaccountable.'' ''The lightning of his eye,'' said Hazlitt, precedes the hoarse thunder from his voice.''[13]

The reference here to ''hoarseness'' of voice points to another particular in which Kean exceeded the naturalism of Garrick. The hoarseness seems to have been not a physical defect or a failure of technique on Kean's part, but the result of conscious surrender to the force of strong emotion, a surrender in which he willingly sacrificed beauty of sound to verisimilitude. That seems to be Hazlitt's view, at any rate, and Fanny Kemble's; she described Kean's voice as ''exquisitely touching and melodious in its tenderness, and in the harsh dissonance of vehement passion terribly true.''[14] Others—those for whom art counted more than nature—simply complained of ''discordance.''[15]

Hazlitt does not say so explicitly, but it is clear that the necessity for observing closely the working of Kean's face applied to another characteristic which the actor held in common with Garrick: a penchant for abrupt vocal transitions. Kean appears to have used the technique in a more specialized way than Garrick had, and with less success. His most favored maneuver was to drop precipitously from ''the lofty vehemence and romantic tone of tragic elocution, to the easy and placid utterance of colloquial level speaking''[16] or, as Coleridge put it, ''from the hyper-tragic to the infra-colloquial.''[17] Evidently not everyone perceived the corresponding shifts of expression which made the vocal shifts ''accountable''—in the manner Hazlitt describes; certainly they did not always please. Coleridge found that ''though sometimes productive of great effect, [they] are often unreasonable.''[18] Ludwig Tieck would not grant nearly so much, declaring testily that "on the artist's part all this is done in mere caprice, with the deliberate purpose of giving a great variety of light and shade to his speeches, and of introducing turns and sudden alternations, of which neither the part nor the author has for the most part afforded the most remote suggestion."[19]

Tieck's was a minority view, however; most observers found Kean's use of chiaroscuro more often powerfully effective than otherwise. But even his most fervent apologists recognized that Kean's art was characterized by great unevenness. In this he differed radically from Garrick. Whereas Garrick excelled in creating fully articulated characters, true in every particular, a Kean portrayal was typically an affair of brilliant but isolated moments, set off from each other by more-or-less lengthy stretches of irrelevance or outright badness. Watching him act was, in Coleridge's celebrated phrase, "like reading Shakespeare by flashes of lightning." One deplored the great patches of darkness, but all was forgiven when the light came again. He was "tricky and flashy," said George Henry Lewes, but "he stirred the general heart with such a rush of mighty power, impressed himself so vividly by accent, look and gesture, that it was as vain to protest his defects as it was for French critics to insist upon Shakespeare's want of *bienséance* and *bon goût*."[20]

It was not that Kean deliberately neglected certain passages in favor of others—as an earlier generation of actors had regularly done—but that he simply failed at some moments while succeeding masterfully at others. Hazlitt attributed the lapses to "want of physical adaptation, or sometimes of just conception of the character" and, echoing Lewes, pointed out that "if at any time . . . the interest has flagged for a considerable interval, the deficiency has always been redeemed by some collected and overpowering display of energy or pathos, which electrified at the moment, and left a lasting impression on the mind afterwards."[21]

Kean's proneness to wild vacillation between the superb and the insupportable naturally manifested itself more strongly in some roles than in others, depending on the degree to which a given character allowed him to sound those emotional notes of which he was most completely the master. As Fanny Kemble's comparison with "Niagara," Coleridge's "lightning" metaphor and Lewes' talk of "a rush of mighty power" vividly illustrate, Kean's greatest talent was for the expression of emotions of elemental force—human passion "taken at the flood" or warmed to the white-heat of the heavens' fire. Hence, his most ad-mired characterizations were Othello, Richard III and Shylock.

His genius for passionate expression served him less well in his por-trayal of Hamlet, at least in the eyes of the Romantic critics. Hazlitt, for example, found Kean's Hamlet ''as much too splenetic and rash as Mr. Kemble's is too deliberate and formal. His manner is too strong and pointed.''[22] This charge must, of course, be judged in the light of Hazlitt's conviction, stated immediately thereafter, that Hamlet is a man largely incapable of ''severity,'' an introvert utterly uninterested in at-tempting ''to impress what he says on others,'' a ''gentleman and scholar'' who merely ''thinks aloud'' throughout most of the play.[23]

But even when proper allowance has been made for Hazlitt's Ro-mantic bias in favor of an essentially contemplative Prince, it seems safe to conclude that Kean presented an uncommonly tempestuous Hamlet, one given more to vehemence and vitriol than to the more tranquil motions of the soul. A critic for *The Stage* wrote in 1815: ''Mr. Kean does not shine in soliloquies. Give him the actions of the mind, and he can exhibit them—the silent solemn cogitations of the soul may not be beyond his reach; but he has not yet evinced that he possesses the secret of displaying them.''[24] Six years later *The Drama* observed that ''the turgidity which sometimes hangs around Mr. Kean's enun-ciation . . . always *heightened* his turbulent delineations of passion, . . . but occasionally *obscured* his calmer soliloquies.''[25] Similarly, Henry Crabb Robinson found Kean's Hamlet more ''cynical and pas-sionate'' than quietly philosophic.[26]

But this is not to say that Kean simply played the part on one un-varying note of unbridled feeling from start to finish. Although he ex-celled in the revelation of elemental passion, it was by no means his only talent. Keats was moved to tears by the gentle pathos with which, as Richard, Duke of York, Kean bade farewell to his son, and many others speak also of his great gift for portraying tenderness;[27] in *Ham-let* it made his parting with Ophelia the most admired part of his per-formance. He was also a master of sarcasm, both genial and abrasive. With Polonius, Rosencrantz and Guildenstern, and the Clown, he ''threw away the tragic stilts entirely'' and delivered both the playful and the cutting passages in an easy, conversational and familiar style.[28]

Kean seems also to have made the Prince appropriately pleasing to the eye, overcoming his physical deficiency, in the view of many spectators, very much as Garrick had done—by the sheer force of other qualities. Lewes wrote that, though "small and insignificant in figure, he could 'at times become impressively commanding by the lion-like power and grace of his bearing,"[29] and Hunt found that, owing to his "exceeding grace [and] measureless dignity . . . his little person absolutely becomes tall, and rises to the height of moral grandeur."[30]

Kean dressed the character in the pseudo-Elizabethan costume Kemble had introduced, but in keeping with his tendency to informality he left off the usual adornments; the St. James's Chronicle, reviewing his Drury Lane debut, treated the omission as nothing less than a breach of etiquette: "He was far from being well dressed, and came to the court without his ornaments and insignia" (15 March 1814).

It is difficult to say precisely what tone Kean brought to the first soliloquy (I.ii.129–59). Speaking of the performance in general, Hazlitt said that Kean missed Hamlet's "strong tincture . . . of tender melancholy, of romantic thought and sentiment,"[31] but these qualities were perhaps not altogether absent from this and later soliloquies; one member of Hazlitt's circle, Thomas Barnes, substituting as Examiner critic for his imprisoned colleague Leigh Hunt, declared that Kean "played the part to the understanding and not to the eye: he never forgot that he was personating a philosophic Prince, so immersed in the depth of melancholy reflections, as to become indifferent to all earthly matters" (20 March 1814).[32] One observer was struck by Kean's handling of a particular line of the speech in such a way as to bring out another aspect of Hamlet's character; in his Authentic Memoirs of Edmund Kean, published in 1814, Frances Phippen recalled that his delivery of "my poor father's body" was "so powerfully reverential that it strongly marked the pious respect he had for his departed father."[33] With his talent for "splenetic" utterance, Kean could no doubt have done much with "a beast that wants discourse of reason" and "Oh, most wicked speed . . . ," but those lines were omitted from his acting text.[34]

But despite his natural propensity, it appears that Kean did not always give way to explosive, overheated delivery even when the text allowed it; Phippen describes an instance, in his talk with Horatio about the apparition, when he deliberately shunned such an opportunity:

At the close of the scene, where he says, "If it assume my noble father's person, I'll speak to it though hell itself should gape . . . " [I.ii.243–44], Mr.

Kean gave it in a quick and low tone, which was in total opposition to the manner of every other actor. This passage has been invariably given by other actors in a bold style of elocution.[35]

Kean met the Ghost with the obligatory Garrick start and received for it the critical wrist-slapping which by now had become as much a tradition as the business itself:

Mr. Kean's astonishment at seeing the Ghost was nothing more than is usual upon *all* such occasions, and with *all* actors; it was mechanically just; therefore Mr. Kean has great authorities before him to indulge in such reveries. But we know not why any being who is visited by a supernatural power, should strut about until his hat falls from his head, for he is equally liable to throw off his shoes in such a rencontre; and for this reason, we do not see the expediency of a tragedian resorting to such a mechanical change (a change which carries with it neither truth nor probability), remaining as inconsistent in the minds of the judicious, as it is astonishing to the vulgar.[36]

But if he could follow tradition, Kean could also break with it. Every Hamlet since Thomas Betterton—or, for all we know, since Richard Burbage—had stood before the Ghost in ashen-faced, unnerved wonder, blasted almost into derangement by the awesomeness of the supernatural visitation. Kean was not only uncowed but at first openly antagonistic; he laid violent stress on ''goblin damned,'' as if warning off an evil spirit. As he continued he seemed to become convinced that this was indeed his father and therefore a welcome ally, ''dead corse'' or not. He spoke calmly and confidently and followed after him eagerly. As a mark of his trust he pointed his sword not at the Ghost but menacingly toward his friends (London *Morning Chronicle*, 14 March 1814).

He maintained his self-possession throughout the ensuing colloquy, armed, Phippen surmised, ''with a familiar philosophy, necessary to imbibe and execute the admonitions of the sacred phantom.'' Left alone, he gazed for some time at the spot where the Ghost had disappeared, and then ''came forward with an eye of supplication, as if he implored the sacred Deity to aid him in his purpose.'' ''Remember thee!'' (I.v.95) was spoken with a firmness that was ''evidently new.''[37]

No commentary survives concerning Kean's playing of the final moments of this scene. He is next observed walking in the lobby, book in hand, bandying words with Polonius. He introduced some new business here: The line "For if the sun breed maggots in a dead dog, being a god kissing carrion" (II.ii.181–82) he gave as a passage from the book he held in his hand, and then, stopping short, asked Polonius, "Have you a daughter?" [38]

There was new business also in Hamlet's reunion with his schoolfellows (II.ii.223ff.). Kean introduced a note of subtle mockery by "taking Rosencrantz and Guildenstern under each arm, under pretence of communicating his secret to them, when he only [meant] to trifle with them." Hazlitt judged it "exactly in the spirit of the character" and took the same view of "the suppressed tone of irony" with which Kean delivered the line about the King's picture "in little." [39]

Hazlitt was less sure that Kean's device of having Hamlet make several attempts to recollect the "rugged Pyrrhus" line (II.ii.451) was "in perfect keeping," but he concluded that "there was great ingenuity in the thought; and the spirit and life of the execution was beyond every thing." [40] The majority of the spectators gave the new reading their unqualified endorsement, as John Finlay contemptuously recalled: "The house shouted applause, but they should have shouted long before '— good Hamlet, cudgel thy brains no longer.' " [41]

Kean gave the "Guilty creatures sitting at a play" soliloquy (II.ii.588–602) in the drastically truncated version introduced by Kemble and evidently made little impact with it; his performance of it prompted no comment.

In his reading of the "To be or not to be" soliloquy (III.i.55–87), Kean made one of his most radical departures from convention. Instead of delivering it in the hushed tones of melancholy philosophic reflection, he made it the occasion for an energy-charged display of strong feeling. As already noted, Hazlitt and others lamented Kean's failure to reveal, in sufficient degree, "the sublimer pathos of thought," [42] and his handling of this speech must have been for them a crucial case in point. Barnes, however, offered a subtle analysis and energetic defense of Kean's reading, pointing out that Hamlet's examination of "all those arguments which withhold the wretched from dying" is prompted by his own desire for death, which is in turn prompted by a passionate loathing of those about him; Kean was thus correct in playing the speech not as "a tedious harangue" but as "a series of impassioned and heart-breaking reflections" (London *Examiner*, 20 March 1814).

The irascible critic for the London *Herald* (14 March 1814), so se-

vere with Kean on so many counts, apparently found nothing to censure in this instance but his pronunciation, which on one word seems
to have taken an oddly Kemble-like turn:

In pronouncing the word *contumely*, he chose to divide it into four distinct
syllables, that seemed to hop after each other like limping relatives; as thus:
Con-*tu*-me-ly! This was another effort of new reading, and certainly did not
pass off without exciting a burst of ''bravos'' from many of the auditors.

Kean's playing of the interview with Ophelia (III.i.88–149) was by
all accounts the capstone of his Hamlet portrayal. Hazlitt named it with
his murder scene in *Macbeth*, the third act of his *Othello* and his death
scene in *Romeo and Juliet* as one of those overpowering displays of
''energy or pathos'' by which Kean redeemed himself for deficiencies
shown elsewhere in his characterizations. In this case, it seems to have
been a mixture of energy *and* pathos, and in that remarkably original
approach lay the source of Kean's great power in the scene. He began
by appearing ''surprised and vexed to find that he has been overheard
[during the soliloquy],'' but instead of giving way to ''bitterness or
paltry pique,'' he addressed Ophelia tenderly, ''as so pure a being ought
to be addressed.'' At this point, Barnes reminded his readers, it was
customary for stage Hamlets ''to become all at once stark staring mad,
to stamp, and rave, and almost fight with Ophelia.'' Kean went his
own way, treating her ''with mournful gravity, and not with noisy rail-
ing'' (London *Examiner* 20 March 1814). The critic for the London
Sun (14 March 1814) thought that in taking such an approach Kean
too much neglected Hamlet's pretense of madness, but most seem to
have felt, with Finlay, that ''the slapping of doors, and a great part of
Hamlet's cruel deportment [was] . . . properly rejected.''[43] In keeping with his general conception of the character, Hazlitt suggested that
Kean could properly have softened the scene still more (London *Morning Chronicle*, 14 March 1814). He perhaps had in mind the scream
of menacing vehemence with which Kean delivered the final ''To a
nunnery, go.''[44] Much more to his liking was the pantomime with which
Kean ended the scene. Tieck described it fully:

He retires hurriedly, and has already grasped the handle of the door, when he
stops, turns round, and casting back the saddest, almost tearful look, stands
lingering for some time, and then, with a slow, almost gliding step, comes

back, seizes Ophelia's hand, imprints a lingering kiss upon it with a deep-drawn sigh and straightway dashes more impetuously than before out at the door.[45]

Tieck was no more than coolly tolerant of the stratagem, and Phippen objected that such an overt display of affection ran counter to Claudius' following line: "Love! his affections do not that way tend . . . " (III.i.162).[46] The London *Herald* critic made the same argument, in the midst of a nearly apoplectic denunciation:

Mr. Kean became *practically amorous*, and kissed the lady's hand, for which deviation from rectitude many thoughtless spectators cheered him! We do repeat, that they absolutely cheered him, though the deed should have been reprobated, because it tended to give *the lie circumstantial* to what the King is made to utter to Polonius immediately after. (14 March 1814)

Finlay thought that Kean's "pantomimical exhibition of repentance" was simply superfluous, since his playing of the scene proper had been such as to convey to all but the dullest spectators the idea that Hamlet's "severity to Ophelia is involuntary, and a violence to his own feelings."[47] But such voices of doubt and denial were scarcely heard above the roars of approbation. Nor was it only "thoughtless spectators" who were captivated. Hazlitt dutifully reported that "it had an electrical effect on the house" and then turned to uncharacteristic hyperbole to record his own opinion: "It was the finest commentary that was ever made on Shakespear" (London *Morning Chronicle*, 14 March 1814). Thus certified by both popular and critical acceptance, Kean's kiss took up its place in the storehouse of stage tradition, where it remained, with the inevitable modifications and embellishments, to the end of the century.

There was a characteristic touch of "common life" in Kean's staging of the speech to the players (III.ii.1–45). He entered with them "at his heels, speaking to them with his back to them . . . as if it had been the continuation of an easy mannered conversation in which he had been engaged with them along the corridor."[48] But there was nothing "easy" about his conduct during the play scene. Hazlitt called his manner of playing it "the most daring of any," and though he felt compelled to say that "its extreme boldness 'bordered on the verge of all we hate,' " he conceded that "the force and animation which he gave to it cannot be too highly applauded" (London *Morning Chroni-*

cle, 14 March 1814). Hazlitt gives no specifics, but other accounts reveal precisely in what Kean's daring and boldness consisted. Instead of restricting himself to covert observation of the King from behind a screen of feigned attendance on Ophelia—Kemble's much-admired approach—Kean openly stalked his prey. Throwing himself to the ground, he crept to center stage and insolently scrutinized Claudius, as if "bullying the King into confusion" (London *Sun*, 14 March 1814). For some this descent of the Prince to the horizontal went well over that border between good taste and bad taste to which Hazlitt alluded. Phippen decried the crawl as "a vulgarity which abuses both common sense and decency."[49] The London *Herald* critic, whose attendance at Kean's performance seems to have brought him all the pleasure of a fortnight in hell, spluttered with rage at this fresh assault on his sense of propriety:

During the mimic representation, Mr. Kean so far forgot that inalienable delicacy, which should eternally characterize a gentleman in his deportment before the ladies, that he not only exposed his *derrière* to his mistress, but positively crawled upon his belly towards the King like a wounded snake in a meadow, rather than a Prince openly indulging himself in moral speculation in the salon of a royal palace.

But like the kissing of Ophelia's hand, the crawl was an idea whose time had come. Audiences liked it, and two generations of subsequent Hamlets eagerly followed Kean to the floor. There was great vocal as well as physical animation in the scene. At the end, Kean greeted the King's headlong flight with an exultant shout. Finlay thought it imprudent for Hamlet to thus risk being "overheard," but another commentator held that one of the great beauties of Kean's portrayal was "the brilliant expression of internal feeling which he seemed unable to repress in the scene where the Court witness the play."[50]

Kean apparently retained the tone of feverish excitement during Hamlet's laceration of Guildenstern and Rosencrantz and mockery of Polonius, but he was relatively calm when he reached Gertrude's apartment, and remained so throughout that scene (III.iv). Mrs. Garrick reminded him that that had not been "Davy's" way and, schooled by her, Kean seems to have abandoned tameness in later performances in favor of the Garrick manner, even though in so doing he "never satisfied himself or others."[51] His initial preference for using all gently also set him apart from Kemble, a fact to which Barnes, in the London *Examiner*, ever on the alert for "odorous" comparisons, pointed with great satisfaction: "He did not shake his mother out of her chair, nor wave his handkerchief with a dignified whirl, nor spread his arms like a heron crucified on a barn-door, when he cries out, 'is it the King?' The omission of these singular beauties made many people shake their heads and prophesy that his fame could not last long." Kean made the comparison of Gertrude's past and present husbands appear somewhat more natural than its usual representation by bearing on his person only the miniature of his father; Gertrude wore a similar miniature of Claudius, and Hamlet's catching sight of it prompted the speech (London *Sun*, 14 March 1814). But not all the rough spots of established methods could be smoothed out. The Ghost slammed the door in the face of Kean's Hamlet as he had so unceremoniously done with Kemble and others.[52]

Kean apparently failed to make much of an impression in the first part of the graveyard scene (V.i.), if the total absence of commentary on it is any indication. Perhaps, as Lewes was later to suggest, he scarcely knew what to do with the scene's soft-toned banter and leisurely meditation on the human condition.[53] Given his reputation for command of thunder and lightning, the hurly-burly of the graveside challenge to Laertes should have been a strong scene for Kean. It is therefore surprising to hear Hazlitt—of all people—complain that "the scene with Laertes, where he leaps into the grave, and utters the exclamation, 'Tis I, Hamlet the Dane,' had not the tumultuous and overpowering effect we expected from it" (London *Morning Chronicle*, 14 March 1814). It appears from this and similar instances—the "gentle" playing of the nunnery and closet scenes—that Kean valued originality so highly that he sometimes eschewed conventional effects even when they were most compatible with the strongest facet of his talent.

The London *Herald* critic at last found something to admire in the "grace and address" with which Kean conducted himself in the fencing match, but he thought the "scarlet cloak" Kean wore in the scene "approximated strongly to the ridiculous."

Kean died as no other Hamlet had before him. Reasoning that death comes not from the rapier wound itself but from the poison with which the weapon is anointed, Kean simulated with clinical precision the fatal progress of the venom through "the natural gates and alleys of the body.'' Apparently, however, this was one of those instances when his fidelity to naturalistic detail was too subtle to be perceived by any but those nearest the stage. At any rate, this was the explanation Leigh Hunt gave, as late as 1831, for the fact that he had never yet seen a criticism of Kean's acting "that has done justice to the beauty and fidelity of his dying scenes." Writing to the *Tatler*, in the guise of "An Actor" who has "had the most favourable opportunities of observation, having had the pleasure of performing with that gentleman in different parts of the United Kingdom," Hunt described what many spectators had allegedly been missing:

What are the effects of such a poison? Intense internal pain, wandering vision, swelling veins in the temple. All this Kean details with awful reality: his eye dilates and then loses lustre; he gnaws his hand in the vain effort to repress emotion; the veins thicken in his forehead; his limbs shudder and quiver, and as life grows fainter, and his hand drops from between his stiffening lips, he utters a cry of expiring nature, so exquisite that I can only compare it to the stifled sob of a fainting woman, or the little wail of a suffering child.[54]

Hunt had apparently not seen a warm appreciation of Kean's skill in dying penned more than a decade earlier by Keats: "The bodily functions wither up,—and the mental faculties hold out, till they crack. It was an extinguishment, not a decay. The hand is agonized with death; the lip trembles, with the last breath,—as we see the autumn leaf thrill in the cold wind of evening. The very eye-lid dies."[55]

The play ended with Hamlet's death, following "the rest is silence," Horatio's closing speech having been cut.

Kean's own death came in 1833. He had acted Hamlet regularly for just under two decades—an impressive record by modern standards, but well short of the thirty- and thirty-four-year runs of Garrick and Kemble, to say nothing of Betterton's prodigious half-century. His chief rival in the role, Charles Mayne Young (1777–1856), had retired a year earlier. Young had been a close imitator of Kemble; his departure from the stage and Kean's death cleared the way for William Charles Macready, an actor who sought to combine the styles of Kemble and Kean.

NOTES

1. Kean ascended to the highest rank of London actors when he played Shylock at Drury Lane on 26 January 1814; Richard III followed on 12 February, and Hamlet on 12 March.

2. John Genest, *Some Account of the English Stage* (Bath: H. E. Carrington, 1832), 8:432.

3. William Hazlitt, *The London Magazine*, January 1820, in *The Complete Works of William Hazlitt*, ed. P. P. Howe (London: J. M. Dent, 1930), 18:277.

4. *Dramatic Essays by Leigh Hunt*, ed. William Archer and Robert W. Lowe (London: W. Scott, 1894), p. 222. For a similar contrast, see Hazlitt, *Works*, 18:278–79.

5. The first line of a verse said to have been inscribed by Byron on a snuffbox presented to the actor; see James Hackett, *Notes, Criticisms and Correspondence upon Shakespeare's Plays and Actors* (1863; reprint, New York: B. Blom, 1968), p. 128.

6. Frances Anne Butler [Kemble], *Journal* (1835; reprint, New York: B. Blom, 1970), p. 184.

7. Hunt, *Dramatic Essays*, p. 224.

8. As a mark of her favor, Mrs. Garrick made Kean a present of her husband's stage jewels; see John Doran, *Annals of the English Stage* (New York and London: Harper, n.d.), 2:392.

9. *Collected Letters of Samuel Taylor Coleridge*, ed. Earl Leslie Griggs (Oxford: Clarendon Press, 1971), 5:179.

10. William Hazlitt, "A View of the English Stage," in *Works*, 5:378.

11. Hackett, *Notes*, p. 126.

12. Kemble, *Journal*, p. 183.

13. William Hazlitt, "Whether Actors Ought to Sit in the Boxes," in *Works*, 8:277.

14. Kemble, *Journal*, p. 183.

15. The London *Morning Herald* said, "His upper tones are unmanageable, and not unfrequently discordant" (14 March 1814).

16. Samuel Taylor Coleridge, *The Drama, or Theatrical Pocket Magazine* 4 (1823): 151.

17. *The Table Talk and Omniana of Samuel Taylor Coleridge*, ed. T. Ashe (London: G. Bell, 1888), p. 25.

18. Ibid.

19. Ludwig Tieck, quoted in Theodore Martin, "An Eye-witness of John Kemble," *The Nineteenth Century* 7 (1880), 292.

20. George Henry Lewes, *On Actors and the Art of Acting* (London: Smith, Elder, 1875), p. 2.

21. Hazlitt, *Works*, 5:208–9. Fanny Kemble wrote: "Kean, the only actor whose performances have ever realized to me my idea of the effect tragic acting ought to produce, acted part of parts rather than ever a whole character"; see Frances Anne Kemble, *Records of a Girlhood* (New York: H. Holt, 1879), p. 477.

22. William Hazlitt, "Characters," in *Works*, 4:237.

23. Ibid. Coleridge and Lamb do not comment specifically on Kean's Hamlet, but their conception of the character, so similar to Hazlitt's, must have prompted in them a similar response.

24. Quoted by William Buell, *The Hamlets of the Theatre* (New York: Astor-Honor, 1968), p. 48.

25. *The Drama* 1 (1821): 3.

26. *The London Theatre, 1811–1866: Selections from the Diary of Henry Crabb Robinson*, ed. Eluned Brown (London: Society for Theatre Research, 1966), p. 90; entry dated 13 December 1819.

27. *The Poetical Works and Other Writings of John Keats*, ed. H. Buxton Forman, rev. ed. (New York: C. Scribner's Sons, 1938–39), 5:243.

28. George Vandenhoff, *Leaves from an Actor's Note-Book* (New York: D. Appleton, 1860), p. 23.

29. Lewes, *On Actors*, p. 3.

30. Hunt, *Dramatic Essays*, p. 224.

31. Hazlitt, *Works*, 5:209.

32. Elsewhere in his review, as will be seen, Barnes seems to qualify somewhat this view of Kean's interpretation.

33. Frances Phippen, *Authentic Memoirs of Edmund Kean* (London: J. Roach, 1814), p. 98.

34. Kean followed Kemble's version of the text with only superficial changes, as can be seen from Oxberry's 1818 edition of the play, listing Kean as Hamlet. The Kemble text was also adopted by subsequent actors until the last quarter of the century.

35. Phippen, *Authentic Memoirs*, p. 98.

36. Ibid., p. 99.

37. Ibid., pp. 99–100. Kean's composure before the Ghost was denounced by the London *Morning Herald* (14 March 1814) and by the London *Sun* (14 March 1814). Hazlitt praised the innovation (London *Morning Chronicle*, 14 March 1814).

38. Unsigned letter to the London *Examiner*, 27 March 1814.

39. Hazlitt, in the London *Chronicle*, 14 March 1814.

40. Ibid.

41. John Finlay, *Miscellanies* (Dublin: n.p., 1835), p. 231.

42. William Hazlitt, "Mr. Kean's Romeo," *The Champion*, 8 January 1815, in *Works*, 5:208–10. Hazlitt is here speaking in general terms of Kean's "in-

adequacy'' in the roles of Romeo and Hamlet. His probable dissatisfaction with Kean's playing of the ''To be or not to be'' soliloquy may perhaps also be inferred from his silence on the subject in his review of the performance.

43. Finlay, *Miscellanies*, p. 231.

44. Tieck, ''Eye-witness,'' p. 293.

45. Ibid.

46. Phippen, *Authentic Memoirs*, p. 100.

47. Finlay, *Miscellanies*, pp. 223–24.

48. Ibid., p. 223.

49. Phippen, *Authentic Memoirs*, p. 101.

50. *The Drama* 1 (1821): 3.

51. Barry Cornwall [Bryan Waller Procter], *The Life of Edmund Kean* (London: E. Moxon, 1835), 2:69.

52. Finlay, *Miscellanies*, p. 230.

53. Lewes, *On Actors*, p. 8.

54. Hunt, *Dramatic Essays*, p. 230; the letter is dated 23 September 1831.

55. Keats, *Poetical Works*, 5:244.

6

WILLIAM CHARLES MACREADY

William Charles Macready (1793–1873) was only six years younger than Edmund Kean and made his London debut at Covent Garden just three seasons after Kean's historic first appearance at the rival house. William Hazlitt promptly declared him "the best tragic actor that has come out in our remembrance, with the exception of Mr. Kean."[1] Macready might well have spent his entire career in second place had Kean not cleared the way for him by drinking himself to death at the age of forty-six.

During the seventeen years when they were both acting in London, Macready had little opportunity to measure himself and be measured against Kean in the role of Hamlet. At Covent Garden the part belonged to Charles Mayne Young; Macready did not manage to play it until five years after his debut, and then only by exercising the traditional right of a junior member of the company to take any role in the repertory on his benefit night. His first appearance as Hamlet before a London audience, on 8 June 1821, went almost unnoticed in the press, since benefit performances were not ordinarily subjected to critical scrutiny. The *Literary Gazette* reported that it was "an energetic picture of the character, and in the closet, grave, and dying scenes drew down thunders of applause" (16 June 1821). The London *Morning Herald* also printed a short review, but the rest of the papers were silent.[2]

Macready's next Hamlet, two years later, was also a benefit, this time for the "Necessitous and Deserving Poor," and was totally ignored by the reviewers. Serious critical notice came only after Macready moved to Drury Lane at the beginning of the 1823–1824 season. Having made the right to play Hamlet a provision of his employment, he appeared in what was effectively his London debut in the role on 17 October 1823.

He may have been emboldened to invite direct comparison with Kean on Kean's own stage by the fact that he had earlier scored well against him in a performance of Richard III, universally recognized as Kean's greatest role. This time, however, the results were to prove considerably less gratifying. Without actually naming Kean, the London *Times* described the performance in terms that left no doubt about where Macready ranked by comparison: "It is distinguished by sober and well-matured *talent* rather than by brilliant and impassioned *genius*. There is nothing in the performance unworthy of an accomplished actor, neither is there anything indicative of a truly great one" (18 October 1823). A reviewer for *Mirror of the Stage* took an even more patronizing tone, choosing to compare Macready not to Kean but to John Philip Kemble, who had died just eight months before:

It is no disgrace to Mr. M[acready] that he cannot play Hamlet; for who is there, now KEMBLE is no more, that can truly embody the poet's conception of this strange, yet beautiful character. . . . We could point many faults and innovations but as we presume it was intended *only as a trial*, and as the Manager must by this time be aware that its merits "were not proven," as the Scotch say, we shall refrain from the ungracious task of dissection. (3 November 1823)

In the twenty-eight years that remained of his career on the stage, Macready was able to improve considerably on these early assessments of his Hamlet, but he never succeeded in winning for it the esteem he believed it deserved. "It is very hard," he wrote in 1837, "that this character, which is decidedly the most finished of any I represent, should be so neglected through the ignorance of those who have decried me in it."[3] The situation had altered little when he played it for the last time, on 29 January 1851, as his diary entry for that date reveals:

Acted Hamlet; certainly in a manner equal to any former performance of the part I have ever given. . . . The character has been a sort of love with me. The press has been slow to acknowledge my realization of the man, of the mind, of the nature of this beautiful conception, because they have not understood it. . . . I have in Hamlet worked against prejudice and against stubborn ignorance, and it has been a labour of love with me.

Beautiful Hamlet, farewell, farewell! There was no alloy to our last parting.[4]

Macready seems to be complaining here about rejection of his *interpretation* of the character, and certainly much of the adverse criticism was on that score. But it was style, rather than interpretation, which seems to have weighed most heavily against him in the estimation of so many of his contemporaries. Macready brought to the acting of Sheakespearean tragedy a degree of naturalism which much of his audience was simply unwilling to accept.[5]

Rejection on these grounds at first glance seems surprising, considering the enormous prestige Kean had won for the natural mode, but Macready went beyond what Kean had done and in the process incurred the censure of the very critics who had exalted Kean. Leigh Hunt, it will be remembered, in arguing for the superiority of Kean over Kemble, made the point that although Kemble mistakenly emphasized manner while Kean correctly valued "the real thing, which is the height of the *passion*," both actors were correct in perceiving that "there was a difference between tragedy and common life." Macready, Hunt concluded, failed to pay sufficient attention to that crucial difference, bringing to his tragic characterizations too much of "common" nature, not enough of the "ideal." Reviewing his Macbeth, on 15 March 1831, he wrote:

It wants the Royal warrant. We do not mean the mouthing and strut of the ordinary stage King; which are things that Mr. Macready is above; but that habitual consciousness of ascendancy, and disposition to throw an ideal grace over its reflections, whether pleasurable or painful, which enables the character to present itself to us as an object of intellectual and moral contemplation.[6]

Hazlitt and George Henry Lewes also found him too earthbound in poetic tragedy, too subdued, mundane and vulgarly "domestic." He was real, to be sure, but it was the reality of contemporary bourgeois life and as such out of place in the timeless, abstract world of a great poet's imagination.[7]

That this general tendency of Macready's acting contributed in an important way to dissatisfaction with his Hamlet portrayal seems to be borne out by certain of the statements made in reviews of his 1823 performance. Their authors are, by and large, not as astute and articulate as the masterly Hunt, Hazlitt, and Lewes, but they seem to be reporting much the same response. "Very considerable portions of the dialogue," said the London *Herald* writer, "were, to our perceptions, nothing at all; for they were gossiped over (and the censure includes several parts of the very fine soliloquies) with a total negligence of pause and emphasis, such as a speaker of intellect and susceptibility could not fall into, in discoursing even of matters of any ordinary interest" (18 October 1823). The London *Morning Post* critic confessed that he was taken aback at hearing the scenes with Rosencrantz and Guildenstern given "in the tone and manner of common conversational discourse," and he wondered whether such behavior did not "rob [the Prince] altogether of tragic dignity." But on reflection he conceded that since Hamlet is arguably no hero and "the tragedy stilts are exclusively intended for heroism, . . . Macready's innovation [though] a startling one . . . does not conduce, by the first impression, to any inferior effect in his performance" (18 October 1823).

Ironically, this greatly increased prominence which Macready gave to common nature probably owed something to his having modeled himself not just on Kean but on the Kembles as well. From his observation of their acting, particularly Mrs. Siddons', Macready become convinced of the paramount importance of close study and meticulous attention to detail, so as to achieve a finished portrait, with every facet of the character subordinated to a single unifying conception. But whereas in Kemble's Hamlet this approach had led to formalism and a tendency toward monotony, Macready was able to combine it with the attention to nature and concern for variety which he had learned from Kean. Macready was able to bring about this amalgam by consciously and systematically employing a method of work on a role which scarcely occurred to Kemble and which Kean seems to have practiced only sporadically, in response to untutored instinct. Macready described his method in his *Reminiscences*:

My long experience of the stage has convinced me of the necessity of keeping, on the day of exhibition, the mind as intent as possible on the subject of the actor's portraiture, even to the very moment of his entrance on the scene. He meditates himself, as it were, into the very thought and feeling of the being he is about to represent: enwrapt in the idea of the personage he assumes, he moves, and looks, and bears himself as the Roman or the Dane, and thus almost identifies himself with the creature of his imagination.[8]

It is one thing to work for identification, and another to achieve it, but that Macready had great success in reaching his goal is amply attested. "An advantage attaches to him," said James Spedding, the great Francis Bacon scholar, "which I have observed in no other Hamlet: it is easy to credit him with the thoughts he utters."[9] John Foster Kirk, the American historian, made the point even more forcefully: "He was . . . the only actor I have ever seen who was always under the apparent influence of the emotion he was depicting."[10]

Given this paramount concern for the attainment of psychological truth, it is not surprising to learn that Macready carried still further that tendency to ignore meter which was begun by David Garrick and amplified by Kean. It was said that "in speaking he paid less attention to . . . the rhythmical flow of verse, than any other great actor whom we remember."[11] Fanny Kemble thought he simply lacked "musical ear"; admirers might talk learnedly of "the natural style of speaking," but all she could hear was blank verse chopped up into prose by an actor who had never learned the difference.[12] The admirers were wont to point out in rebuttal that "on the other hand, no false note was ever struck, no shade of meaning was left undiscriminated, no measured or monotonous recitation ever wearied the ear. . . . Even the . . . spasmodic jerks, seemed to aid the effect in the broken utterances of intense and struggling passion."[13] The impression of jerkiness owed something to Macready's imitation of Kean's habit of sudden transitions. But in his concern for the precise discrimination of the meaning of each word spoken, Macready greatly added to the effect by frequently interposing a superfluous syllable between words to be emphasized; in *Hamlet* the result was recorded as "to-er be-er, or not-er to be-er."[14] He further broke up the verse lines by lengthy pauses, designed on some occasions to give the audience time to absorb the full force of a phrase just uttered, on others to give himself time to call up the required emotion prior to utterance.[15]

In the management of vocal tone, Macready made himself considerably more acceptable to those who set great store by the musical component of spoken verse. Hazlitt described his voice as possessed of "great harmony and modulation,"[16] but following Kean's lead and his own bent, he was always ready to sacrifice sonority to the truth of passion. As Lewes said, he had a "tendency to scream in violent passages."[17]

Fanny Kemble was almost certainly wrong in asserting that Macready's failure to please the ear was the result of natural defect rather than artistic choice, but something of that sort seems to have been true of his corresponding failure to please the eye. Macready greatly admired the dignity, grace and sculptural beauty of form which he observed in the Kembles and in the great French actor François Joseph Talma, and he worked hard to make those qualities part of his own art. Unfortunately, nature stood in his way. He was tall, angular and bandy-legged, and he moved awkwardly, in short, quick, springy steps which reminded James Hackett of "the recoil of a cannon upon its carriage."[18] His face too, with its square jaw and ponderous brow, was unprepossessing, suggesting brutishness more than refinement. John Coleman found his unsuitable appearance augmented almost to the point of clownishness by his highly original manner of costuming the character:

He wore a dress the waist of which nearly reached his arms; a hat with a sable plume big enough to cover a hearse; a pair of black silk gloves, much too large for him; a ballet shirt of straw-colored satin, which looked simply dirty; and, what with his gaunt, awkward, angular figure, his grizzled hair, his dark beard close shaven to his square jaws, yet unsoftened by a trace of pigment, his irregular features, his queer, extraordinary nose—unlike anything else in the shape of a nose I have ever seen—and his long skinny neck, he appeared positively hideous.[19]

Such was the filter of style and appearance through which Macready's audience was asked to view his conception of Hamlet's mind and heart. Many found the filter simply too opaque, a barrier to perception of the inner man. Those who did see through it were, in varying degrees, either enchanted or repelled by what they found.

Macready's interpretation, if less dynamic than Kean's, was not so static as Kemble's. He made melancholy prominent but not pervasive, and his suffering was more abject than heroic. "Lachrymose and fretful," Lewes called him. "Too fond of a cambric handkerchief to be really affecting."[20] The burden of an ill-starred life seemed at times to crush his spirit. "The fetters of destiny weighed too heavily; the grief was too oppressive,"[21] Kirk thought.

But there was sterner stuff as well. "In the early acts," Macready told a friend, "I seek to express, among other things, the impetuous rebellion of a generous nature when its trust has been cruelly deceived; in the last act, the resignation of a generous nature when the storm has spent itself; in presenting the striking contrasts of this conception—its passion, its imagination, its irony, its colloquial realism.'' According to John Westland Marston, who reports the statement, Macready was entirely successful in his intention. Marston found him more passionate than sentimental, an idealist turned misanthrope, full of gall and bitter irony through the first three acts and thereafter painfully fighting his way back to the patience and trust which had been driven out of him by his rough encounter with corruption and treachery.[22]

Other evidence also suggests that it was along such lines that Macready both conceived and executed the character. On the night he played the Prince for the last time he is reported to have said, ''It is only now that I am just beginning to realize the sweetness, the tenderness, the gentleness, of the character''—a remark which may be taken to mean that he had earlier stressed Hamlet's darker side.[23] A reviewer in 1849 called him ''rugged and spasmodic'' and could offer only a grudging sympathy ''for the terrible expenditure of violent emotions and feverish exertions he had deemed necessary to give what we think he had erroneously deemed a true representation of Hamlet'' (London *Morning Post*, 11 October 1849). He was flexible and impressionable, by turns furious and lethargic, now philosophic and now eager for revenge. John Forster, Macready's intimate friend and most dedicated apologist, called it ''the Hamlet of our fancies reconciled to our waking thoughts.''[24]

Descriptions of Macready's behavior at specific moments in the play tend to confirm these claims for a pleasing variety in his rendering of Hamlet's complex psychic life, but they also help make clear how some spectators came away with the conviction that this or that emotional hue had been given undue prominence in the completed portrait. Kirk, who over the full course of the play found Macready's depiction of Hamlet's grief ''too oppressive,'' confessed admiration for the actor's first manifestation of it, upon Hamlet's entry in the court scene:

The key-note was struck before he uttered the first words. Advancing slowly to the very front of the stage, he stood for a moment with dejected eyes, then slowly raised them with a look so expressive of profound grief that few hearts, I think, remained untouched. It was a stroke which no actor could have ventured, except at the risk of exciting ridicule, who was not confident of his power to awaken sympathy by the silent expression of emotion.[25]

Forster also remarked on the lasting impression of anguished bereavement which Macready created in the scene but placed it a little later: "The impassioned and heartbreaking sorrow with which Mr. Macready opened the play in the first soliloquy was a noble foundation for the entire structure of the character."[26] But the soliloquy also revealed something of that "credulous faith turned to gall" which Marston described; Macready restored Hamlet's bitter reflection "Oh God, a beast, that wants discourse of reason, / Would have mourned longer" (I.ii.150–51) and the following scornful recollection of his mother's "unrighteous tears." Of incestuous sheets, however, there was still no mention.[27]

At the news of Hamlet's father's ghostly return, Macready was thrown into a state of bustling excitement. He "darted up the stage" on the last words of Horatio's report, "turned suddenly and rushed down to his starting place, and uttered 'Indeed, indeed, sirs, but this troubles me' (I.ii.224)." The enfilade of questions which followed ("Armed, say you?"; "From top to toe?" etc.) was delivered at such a clip as to endanger comprehension. He became so animated that he actually stammered on the last word of "His beard was grizzled? No?"[28]

Macready opened the Ghost scene by pacing up and down in Kemble's manner; Forster avowed that "nothing could be more true." He also followed tradition in shedding his hat and cloak on cue, leaving them to be retrieved and later returned by his companions.[29] But there was nothing routine about his conduct in the Ghost's presence. It was perhaps the most powerfully affecting part of his performance, praised even by those who found little else to praise. Hunt thought he showed a lack of respect for his father's presence in the noisy violence with which he threw off his friends' restraining hands, but he judged that the rest was done "capitally well."[30] Taking a hint from Kean, he remained physically composed, but in his voice there was a quality of preternatural, trance-like strangeness which matched the Ghost's own otherworldly tones and bore no resemblance to "that human voice of nature in which man speaks to his fellow man" (London *Herald*, 9 June 1821). Macready told Lady Pollock that as a young man he had seen in a dream the ghost of a recently deceased friend and that thereafter "whenever he was to act Hamlet, he summoned up the passion of that dream."[31]

When he mounted the play at Covent Garden in 1837, on taking over the management, he staged the scene of Hamlet's reappearance with the Ghost by opening the curtain on a tableau showing the Ghost standing aloft in a turret as Hamlet inches his way up the steep wall toward him. "Striking but a little too melodramatic," said the *Spectator*.[32] The rest of the scene was a mixture of traditional and innovative touches. He let his sword fall on "Murder!" as Henderson had done,[33] and adopted Garrick's misappropriation of "O, horrible, O, horrible, most horrible!" In the soliloquy after the Ghost's disappearance he also followed Garrick in retaining the lines "O most pernicious woman! / O villain, villain, smiling, damned villain!" (I.v.106). (Kemble and Kean had both omitted them.) He did not, however, go so far as to restore the immediately ensuing references to Hamlet's tables, nor did he see fit to utter the saucy nicknames Hamlet applies to the voice from the cellarage. On his exit line, "Nay, come, let's go together," he gave his hand to Marcellus and took Horatio by the arm, thus delicately suggesting, as Marston saw it, "the sense of brotherhood between man and man which the awe of a supernatural visitation would call forth."[34]

In the lobby scene, and elsewhere, Macready handled Hamlet's antic disposition with a nice ambiguity, revealing "a subtle . . . madness, which is not madness, and yet not an assumption." Forster believed no other actor had ever come so close to realizing Shakespeare's intention.[35]

Forster also thought Macready had caught "the true Hamlet" in his meeting with Rosencrantz and Guildenstern. In questioning them about their unexpected arrival at court, he "happily kept up the quiet demeanour of conscious detection, of cool observance yet friendly familiarity, hitting one of the very nicest points in Hamlet, without the intrusion of any violence or severe abruptness." "We shall never forget," Forster concluded, "the tone with which he broke into 'What a piece of work is man!' so earnest in its faith, and so passionate in its sorrow. . . . No wonder the shock of this outraged sense of good should drive him nearly mad."

As for the remainder of Act II, Macready was too aloof with the players for Forster's taste, but he more than redeemed himself with the closing soliloquy. "If Mr. Macready's performance had suddenly closed," Forster declared, "in the soliloquy of 'O what a rogue and peasant slave am I,' at the words—'Bloody, bawdy villain! Remorseless, treacherous, lecherous, kindless villian!' we should have needed no better assurance of the power of his genius to cope with this wonderful character." Forster particularly admired the way in which he "changes his tone upon the epithet 'kindless' . . . and by some tears of anguish at the word, expresses at once both Hamlet's pure and refined nature, and the weakness and sensibility of his temper."[36]

In October 1823, *The Drama* described Macready's delivery of the "To be or not to be" soliloquy (III.i.55–87) as "possessed somewhat of novelty" and went on to give details: "He delivered the commencement of it . . . in a deep pensive and awful tone. His utterance became rapid in the middle of it where there is less of thoughtfulness in the text, and his voice finally became subdued into broken accents happily indicative of the previous perplexities of thought by which the mind of Hamlet is convulsed." Apparently he kept that approach for some years thereafter, because in 1830 Hunt objected that the delivery "was too quick and continuous; not full of thought enough, nor sufficiently broken with pauses."[37] Macready seems to have taken the criticism to heart; his diary shows that three years later he was keenly aware of a need for "a more entire abandonment to thought, more abstraction."[38] Ironically, Forster shortly thereafter described his delivery as "too quiet and deliberate," but Macready seems to have worked on undeterred to achieve the effect of total absorption in thought. In New York, in 1843, he was able to congratulate himself on final success: "The soliloquy . . . on life and death was reality—as my French friends term it, *inspiration*. I never before approached the real self-communing which possessed me during its delivery. The audience fully appreciated, for they applauded until I actually stopped them."[39] Kirk saw a performance about this time and later seconded Macready's assessment:

His delivery of the famous soliloquy seemed to me matchless. It was true "self-communing," to use the phrase he himself applies to it on one occasion, and in this sense was the only real soliloquy I have ever listened to on the stage. He entered from the wings, his hands behind him, the right hand clasping the left wrist like a vice, the eyes fixed in a gaze of concentrated abstraction, the words, when he began to speak, dropping as if involuntarily from his lips, every movement made with the apparent unconsciousness of a mind plunged in the depths of absorbed and momentous introspection.[40]

Marston heard in Macready's playing of the nunnery scene the bitterness of shattered idealism, "yet the agony of his love pierced through the bitterness."[41] Macready seemed to have adopted the view that Hamlet is here executing a painful duty, deliberately alienating Ophelia's affections so as to free himself for the bloody work in hand. He thus showed, according to Forster, "not anger, but grief assuming the appearance of anger—love awkwardly counterfeiting hate."[42] Sometime prior to his second U.S. tour in 1843, and possibly as early as his first in 1826, Macready took up the practice of having Claudius and Polonius inadvertently reveal themselves to Hamlet for a brief moment in their place of concealment, thus prompting his abrupt question "Where's your father?" (III.i.129) and lending new point to his harsh treatment of Ophelia through the remainder of the scene.[43] In what seems to have been a flourish of his own invention, Macready used Hamlet's knowledge of his enemies' presence to offer a naked threat to Claudius; on the line "those that are married already (all but one) shall live" (III.i.148), Macready walked deliberately to the hiding-place and shouted through the protective covering.[44]

In the speech to the players (III.ii.1–45), Macready was more the dour preceptor than the engaging fellow enthusiast, maintaining throughout that wide social distance he had established between himself and the strollers on their arrival.[45] He carried with him a scroll of paper, supposed to contain the speech Hamlet wants added to the play script, and handed it to one of the actors at the conclusion of his remarks—a touch of realism that promptly became the standard practice of the stage.[46]

The new business Macready introduced a moment later, on the line "I must be idle" (III.ii.91), was far less universally admired. Hackett was appalled:

He immediately assumed the manner of an idiot, or of a silly and active and impertinent booby, by tossing his head right and left, and walking rapidly across the stage five or six times before the footlights and switching his handkerchief—held by a corner—over his right and left shoulder alternately, until the whole court have had time to parade and be seated, and Hamlet finds himself addressed. Such behavior was ill-calculated to indicate an "idle" spectator.[47]

Coleman dismissed the business as an example of Macready's occasional lapses into "weird eccentricity."[48] But another member of the acting fraternity, the reigning American star Edwin Forrest, considered Macready's "fancy dance," as he termed it, "a desecration to the scene"; at a performance in Edinburgh on 30 February 1846, he greeted it with a prolonged hiss—touching off a bitter rivalry between the two actors which lead eventually to the disastrous Astor Place Riot of 10 May 1849.[49]

At the time of the historic hiss, Macready had been engaging in his fantastic promenade for over a decade and had reason to consider it one of the brightest adornments of his characterization; in 1835 Forster had declared that "his quick and salient walk up and down the front of the stage, waving his handkerchief as if in idle gay indifference, but ill concealing, at that instant, the sense of an approaching triumph— was one of those things Shakespeare himself would have done had he acted Hamlet."[50] Nor did Forrest's insult shake Macready's faith in the propriety of the business. He retained it when he performed in the United States in 1848 and was rewarded with a resounding vote of confidence from the audience, as his diary reveals: "Acted Hamlet with care and energy; took especial pains to make the meaning of 'I must be idle' clear; which was followed by cheers on cheers after the first applause, when it was understood by the house that this was Mr. Forrest's 'fancy dance.' Oh fie! fie!"[51]

During the Players' performance, Macready brought out Hamlet's seething hatred of the King with great force, perhaps because sarcasm, as an early reviewer suggested, "was more immediately in Mr. Macready's peculiar way than any other quality" (London *Morning Advertiser*, 18 October 1823). His answers to the King's guarded queries about the play's nature were "keen, glittering, and venomous, like the thrusts of a poisoned dagger." Marston thought him "superb" throughout the scene, not least in his execution of the Kean crawl: "With body prone, and head erect, and eyes riveted on Claudius, he dragged himself nearer and nearer to him, till the moment of Gonzago's murder, then sprang up to meet the convicted King, with a burst of mocking exultation."[52] According to a promptbook note, he illustrated his exultation at this point by bringing his handkerchief into service again, this time waving it "triumphantly"—in imitation of Garrick's business at the same moment.[53] It was a moment to which Macready attached the utmost importance, as he told Lady Pollock: "I have conceived the excitement of that most excitable being to be carried to its highest pitch in the effect of the test he applied to the conscience of the King."[54] According to Forster, Macready managed to suggest at this moment that "the success of his experiment was his greatest aim, and that to *act* upon it was as far from his thoughts as ever."[55] Something of this may have been conveyed by his turning to Horatio, at the completion of his outpouring of exultation, and drooping his head on his friend's shoulder, while asking for the recorders "in the tone of a sick man."[56] In the remaining moments he employed two original readings, both designed to emphasize Hamlet's loathing for Claudius and all who served him. The line "With drink, sir?" (III.ii.302) he gave not as a question but "in a tone of exclamation denoting an *unquestionable* conclusion."[57] After "We shall obey, were she ten times our mother" (333–34) he paused at great length before following with "Have you any *further* trade with us?"[58]

Hamlet's lines about killing or not killing the King at prayer (III.iii.73–96) were omitted. Macready moved quickly to Gertrude's closet, where he took the unusual precaution of bolting the doors after him, "unnoticed by the Queen."[59] Having declined to encumber himself with sword and scabbard during the athletic play scene, he now bore a naked weapon with him in his hand and laid it out on a table immediately upon entering, thus making it appear, curiously, that Hamlet had armed himself *expressly* for this visit.[60] Putting the sword to use a moment later, he gave "Dead for a ducat, dead!" (III.iv.24) in a great shout and followed it with "a very fine and effective contrast of tone"[61] in the rapid question—"Nay, I know not, is it the King?" (III.iv.26). Forster interpreted the shout as "loud bullying of himself, to thrust down the thought which would at once have disabled his act."[62]

In 1840 Macready dispensed with the customary miniatures and replaced them with full-length portraits, or what appeared to be portraits. The frame supposed to contain the likeness of King Hamlet was actually occupied by the actor playing the Ghost, who subsequently made his entrance by "coming to life" and moving into the room.[63] Macready was severe with Gertrude, "sterner . . . than his stage contemporaries," according to Marston, but "his indictment of her was delivered with an arresting concentration that had nothing in it of violence or tumult, and with a mien lofty and unrelenting, as if he had been the commissioned angel of retribution."[64] At the Ghost's appearance, he "broke from the most intense and passionate indignation

William Charles Macready. The Closet Scene (III.iv). Princess's Theatre, London, 1845. Harvard Theatre Collection.

to the lost and bewildered air, and with a voice of unearthly horror and tones of strange awe tremblingly addressed the spirit" (*New Monthly Magazine*, 1 July 1821). He softened somewhat toward Gertrude near the end, enough to bid her a gentle and sorrowful good-night, but when she broke off her exit to return in tears for a last embrace, he warded her off with upraised hand, "clearly implying by his action and melancholy countenance that the memory of his dead parent was a sacred thought, and would not allow him to enfold in his embrace her who, *even now*, held communion with his murderer."[65] That action he doubtless borrowed from Kemble; the tears he shed over the fallen Polonius as the scene closed seem to have been his own idea.[66]

Macready cut not only Hamlet's chance encounter with the Norwegian army (IV.iv) but also the two short scenes immediately preceding it, where Hamlet is apprehended by Rosencrantz and Guildenstern, lectures Claudius on worms and graves, and is delivered over for the journey to England. Hence, after leaving Gertrude's room he was next seen in the graveyard. In his handling of Yorick's skull his penchant for realism got the better of him, in the opinion of at least one spectator; according to James Murdoch, "His early manner in returning the skull . . . to its earthly home, was an inadvertent act of juvenile extravagance, founded on the mere physical aversion of the senses to the loathsome object in his hand:—he literally tossed it over his own head up the stage."[67] Murdoch implies that Macready soon abandoned this practice, but he certainly used it in Paris in 1844, and with it an additional sprinkling of pantomimic action; having rid himself of the offending object, he "took from his pocket a beautiful cambric handkerchief, unfolded it, carefully wiped his hands, and continued." Theophile Gautier thought it a fine illustration of the fusion of "the impossible and the real" in Hamlet's character.[68]

Macready received Osric's delivery of the fencing challenge with "a visible sinking of the heart, although bravely defying augury."[69] The "augury" speech (V.ii.219–24) was as usual cut to its opening sentence. As for the fencing itself, Macready "handled a foil like a pitchfork," in the opinion of John Coleman.[70] But that assessment seems difficult to reconcile with another report, which has the actor showing off his skill, in the course of choosing a foil, by "making a spring and a lunge together, hitting the edge of the wing nearest the footlights with unerring certainty."[71]

In his early performances, Macready appears to have invested Hamlet's death with Kean's protracted spasms of physical pain; an 1823 review described it as "an appalling picture of agony in the extreme struggle of human existence" (*The Drama*, October 1823). In later years, however, he made the death "next to an instantaneous one" (*Theatrical Journal*, 12 September 1840). Throughout his career he followed Kean's practice of ending the play on "The rest is silence." Following Macready's retirement in February 1851, another half-century would pass before a British audience would see the play concluded as Shakespeare wrote it. Meanwhile, this and other practices of the British stage had been exported to the United States where they combined with innovations of native origin.

NOTES

1. London *Examiner*, 22 September 1816, in *The Complete Works of William Hazlitt*, ed. P. P. Howe (London: J. M. Dent, 1930–40), 5:334.

2. The London *Morning Herald* piece (9 June 1821) has a faint odor of puffery about it; Macready's performance is called "one of the finest and most completely successful . . . we have ever witnessed."

3. William Charles Macready, *Reminiscences*, in *Diaries and Letters*, ed. Sir Frederick Pollock (London: Trübner, 1875), p. 410.

4. Ibid., p. 649.

5. For the most thorough modern analysis of Macready's style, see Alan S. Downer, *The Eminent Tragedian, William Charles Macready* (Cambridge, Mass.: Harvard University Press, 1966). Downer concludes (p. 65) that his style "underlies the whole tradition of naturalism, of Stanislavsky and his heirs."

6. Leigh Hunt, in the *Tatler*, 15 March 1831; in *Dramatic Essays* [by] *Leigh Hunt*, ed. William Archer and Robert W. Lowe (London: W. Scott, 1894), p. 209.

7. For Hazlitt's assessment of Macready's style, see his *Macbeth* review for the London *Examiner*, 22 June 1820, in *Works*, 18:340. Lewes' very similar description appeared in the London *Leader*, 8 February 1851; see *Dramatic Essays by John Forster and George Henry Lewes*, ed. William Archer and Robert W. Lowe (London: W. Scott, 1894), p. 132.

8. Macready, *Reminiscences*, pp. 86–87. Elsewhere Macready writes in a similar vein with specific reference to Hamlet; see *The Diaries of William Charles Macready: 1831–1851*, ed. William Toynbee (New York: G. P. Putnam's Sons, 1912), 1:62; entry for 12 September 1833.

9. Quoted in Lady Pollock, *Macready as I Knew Him* (London: Remington, 1885), p. 108.

10. John Foster Kirk, "Shakespeare's Tragedies on the Stage: II," *Lippincott's Magazine*, June 1884, p. 613.

11. London *Daily News*, January 1851, quoted in William Archer, *William Charles Macready* (New York: Longmans, Green & Co., 1890), p. 198.

12. Frances Anne Kemble, *Records of Later Life*, 2nd ed. (London: R. Bentley, 1882), 3:376.

13. Kirk, "Shakespeare's Tragedies," p. 613.

14. C. E. L. Wingate, *Shakespeare's Heroes on the Stage* (New York: T. Y. Crowell, 1896), p. 278.

15. In the *Diaries*, Macready repeatedly lectures himself on the importance of pauses; see 1:23, 74, 114.

16. William Hazlitt, in the London *Examiner*, 22 September 1816; in *Works*, 5:334.

17. Lewes, *On Actors and the Art of Acting* (London: Smith, Elder, 1875), p. 40.

18. James Hackett, *Notes, Criticisms and Correspondence upon Shakespeare's Plays and Actors* (1863; reprint, New York: B. Blom, 1970), p. 137.

19. John Coleman, *Players and Playwrights I Have Known* (London: Chatto & Windus, 1888), 1:50.

20. Lewes, *On Actors*, p. 41.

21. Kirk, "Shakespeare's Tragedies," p. 614.

22. John Westland Marston, *Our Recent Actors* (London: S. Low, Marston, Searle & Rivington, 1888), 1:80. After his retirement, Macready told Lady Pollock, "Of all that I have read on Shakespeare, I prefer, though even then with some reservations, Goethe's remarks on 'Hamlet' in his 'Wilhelm Meister' " (*Reminiscences*, p. 692). Goethe's novel may thus have had some slight influence, depending on when he read it, but Macready was never identified with Goethe's anemic Prince in the way that other stage Hamlets were soon to be.

23. Henry Irving told the story in an address at Harvard College, reported in the *Critic*, 4 April 1885, and reprinted by Laurence Hutton and Brander Matthews in *Actors and Actresses of Great Britain and the United States* (New York: Cassell, 1886), 4:20–21.

24. John Forster, in the London *Examiner*, 11 October 1835; in *Dramatic Essays by Forster and Lewes*, pp. 7–9.

25. Kirk, "Shakespeare's Tragedies," p. 614.

26. *Dramatic Essays by Forster and Lewes*, p. 9.

27. Macready made only minor alterations in the acting text established by Kemble in 1800. His cuts and restorations were marked by him, probably in 1821, on a copy of Oxberry's 1820 edition, now in the Folger Shakespeare Library in Washington, D.C. (This text is designated "*HAM*, 14" in Charles Shattuck, *The Shakespeare Promptbooks* [Urbana and London: University of

Illinois Press, 1965]; Shattuck's designations will also be employed in all subsequent references to promptbooks.) In addition to *HAM*, 14, I have consulted two other promptbooks (*HAM* 37, 44) for business and line readings (see the following notes). For descriptions of five additional Macready promptbooks, see Shattuck, *HAM*, 15, 28, 29, 30, 40.

28. Hackett, *Notes*, pp. 145, 147.

29. *HAM*, 14.

30. *Dramatic Essays* [by] *Leigh Hunt*, p. 160.

31. Pollock, *Macready as I Knew Him*, pp. 105–6.

32. *Spectator* 10 (1837): 946.

33. According to a promptbook prepared by John Moore in New York for the period 1850–1870, now at the Folger Shakespeare Library (*HAM*, 44).

34. Marston, *Our Recent Actors*, 1:82.

35. *Dramatic Essays by Forster and Lewes*, p. 10. Hunt, on the other hand, complained that Macready was "too real" in "the whole of the supposed mad or flighty scenes" (in the *Tatler*, 22 October 1830; in *Dramatic Essays* [by] *Leigh Hunt*, p. 162).

36. Forster, in the London *Examiner*, 14 January 1838; in *Dramatic Essays by Forster and Lewes*, p. 46. It seems clear from these remarks that Macready did not follow the Kemble-Kean practice of beginning the soliloquy at "I have heard that guilty creatures." His marked text, however, shows no restoration (see n. 27).

37. *Dramatic Essays* [by] *Leigh Hunt*, p. 161.

38. Macready, *Reminiscences*, pp. 283–84; entry for 28 May 1833.

39. Ibid., p. 535.

40. Kirk, "Shakespeare's Tragedies," p. 614.

41. Marston, *Our Recent Actors*, 1:81.

42. *Dramatic Essays by Forster and Lewes*, p. 10.

43. According to Arthur Colby Sprague (*Shakespeare and the Actors* [Cambridge, Mass.: Harvard University Press, 1944], p. 153), the business originated sometime in the 1820s, possibly with Junius Brutus Booth's performance in New York on 15 October 1821. Hackett is the only commentator I have found who connects the business with Macready, and he does not make clear whether he saw him use it in 1826 or in 1843 (Hackett, *Notes*, p. 156).

44. Hackett (*Notes*, pp. 156–57) objected, on the not unreasonable grounds that such a revelation of feeling was inconsistent with Hamlet's earlier efforts to avert suspicion.

45. Ibid., p. 157; *Dramatic Essays* [by] *Leigh Hunt*, pp. 161–62.

46. The paper is called for in Macready's marked copy (*HAM*, 14) and is also named in an updated promptbook, now in the Folger Shakespeare Library (*HAM*, 37), used by Macready, Vandenhoff, Anderson, Charles Kean, Hackett, Kemble, Booth, and Forrest.

47. Hackett, *Notes*, p. 158.

48. Coleman, *Players and Playwrights*, 1:32.

49. Forrest used the phrases in a letter to the *Times* of London (4 April) in which he confessed the hiss and defended it as a "legitimate mode of evincing . . . disapprobation in the theatre." For a full account of the riot, see Richard Moody, *The Astor Place Riot* (Bloomington: Indiana University Press, 1958).

50. *Dramatic Essays by Forster and Lewes*, p. 11.

51. Macready, *Reminiscences*, p. 606, entry for 2 December 1848, New York. A similar note, for 12 October 1848, reads: "There was spontaneous applause, and after a short interval, as if it were remembered that this must have been the point of Mr. Forrest's exception, another confirmatory round" (ibid., p. 603).

52. Marston, *Our Recent Actors*, 1:82.

53. *HAM*, 44.

54. Macready, *Reminiscences*, p. 717; letter of 9 May 1861.

55. *Dramatic Essays by Forster and Lewes*, p. 11.

56. Pollack, *Macready as I Knew Him*, p. 107.

57. Hackett, *Notes*, p. 159.

58. *HAM*, 37.

59. *HAM*, 44.

60. Clement Scott, *The Drama of Yesterday and Today* (London: Macmillan, 1899), 1:562.

61. *Dramatic Essays* [by] *Leigh Hunt*, p. 161.

62. *Dramatic Essays by Forster and Lewes*, p. 11.

63. *HAM*, 44. Macready introduced the change at the Haymarket Theatre on 16 March 1840 and that night congratulated himself on its being "a very great improvement on the old stupid custom" (*Diaries*, 2:52).

64. Marston, *Our Recent Actors*, 1:82.

65. *Theatrical Journal* 1 (1839): 126. Macready's promptbook reads: "The Queen goes to the R wing—stops, looks back at Hamlet, clasps her hands and raises her eyes to Heaven, and rushes back to throw herself round Hamlet's neck—he repels her, and she exit sorrowfully R. H." (*HAM*, 14).

66. Pollock, *Macready as I Knew Him*, p. 107.

67. James Murdoch, *The Stage; or, Recollections of Actors and Acting from an Experience of Fifty Years* (Philadelphia: J. M. Stoddart, 1880) p. 256.

68. Theophile Gautier, "Feuilletons: *Othello et Hamlet*," *La Presse*, 23 December 1844, quoted in B. Juden and J. Richer, "L'entente cordiale au théâtre: Macready et *Hamlet* à Paris en 1844," *La revue des lettres modernes* 74–75 (1962–63): 20; my translation.

69. Pollock, *Macready as I Knew Him*, p. 107.

70. Coleman, *Players and Playwrights*, 1:50.

71. Godfrey Turner, "Scenery, Dress and Decorations" *The Theatre*, 1 March 1884, p. 128.

7

EDWIN FORREST

When Edwin Forrest hissed William Charles Macready in Edinburgh and thereafter entered into open rivalry with him, he was, among other things, asserting the superiority of homegrown American theatrical art over the English imports on which the young nation had been dependent since colonial times. Edwin Forrest (1806–1872) was America's first native-born tragedian. Prior to his appearance as Hamlet on 27 August 1829,[1] the United States had seen only English actors in the role.

The qualities which had brought Forrest to preeminence among American actors, beginning with his portrayal of Othello at the Park Theatre in June 1826, were such as to render him a most unlikely candidate for success in the role of Hamlet. A major factor in his enormous popular appeal was his physical person, which in its massive muscularity seemed to many to embody the vast untamed power and beauty of the American continent itself. His vocal power was also prodigous and regularly set commentators to work framing comparisons with cataracts and hurricanes.

That was all very well for such a paragon of noble savagery as Metamora, Forrest's most admired impersonation, and it could even be used to good effect for the warrior heroes Othello, Macbeth and Coriolanus, but Hamlet was another matter. For John Coleman, Forrest's gladiatorial physique produced, in Hamlet's very first soliloquy, "a note of dissonance which pervaded the entire assumption. When he exclaimed, 'My father's brother, but no more like my father / Than I to Hercules' [I.ii.152–53], the exclamation appeared absurd, for he was Hercules—the Farnese Hercules incarnate!"[2] Another observer said he played both Lear and Hamlet "like enraged Titans,"[3] and another spoke of the constant struggle between mind and muscle, with the latter always the victor.[4]

The impression of "animal coarseness" (the phrase is William Winter's), which his natural endowments did so much to foster, was abetted, some thought, by a corresponding coarseness in his acting style. Forrest took Edmund Kean as his idol and model, after acting second parts with him in Albany in his apprenticeship days, but when John Forster saw him perform in London in 1836 he concluded that he had managed to take from Kean only "the more vulgar and obvious points." Lacking Kean's imagination, intelligence and subtlety, he relied almost entirely, Forster argued, on the merely mechanical "alternation of senseless tones," sacrificing meaning and character identity to "such coarse effects as may happen to lie on the mere surface of words wrenched from the general text; . . . where a tender word occurred, it was spoken tenderly; where a fierce word, fiercely." Forster further charged him with an irritating propensity to reduce poetic imagery to the most vulgar literalness, as when he vigorously shook drops of blood from Richard of Gloucester's sword on the line "See how my sword weeps for the poor king's death!"[5] Winter took much the same view: "He lacked spirituality, and, as a general thing, he lacked poetry. His acting was radically literal."[6] John Foster Kirk, in what seems an implied comparison with Kean, also declared that Forrest's vaunted "fire" was only empty fulmination. He had the look and sound of mighty nature in furious upheaval, but there was "no electric current passing along the veins," fomenting disturbance from within.[7]

Or so it seemed to the discerning and fastidious few. The vast majority thrilled to Forrest's interpretations, Hamlet among them. Most of his fervent partisans simply did not value, indeed, they were inclined to disparage, those qualities of subtlety and refinement which his critics found lacking, and they therefore dismissed all such criticism as flatly perverse. Perhaps the most eloquent apology for their point of view was made by one not entirely sympathetic to it; the writer for the *Albion*, who called Forrest's Hamlet an "enraged Titan," went on to observe:

The courtly guise, the old-world conventionalism, which "hedge in the divinity of kings," and the polished graces that surround the great and highborn— are not held by Mr. Forrest as the imperative auxiliaries of his acting. His graces and dignity have been founded on other models—the free aboriginal of his country, erect and fearless in the freedom with which nature has endowed him, has afforded to this great actor lessons in the histrionic art, which the finished artists of Europe take only from the Court or the Salons. And in striking out this originality, Mr. Forrest has touched the hearts, and jumped with the tastes of a majority of his countrymen.[8]

It does not seem to have bothered these spectators—probably it never occurred to them—that there is little ground for thinking of Hamlet as a "free aboriginal." They went to the theater to see Forrest, not Hamlet, and they liked what they saw. Kirk maintained of Forrest: "Not only did he not seem to lose his own individuality, but he did not seem to find it in that of any personage that he represented. One could not perceive that he had more affinity with one character than another: to his admirers he seemed equally great in each."[9] The quality of greatness they perceived in him, whatever the character he might be nominally representing, was vividly described by Winter, himself by no means an admirer, as "a puissant animal splendour and ground-swell of emotion. He was tremendously real. He could be seen and heard and understood . . . and in moments of simple passion he affected the senses . . . like the ponderous, slow-moving, crashing, and thundering surges of the sea."[10]

Winter concluded that Forrest's primary appeal was to "the lower order of public intelligence," and that certainly seems to have been the case. But in addition to the *hoi polloi* who simply did not demand of a Shakespearean actor what Winter and other sophisticates demanded, there were those devotees of Forrest's artistry who insisted that he did in fact bring to his characterization of Hamlet not just brute power but the intellectual and emotional complexity with which Shakespeare had invested his most fascinating creation. George Becks, who played supporting roles in Forrest's *Hamlet* company through four seasons, described him as "Too heavy for ideal princeliness—but great and *grandly* philosophic."[11] Forrest's friend and biographer, the Rev. William Rounseville Alger, also acknowledged that the actor's Herculean frame was a hindrance to ideal representation of the introspective Prince but argued that it was a handicap successfully overcome. He "laid aside the massive hauteur of his port" and assumed the refined and cultivated manner of a scholar.[12]

Alger and Becks both saw Forrest's Hamlet quite late in the actor's career, by which time he had evidently brought to it a degree of intellectuality not present in the beginning. James Rees, another biographer, saw one of the very early performances and recalled later that

"it was a beautiful but not a philosophical Hamlet." [13] His performance seems to have grown also in beauty over the years. In 1848 a
critic reported, "He has acquired a depth of pathos, and a finish in the
expression of the softer passions, eminently marked and beautiful. His
attitudes too are more graceful, picturesque, and artistical." [14] Twelve
years later another observer detected still greater modulation: "His
manner is graver, more sedate, more gracious. The man has been, to
use a painter's phrase, 'toned down.' At the same time his voice has
not lost its old-time ring and can still sound the trumpet call" (New
York *Herald*, 18 September 1860).

All this commentary, from friend and foe alike, suggests that however much he might succeed in temporarily directing audience attention away from it, Forrest's sinewy virility remained a crucial part of
his impersonation, producing a highly original interpretive slant to the
character. The restless cerebration and fine-tuned emotionality evident
in so many of Hamlet's utterances were so much at odds with the image of adamantine strength conveyed by the voice and body of the
speaker as to make these qualities appear subversive, like fatal hairline
cracks in the foundations of a great stone edifice. The play thus became, in Forrest's hands, a sort of cautionary tale of vibrant health
undermined and ruined by a malignant excess of thought and feeling.
The ruin was signalized by mental breakdown. Forrest moved past affected madness into episodes of real distraction. He played the part,
said Rees, "from the mad point of view," and in that respect "soared
above all the other Hamlets of the day." [15]

Forrest's costume, designed to mask his bulk, consisted of a knee-
length doublet, worn with black silk tights, and over that a short black
cape fastened across the chest by a double cord from which hung several tassels. He wore no jewelry, and the only relief from the solid
black of the costume was a narrow edging of white at the neck. During
his first decade or so in the role, he was clean-shaven; later he grew a
mustache and a small tuft of hair under his lower lip. He wore no wig,
but curled his own hair slightly. His face was pale and his eyebrows
artificially darkened. [16]

For his first appearance he usually chose to be discovered seated at
the rear on a chair conspicuously smaller than the "states" occupied
by Claudius and Gertrude. Alger thought this showed "a delicate perception that the deep melancholy and suspicion in which he was plunged

would make him adverse to ostentation,"[17] but Winter saw something quite different:

His head was held erect, his dark, glowing eyes were fixed defiantly on the King, his hands were clenched on the arms of his throne chair, his demeanor was that of menace, not of melancholy, and it was evident that if any "clouds" hung upon him they were thunder clouds. His delivery of Hamlet's first line, "A little more than kin and less than kind," was firm, deep, reverberant, and it needed only a sonorous profane expletive to make it superlatively Forrestian.[18]

Hamlet's reply to his mother's gentle chiding about the "particularity" of his grief provoked a typically rhapsodic appreciation from Alger: "His grief and gloom appeared to embody themselves in a voice that wailed and quivered the weeping syllables like the tones of a bell swinging above a city stricken with the plague."[19] Some Hamlet of the day, perhaps more than one, must have been in the habit of emphasizing "you" in the line "I shall in all my best obey you, madam" (I.ii.120), because Forrest was complimented for having "the good taste" not to do so.[20]

The soliloquy (I.ii.129–59) he delivered as an intricately orchestrated revelation of the succession of emotions battering wave upon wave against Hamlet's consciousness; Becks sought to record its every note and chord:

" 'gainst self-slaughter"—almost one sibilant

"So excellent a king"—retrospective love

"that was, to this"—disgust

"loving to my mother"—tender

"Heaven and earth"—angry

"would hang on him"—loathly [sic]

"A little month"—unbelievable [sic]

"shoes were old"—grief

"poor father's body"—tender

"married with mine uncle"—disgust

"My father's brother"—contempt

"cannot come to good"—scornful

Forrest restored "O most wicked speed: to post / With such dexterity to incestuous sheets" (I.ii.156–57), but Becks does not reveal the tone in which it was delivered.[21] Alger said of the soliloquy as a whole, "These phrases of his unhappiness were painted with an earnest truthfulness which seized and held the sympathies as with a spell."[22]

On the line "Would I had met my dearest foe in heaven / Or ever I had seen that day, Horatio!" (I.ii.182–83), Forrest put his hand to his head "to soothe the pain," then stepped forward, dropping his hand, and "with a faraway look and *such* love in the voice" continued with "My father—methinks I see my father!" (Becks). Alger, whose desire to pay tribute to Forrest's portrayal seems occasionally to have got the better of his judgment, attributes powers to him in this scene which are barely to be reckoned among the humanly attainable. In his manner of listening to Horatio's account of the apparition, Alger alleges, Forrest showed "obscure presentiments of the invisible state and supernal ranges of being in hidden connection with the scene in which he was playing his part." "Yet more forcibly," Alger continues, "a sense of a providential, retributive, supernatural scheme mysteriously interwoven with our human life was breathed . . . in his soliloquizing moods after agreeing to watch with them that night."[23] We may safely conclude from this that Forrest powerfully conveyed a strong sense of foreboding on Hamlet's part.

He did not pace the stage while waiting for the Ghost, but he gave a "violent start of amazement" on seeing it, and lost part of his costume in the process, his cloak slipping off his shoulders "by the action of his surprise" and his hat dropping "unconsciously . . . from his hand" (Becks). In the catalog of names which Hamlet applies to the specter (I.iv.44–45), Forrest came to a full stop after "Father" and linked "Royal Dane" with the following phrase, "O, answer me!" Since it occasioned comment, it was apparently a new reading.[24] He accented the transition by kneeling before "Royal Dane" and remained in that position until the end of the speech, when he rose slowly and followed the Ghost with his eyes as it crossed the stage. Restrained by his friends from obeying the spirit's beckoning hand, he broke free and drew upon them, stepping forward and thrusting "two or three times backward at Horatio and Marcellus" (Becks). That use of the sword sounds like a magnification of Kean's menacing way with it, but his subsequent employment of the weapon was apparently his own invention; he remained "*en garde* with his sword pointed at the ghost during the whole scene." "It is proper enough," said the New York *Herald*, "but it seems a little strained" (18 September 1860). The defensive posture must also have added a note of awkwardness to the bow of filial respect he made on "I am thy father's spirit . . . " (I.v.9).[25]

Not content to stand silently until time to speak the purloined line, "O, horrible! . . . " Forrest gave himself a cry of "Oh!" at mention of the death-dealing "leprous distillment" (I.v.64; Wright). In a display of that literalness which Forster and Winter deplored, he accompanied "sweep to my revenge" (I.v.31) with "action . . . as if *darting* to his thrust." Similarly, he went down on one knee when the dead King spoke of his "most seeming-virtuous queen" (I.v.46), so as to be able to rise on "my sinews, grow not instant old, / But bear me stiffly up" (I.v.93–94; Becks). He must have given the line with a great show of feebleness in body and voice, because Alger wrote that at this point "a withering spell seemed to have fallen on Hamlet and instantly aged him. He looked as pale and shriveled as the frozen moonlight and the wintry landscape around him."[26] A writer in the New York *Tribune* of 20 March 1855, reviewing Forrest's performance at the Broadway Theatre the night before, accused him of delivering the rest of this speech with "the coarse rage of a ruffian told of a rival bully's murder, of some butchery of one of his gang, and thirsting to glut his fury."[27] He ended the soliloquy with "Yes, by heaven, / I have sworn it," thus omitting "most pernicious woman," "smiling, damned villain" and the cryptic memorandum confided to his tables (I.v.105–9). As if sensing a need for some other piece of business to cap the speech, Forrest knelt yet again and kissed the cross of his sword (Wright).

When joined by his anxious and inquisitive companions, he adopted Kemble's plan of suspecting Marcellus' loyalty—a device which made it possible to suggest that Hamlet's disjointed speech is designed to mask his unwillingness to speak frankly in the sentinel's presence. Forrest introduced it earlier than Kemble had, however. At "But you'll be secret?" (I.v.122), Marcellus was seen "peering close to his face for the news," whereupon Hamlet, having caught a glimpse of something disquieting in his eyes, "turned the subject" with "There's ne'er a villain . . . " (I.v.124). By way of further elaboration, Horatio was "a little piqued" at this and turned away to show it; there was, moreover, "a little nettle" in his next line, "These are but wild and whirling words, my lord'' (I.v.133), and that prompted Forrest to give ''I am sorry they offend you, heartily'' (I.v.134) ''as if pained at having caused pain.'' Brushing aside Horatio's disclaimer (''There's no offence, my lord'' [I.v.135]), he sought to ''assuage that pain'' by again beginning to unburden himself on ''Touching this vision here'' (I.v.137), only to be again deterred by a repetition of Marcellus' hot-eyed anticipation. This time, however, he ''quietly put them from him'' and spoke in a manner ''so princely—as if not wishing to give pain or again offend'' (Becks). The usual cuts were made in Hamlet's jaunty responses to the subterranean injunctions of the Ghost, and the swearing was otherwise conducted along orthodox lines. In what was apparently a new reading, Forrest emphasized the word ''philosophy'' in the famous comment on Horatio's education, rather than ''your.'' [28] Reinvested with cloak and hat, he was led off by his friends to close the scene.

Forrest played the opening lines of the fishmonger scene seated on the throne chair, rising at ''Ay, sir! to be honest . . . '' (II.ii.178). Like Kean, he treated ''For if the sun breed maggots . . . '' (II.ii.181) as a passage in the book he held (Wright). He made a ''positive insult'' of ''You cannot, sir, take from me . . . '' (II.ii.215) by turning full toward Polonius and delivering it in ''a very quiet and positive manner'' (Becks).

There was close attention to shading and nuance also in his encounter with Rosencrantz and Guildenstern. ''I know the good king and queen have sent for you'' (II.ii.281) was spoken with guarded irony, and ''But let me conjure you, by the rights of our fellowship . . . '' (II.ii.283) had a ''feeling in it—as if past liking the boys and now dubious.'' The hymn to man, paragon of animals, was taken in a ''low, adorative tone—and became abstracted'' (Becks). Alger was reminded of ''the grandest chords in the Requiem of Mozart, thrilling [the soul] with sublime premonitions of its own infinity.'' [29] Brought back to earth by a movement from Rosencrantz, Forrest added ''a little ugh—of playful contempt'' to ''no, nor woman neither . . . '' (II.ii.309; Becks). He seems to have been partial to these impulsive interjections. News of the approach of the players brought forth a ''joyous 'ah!' '' and talk of the fickleness of their patrons, so like the faithlessness of his father's subjects, provoked ''a bit of a sigh of upset'' (Becks). To show his contempt for the two supposed turncoats now in his presence, Forrest drew them close to him, as if about to take them into his confidence, on "But my uncle-father and aunt-mother are deceived" (II.ii.376) and then unceremoniously put them from him with "I am but mad north-north-west . . . " (II.ii.378–79; Becks). He was contemptuous also of Polonius upon his reappearance, turning from him in irritated impatience on "Buzz, Buzz!" (II.ii.393), bidding him "Hush!" after "the 'mobled queen' is good" (II.ii.504; Wright) and adding "cautionary smiles" to his command that he see the actors well bestowed (Becks). In pointed contrast, he behaved toward the actors with "thoughtful and gracious kindness." Their leader he dismissed, following their whispered conference, "with a sympathetic touch on his shoulder and a smile." [30]

Forrest nearly always spoke the "rogue and peasant slave" soliloquy (II.ii.550–605) in its entirety, rather than the scant half of it preferred by most actors since Kemble. No doubt he saw in it an opportunity to use his mighty voice to the fullest. Becks noted "terrible— *tearful* grief" on "Remorseless, treacherous, lecherous, kindless villain!" but that was followed by immediate recovery and a "subdued" tone on "Why, what an ass am I!" He "burst out again" on "by heaven and hell" and gave "Fie upon't! foh!" in "a whirl of shock," but after a pause he went on calmly and finished in a "low mumbling tone" seated in a chair.

In the meditation on suicide he said "seige of troubles" (III.i.58) for "sea of troubles," an emendation first suggested by Alexander Pope but apparently not before heard on the stage.[31] The New York *Herald* critic (18 September 1860) was offended by a "tinge of cynicism" bordering on the "savage" in Forrest's rendering of the first half of the soliloquy, but vowed that he and all who heard it would never forget the "exquisite pathos" which he threw into the lines beginning "who would fardels bear" (III.i.75). Alger admired "the intense ennui raising sighs so piteous and profound that they seemed to shatter all the bulk." [32]

Forrest made a tender question of "Nymph, in thy orisons . . . " [33] and on that line went to lean on Ophelia's prie-dieu and look down at her as she knelt; he kissed her hand on the next line, and then escorted her down the stage (Wright). Apparently in the belief that Hamlet's tone shifts abruptly to the abusive on his very next line, "No, not I; I never gave you aught" (III.i.95), he caught sight of the eavesdroppers just in time to motivate the shift—during Ophelia's attempts to redeliver his "remembrances" (Becks). He fell back into the melting mood on "I did love you once" (III.i.114) and took her briefly in his arms, but the rest was all physical and vocal assault, with Ophelia "shrinking away from him in fright" (Wright).

Not unexpectedly, given his much-publicized devotion to the American democratic spirit, Forrest delivered Hamlet's remarks on the art of acting (III.ii.1–45) with none of Macready's aristocratic disdain.[34] Alone with the Player King, he spoke in a manner "subdued and wholly conversational. After speaking a few sentences he turned his back on the Player, and walked toward a chair. He then faced him, and again approached, again retired and seated himself, delivering the greater part of the speech in this attitude."[35] Like Macready, he handed over, at the end of the speech, the quatrains Hamlet has composed for insertion (Wright).

He clasped Horatio to his breast on avowing his heartfelt affection for him (III.ii.54) and drew him into his conspiracy against Claudius in "quickish, low, intense urging tones" (Becks). The lewd twitting of Ophelia (112–14) was as usual bowdlerized. Instead of taking his customary place at her feet, Forrest sprawled on a couch nearby.[36] That gave him an opportunity to introduce, or reintroduce, a note of dignity to the scene; because he was not on the floor, there was no occasion for slithering across it to the throne as the pressure on Claudius mounted. A Cincinnati paper, quoted by Becks, rejoiced to see the "miserable crawling" done away with.

Forrest reacted to the King's frantic flight from the scene with "grand, exuberant ecstasy," falling on Horatio's shoulder. The ebullient chatter about qualifying for a "fellowship in a cry of players" and the four lines of verse ending with the nonrhyming "pajock" were omitted as usual, but just thereafter Forrest restored some lines; with an hysterical laugh he called for the recorders and then spoke, in its proper place, the seldom-heard rhyming couplet "For if the king like not the comedy / Why then, belike, he likes it not, perdy" (III.ii.291–94), except that he changed the archaic "perdy" to a proper French "*par dieu*," thus destroying the rhyme (Becks).

Through the remainder of the scene, Forrest scored repeatedly off the absent Claudius and his sycophantic emissaries, now mocking them with an elaborate pretense of courtesy, now jabbing at them with cool contempt. He bowed very formally in burlesque to Guildenstern's bow, on "Sir, a whole history," "drew himself up in disdain" on "Ay, sir, what of him?" attached "an insinuative sneer" to "With drink, sir?"

and inserted "a derisive 'Oh!' " before "Your wisdom should show itself more richer . . . " (298–307). Other business included an illustrative working of his fingers on "pickers and stealers," another parody of a bow on "We shall obey . . . " and a contemptuous hurling away of the recorder on "You cannot play upon me" (III.ii.333, 372; Becks/Wright). The entrapment of Polonius over the cloud formations, glimpsed off in the wings as if through a window, was managed "colloquially—with nice courtesy—and as if pleased to see those shapes." He paused before "like a whale," "as if rummaging for a simile," said "Then I will come to my mother by-and-bye" in a manner "almost childish in its pleasantness," allowed himself a moment of "subdued bitterness" on " 'By and bye' is easily said" and dismissed Rosencrantz and Guildenstern with yet another bow (III.ii.381–87; Becks).

The scene following the soliloquy (III.iii) being given in the eviscerated form sanctioned by Kemble, Forrest was next seen in Gertrude's closet. After stabbing at the arras, he sometimes disappeared completely behind it to ascertain the identity of his victim—apparently an unusual maneuver (Becks). Late in his career he adopted the full-length portraits popularized by Macready, which occasioned some surprise because of the notorious enmity between the two actors. On 18 September 1860 the New York *Herald* critic wrote: "This is much better than the old-fashioned miniature business, but it seems a little odd that Forrest should take lessons from Macready. However, *tempora mutantur*." In directing Gertrude's attention to the portraits, Forrest employed a move which was perhaps his own invention; "He takes her hand," Becks noted, "and swirls her round to face the large panel pictures, her back to the audience." He spoke in "tender, loving, worshipful tones" of his father, and of the usurper of his throne and bed with contempt, interjecting an "aagh" in the middle of "stoop [*sic*] from this—to this (III.iv.71; Becks). At the entrance of the Ghost—which does not seem to have been made through the portrait—Forrest fell back "fully erect with hand aloft" and cried out in terror; the New York *Herald* critic found this and his subsequent business absurdly artificial:

Mr. Forrest came very near obliterating the favorable impression he made in the first two acts. When he first sees the Ghost, Hamlet would naturally be stunned for a moment, but Mr. Forrest instantaneously bursts into his famous guttural exclamation which cannot be represented by types [*sic*]. Take all the consonants and macadamize them—then you have it. Again, at the Ghost's exit, Mr. Forrest exclaiming "Look where he goes, even now, out at the portal!" drags Gertrude down to the corner, and leans gasping against the proscenium box. A most unnatural piece of business, as by no means could he there catch a glimpse of the spiritual intruder. (18 September 1860)

The scene ended in Kemble's way, with blessings proferred and repelled.

The usual cuts followed: no hide-and-seek with Rosencrantz and Guildenstern, no homily on fat kings and lean beggars. He added strong comic emphasis to "He will stay till you come" (IV.iii.38) by imparting the information to Guildenstern after first interrupting his exit and calling him across the stage to his side; Guildenstern laughed and continued on his errand (Wright).

In the graveyard, Forrest sat casually on a stump and conversed "in the same sarcastic vein of the clown digging the grave, . . . keeping up at the same time the even flow of a full understanding with Horatio."[37] James Murdoch greatly admired the way he handled Yorick's skull:

Paragraphists who echo each other's criticisms, without observing for themselves, and who repeat the stale objection to Forrest's style of acting, that it is all physical force, etc., etc., might derive a most impressive rebuke from observing his manner in this instance. He hands, carefully and tenderly, the precious relic back to the grave-digger, like one conveying a frail but precious vessel, which carelessness might drop or injure. The effect is touching in the extreme: it bespeaks all the gentleness and affectionate regard of the prince for him who had "borne him on his back a thousand times."[38]

On learning that the obsequies in progress are for Ophelia, Forrest "staggered, and bent his head for a moment on the shoulder of his friend Horatio. Though so quickly done," Alger noted, "it told the whole story of his love for her and his enforced renunciation."[39] He fought with Laertes outside the grave, Horatio having thoughtfully relieved him of his cloak for that purpose.

The remainder of the performance seems to have been unremarkable, down to the moment of Hamlet's death. In keeping with his fondness for interpolated ejaculation, Forrest uttered three of the four dying "Os" which the Folio authorizes after "The rest is silence"—thus availing himself of a bit of theatricality apparently originated by Richard Burbage but spurned by most actors and editors ever since.[40] In physical action the death was correspondingly elaborate; Becks devoted more space to it than to any other part of the performance:

"hold me in thy heart"—almost embracing Horatio, Horatio supports him

"I die, Horatio"—a little irritant pain in tone; would fall on face to L but Horatio catches him in support and passes behind him; still holds him, then: with the legs giving way falls sideways—Horatio holding R hand and bends left knee to partially support Hamlet in half reclining position

"My spirit"—a sudden convulsive movement, as if parting with a last choking breath and sinking in stages, the features set in death—Horatio lets go the hand as if the last movement of the body has forced it away, then tenderly adjusts it again over the bosom and he and Osric turn away burying their faces in their hands

This sounds tame compared with Edmund Kean's thrashing and throbbing, but Winter nevertheless found it "needlessly 'realistic' "; he was not impressed by Forrest's contention that "a man as strong as himself could not expire without decided manifestations of physical agony."[41] Alger saw nothing amiss; for him it was an end very properly suffused with "philosophic resignation and undemonstrative quietude."[42]

In 1855, when Forrest was past the noonday of his fame and the rough-hewn vigor of his style was being more and more often denounced as a national embarrassment by the refinement-conscious custodians of American taste, a young commentator on the arts for the New York *Sunday Times*, Adam Badeau, published a shrewd and spirited rebuke of the elitists. "When passion arrives at a climax," Badeau argued, "its manifestation is pretty much the same in all classes, and the gods of the gallery are as good critics of the great points in a performance as the wits and blues of the boxes. Because then, Mr. Forrest has triumphed only or mostly over audiences not 'in society,' he has triumphed nonetheless triumphantly."[43] Badeau was himself a certified member of the cultural elite and as eager as anyone to see American art advance to the highest level of European achievement, but his vision of something better did not blind him to the solid worth of Forrest's accomplishment. Forrest's Hamlet impersonation was, in his view, "full of life and spirit. It may not have been sufficiently refined, sufficiently subtle, sufficiently elaborate: but I could not see it without emotion. . . . In what is universal, human, sympathetic, Mr. Forrest excels."[44]

The ideal Hamlet, Badeau implies, would be an actor who could match Forrest's power to move while at the same time supplying all the qualities Forrest lacked. Less than two years later, in May 1857, Badeau announced to his readers that such an actor had appeared: he was the son of Junius Brutus Booth, named, in Forrest's honor, Edwin.

NOTES

1. At the Bowery Theatre in New York; see George C. D. Odell, *Annals of the New York Stage* (New York: Columbia University Press, 1927–49), 3:403.

2. John Coleman, *Players and Playwrights I Have Known* (London: Chatto & Windus, 1888), 1:28.

3. *Albion*, 2 September 1848, quoted in Bernard Hewitt, *Theatre U.S.A.: 1665–1957* (New York: McGraw-Hill, 1959), p. 109.

4. An anonymous critic quoted in William Rounseville Alger, *Life of Edwin Forrest* (1877; reprint, New York: Arno Press, 1977), p. 760.

5. John Forster, *Dramatic Essays by John Forster & George Henry Lewes*, ed. William Archer and Robert W. Lowe (London: W. Scott, 1894), pp. 21, 30, 33, 40. Impelled by a fanatic loyalty to Macready, Forster went out of his way to denigrate Forrest; Macready himself took his friend to task for his unmitigated harshness toward the American visitor, as Richard Moody reveals in *Edwin Forrest: First Star of the American Stage* (New York: Knopf, 1960), p. 150. But Forster was an extremely able and conscientious critic, and his notices of Forrest's Othello, Lear, Macbeth and Richard III, packed with concrete detail and reasoned technical analysis, sound persuasively authoritative. Forrest did not play Hamlet during his 1836 visit, nor during his second London engagement in 1845.

6. William Winter, *Shakespeare on the Stage* (New York: Moffat, Yard, 1911), 1:264.

7. John Foster Kirk, "Shakespeare's Tragedies on the Stage: II," *Lippincott's Magazine*, June 1884, p. 606.

8. Quoted in Hewitt, *Theatre U.S.A.*, pp. 109–10.

9. Kirk, "Shakespeare's Tragedies on the Stage," p. 606.

10. Winter, *Shakespeare on the Stage*, 1:126.

11. George Becks made copious notes on Forrest's "business and manner in Hamlet" on his copy of French's Forrest edition, 1860, now in the New York Public Library (*HAM*, 67); the comment quoted is inscribed on the flyleaf. A substantial portion of my information about Forrest's portrayal comes from this source, referred to hereafter as "Becks."

12. Alger, *Life of Edwin Forrest*, p. 751.

13. James Rees, *The Life of Edwin Forrest* (Philadelphia: T. B. Peterson, 1874), p. 191.

14. *Albion*, 2 September 1848, quoted in Hewitt, *Theatre U.S.A.*, p. 110.

15. Rees, *The Life of Edwin Forrest*, p. 193.

16. Winter, *Shakespeare on the Stage*, 1:334.

17. Alger, *Life of Edwin Forrest*, p. 751.

18. Winter, *Shakespeare on the Stage*, 1:335.

19. Alger, *Life of Edwin Forrest*, p. 752.

20. Unidentified newspaper clipping quoted in Horace Howard Furness *A New Variorum Edition of Shakespeare: Hamlet* (1877; reprint, New York: American Scholar Publications, 1965), 2:255.

21. My account of Forrest's alterations derives from Becks' memorial book (*HAM*, 67); see above, n. 11. The text is in most respects identical to Kemble's 1800 edition; two noteworthy exceptions are that Polonius' advice to Laertes (I.iii.58–80) is restored and the scene between Horatio and the sailors (IV.vi) is eliminated.

22. Alger, *Life of Edwin Forrest*, p. 752.

23. Ibid.

24. Rees, *The Life of Edwin Forrest*, p. 193.

25. The bow was recorded by John B. Wright, Forrest's stage manager in later years, on a copy of *French's Standard Drama* (n.d.), now in the Folger Shakespeare Library in Washington, D.C. (*HAM*, 66). Further references to this memorial book will be identified as "Wright." The Folger has three other Forrest promptbooks (*HAM*, 63, 64, 68); the first is very lightly marked, the second closely resembles Wright's book and the third is a transcription of Becks' memorial book. Another promptbook (*HAM*, 65), fully marked, is on permanent loan from the Edwin Forrest Home to the Rare Book Room of the University of Pennsylvania Library (Philadelphia).

26. Alger, *Life of Edwin Forrest*, p. 754.

27. This was one of several vicious attacks on Forrest written by a man of unsavory character named William Stuart. Born Edmund O'Flaherty, he had recently arrived from Ireland under a cloud of scandal and took advantage of Forrest's declining prestige to advance his own fortunes; see *Between Actor and Critic: Selected Letters of Edwin Booth and William Winter*, ed. Daniel J. Watermeier (Princeton, N.J.: Princeton University Press, 1971), p. 19.

28. Clipping quoted in Furness, *Variorum*, 2:255.

29. Alger, *Life of Edwin Forrest*, p. 757.

30. Ibid.

31. French's Forrest edition of 1860 prints "seige," and the word was underlined by Becks; French's Standard Drama prints "sea." The attribution to Pope is made by Furness, *Variorum*, 1:207.

32. Alger, *Life of Edwin Forrest*, pp. 757–58.

33. Clipping quoted in Furness, *Variorum*, 2:255.

34. According to Lawrence Barrett, Forrest once arrived in a small town to play Hamlet and found the stage decorated by two American flags in lieu of scenery. "Instead of anger and annoyance," Barrett writes, "Forrest only smiled as he saw these preparations, and he declared that nothing could be better. He would show the audience that *Hamlet* could be played in that foreign frame with none of its powers shorn or weakened, while his own patriotism would stimulate his energies, as his eyes rested on the banners of his native land"; see Lawrence Barrett, *Edwin Forrest* (Boston: J. R. Osgood, 1861), p. 6.

35. Clipping quoted in Furness, *Variorum*, 2:255.

36. The scurrilous William Stuart (see n. 27) wrote that Forrest "had far more the air of some huge gypsy watching with roguish glance an opportunity to rob the hen-roost, than a highly intellectual analyser of nature trying to descry on the human countenance the evidence of its guilt" (New York *Tribune*, 20 March 1855).

37. Becks, quoting from a Cincinnati paper.

38. James Murdoch, *The Stage, or Recollections of Actors and Acting from an Experience of Fifty Years* (Philadelphia: J. M. Stoddart, 1880), pp. 256–57.

39. Alger, *Life of Edwin Forrest*, p. 756.

40. The Becks text does not show the interpolation; Wright adds "Oh, oh, oh" in longhand. For the attribution to Burbage, see Harold Jenkins, Playhouse Interpolations in the Folio Text of *Hamlet*," *Studies in Bibliography* 13 (1960): 41.

41. Winter, *Shakespeare on the Stage*, pp. 335–36.

42. Alger, *Life of Edwin Forrest*, p. 760.

43. Adam Badeau, "Edwin Forrest," in *The Vagabond* (New York: Rudd & Carleton, 1859), p. 72. Dates of individual essays are not given in this collection of Badeau's pieces for the New York *Times*, but the Forrest article was probably written in October 1855; Badeau remarks that he saw J. W. Wallack, E. L. Davenport and Forrest play Hamlet "within a short while of each other"; Wallack played it at the Bowery on 17 September, Davenport at the Broadway on 19 September and Forrest at the same theater on 8 October; see Odell, *Annals*, 6:456, 424, 425.

44. Badeau, "Edwin Forrest," p. 74.

8

EDWIN BOOTH

Edwin Booth (1833–1893) had little more than a novice's acquaintance with Hamlet when he first played it in New York at Burton's Theatre on 12 May 1857. He had made his initial appearance in it some four years earlier, at his brother's theater in San Francisco, but had been playing it regularly in repertoire for only a few months.[1] Hence, Adam Badeau noted that "the workman is raw and his tools unwonted," but he nevertheless perceived in the twenty-three-year-old actor "the power of genius." What especially excited Badeau was Booth's capacity for "real feeling," for "enthusiasm." He contrasted him in this respect with two established actors, J. W. Wallack (1818–1873) and E. L. Davenport (1815–1877), whom he described as "clever, careful students," more "finished" than Booth but lacking his "absolute genius."[2] In an earlier essay, he had made precisely the same contrast between these two actors and Edwin Forrest, which reveals that Badeau saw a certain similarity between the great star and the newcomer. But he also saw in Booth the promise of much more. If Forrest had feeling without refinement and Wallack and Davenport had refinement without feeling, Booth had it in him to unite the two in a new and powerful "poetry of the stage."[3]

Badeau was not the first to discern in Booth's early tentative efforts the makings of a Hamlet of rare beauty and power. Ferdinand Cartwright Ewer, a young writer for the San Francisco *Times and Transcript*, marked him down for future glory after witnessing his debut appearance in the role. Booth was awkward in places, he had not yet learned to "measure time and arrange effect on the stage," he did not have his father's finish and "grace of gesticulation" and he was not "sufficiently settled into manhood to impart to the character its proper weight and dignity," but these were faults which, Ewer predicted, time would inevitably cure. Meanwhile, even in its imperfect state, Booth's performance had "a style of excellence which put to the blush any attempt in the same character" that Ewer had yet seen, including the impersonation of Booth senior, Junius Brutus Booth (1796–1852).[4]

For Ewer and Badeau, and in time multitudes of others, Booth's Hamlet was something like a dream come true. It was the Hamlet of their imaginings, made flesh upon the stage. They had read of such a Hamlet, chiefly in the criticism of William Hazlitt, but had scarcely dared hope ever to see and hear him. Had not Hazlitt himself declared his conception "hardly capable of being acted"? Could Booth do what in Hazlitt's estimation John Philip Kemble and Edmund Kean had been unable to do? It seemed so. Ewer's description of Booth's maiden effort was a close paraphrase of Hazlitt; his Hamlet, said Ewer, had "all the easy motion and peaceful curves of 'a wave of the sea.' " He was "melancholy without gloom, contemplative yet without misanthropy, philosophical yet enjoying playfulness in social converse, a man by himself yet with ardent feeling of friendship, a thorough knower of human nature . . . the type of all that is firm, dignified, gentlemanly and to be respected in a man."[5]

Badeau's thoughts also turned promptly to the great Romantic critic. Having undertaken to tutor Booth to the perfection he believed lay so nearly within his grasp, he directed him to Hazlitt's "Characters of Shakespear's Plays."[6] There Booth found articulated the conception toward which his own instincts were already drawing him:

It is not a character marked by strength of will or even of passion, but by refinement of thought and sentiment. Hamlet is as little of the hero as a man can well be: but he is a young and princely novice, full of high enthusiasm and quick sensibility. . . . He seems incapable of deliberate action, and is only hurried into extremities on the spur of the occasion.[7]

This view of Hamlet as a bark too frail for the rough seas of painful experience had in recent years become well known and enthusiastically embraced, among the cognoscenti, as a result of its having also been eloquently set forth in Goethe's widely read novel, *Wilhelm Meister's Apprenticeship*. Goethe's protagonist there describes Shakespeare's protagonist as a "soft . . . royal flower" possessed of "tender soul." "Shakespeare meant," says Wilhelm Meister, "to represent the effects of a great action laid upon a soul unfit for the performance of it. . . . There is an oaktree planted in a costly jar, which should have borne only pleasant flowers in its bosom; the roots expand, the jar is shivered."[8] Introduced to Goethe's compelling metaphor by his wife, Molly Devlin, Booth found in it final confirmation of his own intuitive approach to the character.[9]

It was, moreover, a conception which Booth's physical person seemed to have been expressly fashioned to embody. "He looks like Hamlet," his father had said on seeing him costumed for his first tragic role, and it was a sentiment many times emphatically repeated as the years passed. He was slightly taller than Kean, and his broad shoulders, narrow waist and perfectly proportioned limbs made him appear vulnerable but neither puny nor mean. A high forehead, dark, loosely flowing locks and lustrous, deep-set eyes completed the picture of a man "woeful beyond tears."[10] His voice too, "with bird notes in it, . . . the song of the rain, the soul of the 'cello," seemed the perfect instrument for revealing the soul of a beleaguered poet-prince.[11]

Popular acceptance of this new image—new on the stage—was slow in coming. When Booth ventured into New York a second time, opening in *Hamlet* at the Winter Garden on 26 November 1860, attendance was so poor that he had to abandon the role after only three appearances. Forrest was then performing at Niblo's Garden, and the masses clearly preferred the familiar impersonation of the established favorite. By contrast, a number of critics energetically took up the cause of the newcomer. "Unquestionably the greatest actor we have now upon the American stage is Edwin Booth," said the *Spirit of the Times*. He is much superior to Forrest who, in playing Hamlet, "loses all the tenderness and all the dignity . . . destroys every feeling save that of violence" (8 December 1860). The *Albion* made the same comparison, with devastating succinctness: "Mr. Booth is as unlike Mr. Forrest as Mr. Forrest is unlike Hamlet" (8 December 1860). The New York *Times* thought Booth was so eager to separate himself from "the loud-voiced Forrest school" that he lacked "muscular force" and too often fell into a whispering timidity. But for all that, he had "a decided and discriminating intellectual talent" and was to be preferred to "all tragedians of the present time" (27 November 1860).

Three more seasons passed before Booth got an unbreakable grip on the crown to which his early champions considered him the rightful heir. In 1861–1862 he was in England, where he played Hamlet only in the provinces. When he was next seen in the role in New York, on

Edwin Booth. Soliloquy, the Nunnery Scene (III.i). Booth's Theatre, New York, 1870. Harvard Theatre Collection.

29 September 1862, he was praised for having polished to still brighter luster the facets of his performance which had earlier attracted praise. He rendered "that which was natural still more natural," said the New York *Evening Post*, and imparted "additional grace to what was always graceful" (30 September 1862). But the embrace of the great public still eluded him.

When he returned the following September, he appears to have tried to remedy that situation by including in his performance some of that "muscular force" which he was said to lack and which the popular Forrest possessed in abundance. The New York *Herald* critic warned him that in going in for excessive gesticulation and "unnatural shapes" he was pursuing a mistaken course: "[Mr. Booth] may be the greatest actor in the country, if he will. But, to become so, he must now act for the intellectual, and not for the gallery, portion of his audience" (22 September 1863). William Winter, whose admiration for Booth's acting was already fast approaching the near-idolatory it would later become, was also pained to see him apparently playing to the gallery, but he argued that the deplorable taste of these latter-day nutcrackers left an actor no choice (New York *Albion*, 26 September 1863).

If Booth *was* at this time consciously currying favor by using uncharacteristically robustious effects—and he may, after all, simply have been having a few "off" nights—he might have saved himself the trouble. The Mountain was about to come to Mohammed. In the following season he took over the management of the Winter Garden Theatre, and there, on 26 November 1864, he again offered New York theatergoers the refined, intellectual, delicate, sensitive Hamlet he had been painstakingly molding and polishing for so many years. This time they came and came again and kept coming, gallery gods and all. They came for one hundred nights, conferring on Booth a mark of public favor such as no other actor of Hamlet had ever received.[12] Because no one had any way of knowing when the play opened that history was in the making, the critical community did not turn out in force. But those most keenly interested in Booth's career were in attendance and were pleased to announce that the brilliant apprentice had now taken his place among the masters. "Mr. Booth surpassed his former successes in the character," said the New York *Herald* on 28 November 1864. "He gave to the very life the picture of a reflective, sensitive, gentle, generous nature, tormented, borne down and made miserable

by an occasion and by requisitions [*sic*] to which it is not equal.'' On
3 December the *Spirit of the Times* proclaimed his coming of age:

The sensitively reflective and generously gentle phases of the character were
more prominently developed than heretofore, and its splenetic and revengeful
characteristics kept more in the shade; hence his personation of the part comes
far nearer the standard of excellence than it is wont to be represented by the
majority of actors, Forrest, for instance, who would have frightened the Queen
into fits at the first interview, and spoilt the whole plot.

Even those who did not share Booth's view of the character confessed
great admiration for his execution. Lucia Gilbert Calhoun, recalling
Booth's historic run, wrote, ''It was the fine poetic conception, the
artistic representation of a marvellous character that made the subtlest
of Shakespeare's plays hold the boards for a hundred nights. And that
it was not my notion of Hamlet . . . seems to me of no earthly consequence to anybody.''[13]

The ''Hundred Nights'' run would have secured Booth an honored
place in the pantheon of stage Hamlets had he never acted the part
again. But still greater prestige lay ahead. Nurtured by tireless study
in the rich soil of accumulating experience, his characterization continued to ripen into lush maturity. On 5 January 1870, as proprietor of
an opulent new theater which bore his name, he mounted a spectacular
production of the play that he hoped would effect a final, definitive
conquest of public and critical opinion.[14] He was not disappointed. The
critics turned out in force and, with rare exceptions, returned to their
writing-desks to compete with each other in the coining of fresh su-
perlatives. He was now ''the accepted Hamlet of the American stage,''
''the best Hamlet seen in this country, by the present generation, and
perhaps the best America has produced'' (New York *Herald*, 6 January 1870; New York *Times*, 7 January 1870). Winter was characteristically rhapsodic in his review for the New York *Tribune* (7 January
1870), but not before allowing himself to declare simply that ''the
Hamlet of Mr. Booth seems, in our thought, to be the literal Hamlet
of Shakespeare.'' One enraptured spectator, in a letter addressed to Booth
in the pages of *The Leader* (8 January 1870), took it on himself to
second that opinion in the persona of Shakespeare himself. ''From the
rising of the curtain until the going down thereof, you are *my* Hamlet,'' said the voice from beyond the grave. Several weeks after the

opening, the New York *Evening Post* declared that Booth had defined Hamlet for his contemporaries with the same finality that Kemble and Kean had for theirs: "We of today live in the era of Booth; and Booth, to a majority of us, is Hamlet" (16 March 1870).

To a majority, certainly, but not to all. Badeau and other early votaries had foretold that in the fullness of time Booth would achieve a perfect blend of truth and beauty—genuine human feeling wedded to consummate craftsmanship—and for most that day seemed now to have arrived. But others had reservations. The New York *Times* critic, obviously with Forrest and Kean in mind, said that what Booth offered was "not lightning but steady light" and confessed to a certain nostalgia for the gods of the lightning. He admitted that Booth's "temperateness" was generally commendable and represented a much-needed reform, but he thought that in particular instances the result was a disappointing austerity. Perhaps too much emotional truth had been sacrificed to beauty of form (7 January 1870).

A. C. Wheeler, a longtime partisan of Forrest who wrote for the New York *World* under the name Nym Crinkle, filed the strongest brief against Booth in his review of 9 January 1870. He began by allowing that the new Hamlet was "the perfect expression of the artistic taste of our times" but went on to characterize that taste as "the substitution of finish for feeling, elaborateness for earnestness, accuracy for emotion." Booth's performance, he insisted, "nowhere and at no time answers exactly to the highest requirements of good acting by touching the feelings and swaying the emotions independently of the critical sense." He challenged spectators to put the matter to a test by asking themselves whether they came away from the theater having "been aroused to a keen interest in the individuality, the deep human significance of the central character" or merely with "a certain pleasant recollection of what was skillfully and harmoniously done."

In essence, Wheeler accused Booth of elevating style over substance, of muffling up the character in layers of physical and vocal finery, but in Booth's understanding of things, and in his admirers' perception of things, there was no such distinction to be made: the *style was* the character. Booth's conviction of the pervasive delicacy and refinement of Hamlet dictated a style of stage deportment appropriate to those qualities. If Wheeler found him bloodless and effete he was finding precisely what Booth was attempting to show. Booth wrote to William Winter:

I have always endeavored to make prominent the femininity of Hamlet's character and therein lies the secret of my success—I think. I doubt if ever a robust and masculine treatment of the character will be accepted so generally as the more womanly and refined interpretation. I know that frequently I fall into effeminacy, but we can't always hit the proper key-note.[15]

Booth's nice concern for elegance of gesture and tone stemmed not only from his understanding of the character but also from his sense of what was appropriate to the acting of poetic tragedy generally. In his 1857 essay, Badeau praised Booth's "refined ideality" in the last act of *Richard III*: " . . . so different from the animal contortions of Mr. Forrest. . . . There is no cold, debasing realism here: There is the poetry of the stage, the realization of your ideas of the Richard of Shakespeare." During that same formative period, Booth told Molly Devlin that while he favored a judicious amount of the conversational and colloquial in his acting, too much nature was "dangerous," and she strongly reinforced that opinion: "Acting is an imitation of Nature, is it not? Then 'tis Art; and the Art must be seen too, for nature upon the stage would be most ridiculous."[16]

This was the faith that sustained Booth and carried him to the heights. What Wheeler saw as weakness, most others celebrated as the actor's greatest strength. Said Winter, "Mr. Booth does not labor to unpoetize and drag down to the plane of ordinary, every-day life, an ethereal, exalted, poetical creation, the rarest fruit of the grandest imagination that was ever vested in mortal clay" (New York *Tribune*, 21 March 1870). Winter's intemperateness of phrase detracts somewhat from the authority of his opinion, but there can be no doubt about its essential soundness. Another observer put the case with a degree of lucidity and sobriety which compels belief:

Booth's Hamlet is not natural. Shakespeare's Hamlet is not natural. Shakespeare's Hamlet is full of art, full of rhetoric, full of versification. Booth's Hamlet is full of art, full of mechanical rhetoric, full of that poetry of way and method which in the actor is akin to the versification of the poet. Both are ideal—too ideal for life. Yet both are full of human nature.

It is unsafe and false to play Hamlet *practically*. . . . No piece that is written in poetry can be played prosaically. It must be expressed in a higher form than the literal and commonplace expression of matter of fact. It represents possibility—not reality. It appeals to one's sense of what might be—it does not represent actual occurrence.

Booth's Hamlet is poetical; essentially life-like, but life elaborated and thrown into rhythmical shape.

The author of this exemplary piece of theatrical reporting was not a working journalist or even a seasoned playgoer, but a twenty-one-year-old clerk named Charles Clarke. When he first saw Booth's Hamlet, on 18 January 1870, Clarke was so moved by the experience that it became something of an obsession. He memorized the entire play, read all the criticism of Booth's portrayal he could lay his hands on, and then returned to the theater for eight more performances. He took copious notes in the ensuing months and shaped them into a 60,000-word manuscript in which he sought to describe every nuance of Booth's performance: every move, every gesture, every facial expression, every shift in vocal emphasis, inflection and intonation. In addition, Clarke set down a number of general assessments of Booth's style and interpretation—of the kind and quality quoted above. It will not be possible to reproduce here Clarke's full account, but even a condensation of it, supplemented by material from other sources, provides a strikingly vivid recreation of Booth's portrayal.[17]

Booth entered with a slow, unvaried "monotread," which seemed to say that his presence was "in sullen obedience to the courtesy of the occasion." The little bow he gave the King after the first solemnly scornful aside had something of the same quality. Throughout the play, in keeping with his emphasis on Hamlet's gentility, he took great care to mask Hamlet's scorn from those toward whom it was directed, but on "too much 'i the sun" he permitted himself a gesture, "raising his left hand with the palm toward the King," designed to emphasize the line's hidden abusiveness. In his reply to Gertrude (I.ii.76–86) he employed a number of illustrative gestures which were typical of his general manner; he raised the hem of his cloak on "suits of solemn black" and again on "trappings," struck his breast "gravely" on "that within" and pointed to his eye when he mentioned that organ's "fruitful river." Clarke explained, perhaps defensively, that the many gestures "were delivered with so much ease and in so natural a manner that one would scarcely notice them especially. There was no vivacity in them; they were full of languor, but so conversant with Hamlet's meditative, mournful demeanor that they appeared highly natural."

No doubt these and the many similar manual signs which Booth used contributed much to the impression of crystalline clarity which was such an admired part of his portrayal. During the 1864 run, the critic for the New York *Herald* (28 November 1864) wrote: "The performance of Hamlet by Mr. Booth is a continual elucidation of Shakespeare. . . . All is as clear as daylight. To see it inevitably excites the wonder that this part should have been so misunderstood by so many able writers."

When the King said "think of us as a father," Booth gave a start and looked at him with "repugnance speaking from his eyes." A London critic, writing of the 1880 performance there, called it "a spasm of hatred . . . [an image] of disgust that seemed to pervade his whole frame." [18]

He paced the stage during the soliloquy (I.ii.129–59). Clarke noted that despite his busy movement there was "no abrupt vehemence, bluster, or violent transition from rage to grief. His Hamlet is too well tempered for that. It is the Hamlet of a gentleman and a scholar, of a man not apt to fly into a passion spontaneously. . . . And so in this speech, Booth's fitfulness of delivery, which was very great, never was savagely abrupt but was always gradated." There was more illustrative gesturing during the speech. He tapped his breast lightly several times on "increase of appetite." In the notebook he prepared as a record of his performance, Booth wrote opposite this line: "Touch your heart to indicate what kind of appetite." [19] In later years he illustrated the line "she followed my poor father's body, / Like Niobe, all tears" (I.ii.148–49) by taking a few slow steps in the attitude of a disconsolate mourner (London *Morning Post*, 8 November 1880). The lines characterizing Gertrude as a dumb beast rushing to the pleasure of an incestuous bed were incompatible with Booth's idea of the character and were duly omitted. [20]

On being hailed by Horatio from offstage, Booth at first gave a look of "partial displeasure and of enforced toleration," but when Horatio came near enough to be recognized he greeted him with "kindliness and heartiness," though not so much as to "overbear his consciousness of grief." A London critic thought he made too much of "We'll teach you to drink deep ere you depart" (175), delivering it "not with a simple air of good fellowship, a careless reference to the custom 'more honored in the breach than in the observance,' but with deep intention, much raising and lowering of the eyebrows, as if great events were destined to spring from some future drinking bout, and Hamlet wished to convey a premonitory hint of it'' (London *Evening Standard*, 8 November 1880). During Horatio's description of the Ghost's departure, Booth stared into his face ''in extreme agitation, his breath coming short, and a movement of the lips or throat hinting of a tremor running through him.'' Before ''Indeed, indeed, sirs, but this troubles me'' (I.ii.224) he moved upstage ''with both hands on his forehead, his head thrown back, his elbows reaching out on both sides over his shoulders.'' In ensuing scenes, Booth used this gesture of hands to forehead (sometimes it was only one hand) over and over again—in moments of mental anguish or intense cerebration, building it up as an external sign of Hamlet's intellectuality and sensitivity. In the close questioning of his informants he delivered ''Pale or red?'' in a ''soft, feminine voice, full of stops, eager almost to anguish; a little too masculine for a woman's tongue,'' Clarke remarked, ''but had a woman spoken it so one would have thought the tears close behind.'' His treatment of the closing couplet (256–57) was an example of his characteristic ''poetry of way and method.''

He takes a step toward the . . . passage. Stops, reaches out right hand pointing down with it, fingers closed: ''Foul deeds WILL rise (lifting his hand above his head and outward toward the audience), 'though all the *earth* o'er-whelm them'' (his voice drops from a sonorous pitch to one of lesser force, but quite as earnest; brings down his arm with energy in a rounding sweep) ''*to* men's eyes'' (partial upward accent of eyes, but final recognition of the period. Exit.).

The ''sweep'' carries the mind back to Kemble's delivery of ''The play's the thing.'' In general, says Clarke, Booth revealed in this first scene ''deep philosophical and emotional perplexity; . . . thought always overweighs his actions.''

The critic for *Appleton's Journal* (5 February 1870) declared that Booth's playing of the Ghost scene ''more than any other feature of the play, wins for the actor the popular identification of his name with the character.'' Badeau had singled out this moment for special praise as early as 1857; apparently unfamiliar with Kean's way of playing the scene, he commended Booth for not ''representing Hamlet as overcome by animal fear, as most, if not all, actors have done.''[21] The generally hostile Nym Crinkle was quick to point out the debt to Kean, but even he acknowledged that Booth's demeanor during the ''tremendous visitation'' was ''superior in refined ideality to nearly all else in the play, as we now have it, and so much better than the superstitious terror of all our other Hamlets" (New York *World*, 9 January 1870).

He staggered and fell into Horatio's arms on catching sight of the apparition, dislodging his hat so that it was left hanging down his back; his cloak he retained until later. "Angels and ministers of grace" (I.iv.39) was taken in "a whisper of fear." The London *Post* critic heard in it "no idle exclamation" but a genuine invocation of "supernatural assistance in his terrible extremity" (8 November 1880). Like Forrest, he came to a full stop on "Father" and, also like Forrest, went to his knees and remained in that position until beckoned to follow. On "Royal Dane" his hand "trembled so violently as to be noticed in all parts of the theatre." "This speech was delivered slowly," Clarke says, "with a marvellous amount of pathos, fear, and longing. . . . His voice was very low, yet distinct and clear."

To his friends' entreaties not to follow, he replied distractedly. In breaking loose from them he was thrown forward almost into the arms of the Spirit and so stopped abruptly, his iron resolve deserting him momentarily. At a performance early in his career, Booth reveals in his Notebook, he lost control of his sword in the scuffle and, taking advantage of the lucky accident, "held the weapon up as a moral guard against the spirit—the hilt and handle forming the sign of the cross." Thereafter he used the business regularly. Clarke describes this moment as "one of the most commanding situations of the whole play, and during his exit the whole theatre was in such a hush that it seemed as if even to wink would have made a noise audible throughout the place."

Booth did not go in much for new readings, but he introduced one in the way he said "What?" in reply to the Ghost's "So art thou to revenge, when thou shalt hear" (I.v.7). Clarke says he made it mean not "What do you say?" but "What am I to revenge?" When the Ghost began his recital, Booth sank slowly to his knees in an attitude of reverence, leaned on his sword, averted his gaze somewhat, "as if in fear of the Ghost's narration," and raised his right hand a little "as if to shield his ears from the suggestion of such terrible things." "Face and hands play their part so perfectly," said the *Metropolitan* (15 January 1870), "that the mastery of the subject by the artist is at once established, and every auditor knows that the performance will be perfect to the end." He got to his feet on "Murder," dropping his sword in the process, and remained standing to the end of the Ghost's tale, which he interrupted in the usual way with "O, horrible, O, horrible, most horrible." As the Spirit drifted off to heed the summons of the dawn, Booth fell to the floor in an elaborate display of emotional agitation. Richard Grant White criticized the action severely in the *Galaxy* (March 1870) a few weeks after the opening:

He lies still a moment, and then, tossing about as a man might who had been so disturbed and was so exhausted, he begins the following soliloquy before he rises, and actually speaks the first lines . . . lying flat on his back looking up to the sky, and with his head toward the audience. . . . We may be sure that Shakespeare had no such delivery of this soliloquy in mind when he wrote it; for there is so great an incongruity between the realism of the actor's treatment and the ideal and romantic conception of the scene as to void the performance of all dignity, and to make it approach as nearly to the ridiculous as is possible in the hands of an artist of Mr. Booth's histrionic power.

Appealed to on aesthetic principles that were so nearly his own, Booth promptly modified the business, eliminating the "tossing." Thereafter, as Clarke reports, he began the soliloquy lying on his side, his hand on his head and covering his face. He made the traditional cuts in the speech ("Damned villain," "pernicious woman" and "my tables . . . ") ending it by linking "yes by heaven!" and "I have sworn't."

As his friends approached, Booth employed a bit of business which recalls Macready's celebrated action in a later scene. He took out a handkerchief and mopped his brow, then twirled it above his head on "Hillo, ho, ho, boy!" It was apparently designed to show a true fever of the brain rather than feigned "idleness" since he was already tucking the item away in his bosom when his companions joined him. He was in "a state of high excitement. . . . His new duty bewildered him by its solemn magnitude. He acted like one barely capable of coherence." In what followed he was "restless, secretive, wild, only bent on securing the silence of his friends regarding the spirit." The secretiveness he showed in the traditional way, by breaking off abruptly in the face of Marcellus' curiosity. The wildness he brought out in a most untraditional way, by restoring "boy," "truepenny," "this fellow in the cellerage," "old mole" and "worthy pioneer," spoken in a tone of "ghastly levity." But the world was still not ready for Shakespeare unimproved. Nym Crinkle complained that such language on Hamlet's lips was out of keeping with "the ineffable tenderness with which he has just addressed the dread visitant'' (New York *World*, 9 January 1870). Booth later wrote in his Notebook that he meant the lines ''not as unfeeling levity but the very intensity of mental excitement''; nevertheless, he retained in later productions only the first two of the offending terms. He continued the sword-as-cross motif introduced earlier in the scene by using the hilt rather than the blade for the swearing.[22]

Though thrown into an ''intensity of mental excitement'' by the vision of his father's wandering soul, Hamlet was not, Booth firmly believed, shaken loose from sanity. In his Notebook he urged that point repeatedly. The terse and rather mysterious line ''So be it'' (I.v.114), spoken as Marcellus and Horatio approach, Booth took to be a declaration of Hamlet's decision to *feign* madness. The quality of Hamlet's intelligence is such that ''thought requires no *time* to form its plan of action,'' he wrote. ''Quick as a flash his mind conceives the means of safety in pursuing his revenge.'' The later line, ''shall think it meet to put an antic disposition on,'' he labeled ''undoubtedly the keynote to the character.'' Hamlet's visit to Ophelia's closet was no more, Booth was sure, than skillful ''play-acting.''

This conviction of Hamlet's secure mooring in the safe harbor of reason colored Booth's entire portrayal. ''From this point [the swearing scene],'' said the *Daily Chronicle* of the 1880 London performance, ''it was apparent that Mr. Booth intended to adopt the theory that Hamlet only assumed madness, for throughout the play the soliloquies and asides were spoken in calm, even conversational tones, sometimes to their exceeding disadvantage, while the converse with other personages was embellished with that 'antic disposition' of which Hamlet forewarns his confidants'' (8 November 1880).

Even this assumed madness Booth kept under tight rein. In the scene with Polonius (II.ii.171–219), his first onstage opportunity to employ his stratagem, it was conveyed, Clarke says,

more through insinuation . . . than through intense outbreak at anytime. . . . There was a stoppage of the voice, a slightly frazzled look . . . giving the idea of a mental tack, a veering of the intellect, but not a variable movement of the passional nature. And every one of the barbed ironies which he shot at Polonius, was delivered with a courtesy of action that made outwardly smooth its real rudeness and vigor.

He did not read ''god kissing carrion,'' but he worked the book hard on ''Words, words, words,'' showing it to Polonius, pointing to it and reading in it as he voiced his scorn both for Polonius and for the book's contents. He made "Into my grave?" a question (the Folio reading) rather than the long-preferred and more pessimistic statement of fact authorized by Q2. His face brightened with pleasure when Polonius announced his intention to take his leave. It was an expression rarely seen in Booth's performance.

Turning to the Folio once again, Booth said, "What a piece of work is *a* man" (II.ii.303). He preferred that version to the common stage usage ("is man") because he thought it supported his view that Hamlet does not love Ophelia. His marginal notation here reads: "A man. *Woman* holds a very low place in his estimation; since the very *root* of his veneration for her has been blasted by his *mother's* conduct. . . . *Intellectuality* in him absorbed all trivial fond emotions." He made "He that plays the king shall be welcome" (II.ii.319) a pointed reference to Claudius, then paused as if fearing he had revealed too much and continued in a more relaxed tone. But he was soon thinking darkly of Claudius again; on the reference to "his picture in little," he took hold of such a picture hanging on Rosencrantz's breast and let it go again, "with a short, dry, sarcastic laugh." The First Player kissed the hand Hamlet extended in greeting, and so did "my young lady and mistress," played by a boy who was dressed not for the role of the Player Queen, as was customary, but as befitted his true, offstage sex. The change lent sense to the following pleasantry about the boy's growth, and Booth gave it with an appropriate smile.

He spoke "Now I am alone" (549) while huddled in the corner of a chair,[23] his head hanging dejectedly, but rose impulsively on "O, what a rogue and peasant slave am I!" He accented the line by striking downward contemptuously with his right arm, and repeated the gesture on "What's he to Hecuba?" He moved frequently as he poured out his self-reproach, and when it was spent threw himself down again, after "damned defeat was made," in a "sorrowful, reckless fashion" and buried his face in his arms. "Am I a coward? instantly brought him back to his feet, staring forward into space with a look of "anger, disdain and pain." On "Who calls me villain?" he invited a reply with both arms outstretched. He moved toward the wings as he continued to cover himself with blame, and looking out through an arch he addressed his absent adversary on "Bloody, bawdy, villain" while shaking his arm angrily in that direction. As if again exhausted by the expenditure of feeling, he fell into another chair and repeated the gesture of momentarily covering up his face. He remained seated for the final unpacking of his heart in self-contempt and put his brain to work devising a plan by striking his forehead in his characteristic way. On his feet again at "though it have no tongue, will speak," he stood by the chair, his lips pursed in "sober self-communion" as he continued his calculations. Moving forward, he gave "The spirit that I have seen" almost in a whisper, then drew back with a start on "may be a devil," casting an apprenhensive look behind him. His hand was at his forehead again on "I'll have grounds more relative than this," and he looked around "resolutely" as if to find them. Starting for the exit, he raised his right hand and on "catch" plucked the conscience of the King out of the air and held it in his closed hand as he left the stage.[24]

As if again fearing that his description of Booth's many moves and gestures might give the wrong impression, Clarke closes his account of Act II by remarking, "He is always the *prince*; and although his soul appears to be running a wild zigzag course of self-reproach, philosophy, introspection, strong grief and over-wrought imagination, he never falls into vulgar ways of exhibition in making these things known."

For an actor with Booth's view of the character, the "To be or not to be"soliloquy (III.i.55–87) had a solemn importance that transcended even that sacred character which Georg Christoph Lichtenberg had assigned to it a century earlier, in likening it to the Lord's Prayer. To Booth's portrait of Hamlet it needed to be what the face of the Divine Infant was in a Renaissance painting of the Madonna and Child: the shimmering center of interest, the crucial test of the master's skill. If Hamlet was what Hazlitt and Goethe took him to be, it was here that he would stand most fully revealed. Clarke is at his best in describing what he saw and heard at this moment and what it meant to him:

He comes down to the left hand and drops into a chair. Every movement is replete with thoughtfulness and mental absorption, and his face is almost condensed, so powerful seems the working of his mind. He looks over the side of the chair at his audience with one hand held up to his temple and two or three dark locks of hair falling over it. But although his eyes are resting directly on one he does not see a single external thing. He does not speak for ten or fifteen seconds—not with his tongue; but his eyes proclaim the thought almost as well as the voice could. I forget all about the man then; for the time I see right through his flesh and overlook his *mind*. He speaks—oh wonderful! It is not declamation. It is not recitation. It is the deep thought running right

out at the lips, finding a vocal liberty. The power of it is not in the voice—
though the voice is as apt as it could be—but in the spirit of the man, Hamlet,
that shows itself behind. Every word gives me a shake, and then goes through
me like a lance.

Clarke was not alone in feeling himself pierced to the heart by the
emotive force of Booth's soul-baring. Said the New York *Evening Mail*
(6 January 1870):

There was something deeply touching in the reckless, despondent attitude and
the staring eyes, fixed on vacancy, betokening the complete misery of the man,
while the intensity with which the words were spoken revealed his inmost
thoughts with all the dark gloomy forebodings. . . . The audience seems to
feel that the man was alone with his thoughts, and that they were far removed
from his consideration.

Much of the unusually striking impression of self-communing which
Booth was able to convey seems to have come from the mere fact of
his being seated. Even Nym Crinkle admitted that this "impulsive and
unpremeditated negligence of attitude is infinitely superior to the delivery of the passage at the footlights in oratorical style" (New York *World*,
9 January 1970). After the opening line, delivered in a "subdued,
searching voice, . . . looking down and forward, with a sad, puzzled
pushing look," he remained seated, speaking in "free, almost colloquial . . . yet very sober . . . accents" until "There's the rub" propelled him to his feet. He spoke more rapidly now, "as if he had slipped
into a current of thought that relieved somewhat the earnestness of his
reflections." The meaning of "this mortal coil" he sought to clarify
by striking his breast three or four times with the fingertips of his left
hand.

Booth chose Forrest's early discovery of the eavesdroppers. Re-
pulsed by Ophelia's cold response to his salutation, he turned abruptly
from her on "I humbly thank you, well, well, well" (91), just in time
to spot his foes tardily arranging themselves behind the hangings on
an upstage gallery. He stopped abruptly, clutching his forehead, made
as if to go on, then paused and gave Ophelia a quick look of reproach
over his shoulder (unseen by her because she was busying herself with
his "remembrances"), then continued on a pace or two, his head bowed
in dejection at her betrayal. Booth says in his Notebook that following
the discovery of the hidden auditors Hamlet "*acts* the rest of this scene

with Ophelia principally for the King." It is difficult to see precisely what he had in mind here. In one respect the business was very useful to him, almost indispensable, since it took some of the sting out of Hamlet's ill-usage of Ophelia, turning it into pretense intended to deceive the spies and leaving largely unsullied the image of perfect knightly courtesy which Booth everywhere sought to project.[25] But in another respect it worked to defeat one of his stated aims, since it also seemed to turn into pretense Hamlet's denial of his love for Ophelia, leaving the audience to conclude, contrary to Booth's strong belief, that he loves her nonetheless. Perhaps he did not think the matter through, or, having done so, decided that it was a fair trade-off. One wonders, though, why he did not delay the discovery, as William Charles Macready and others did, until "Where's your father?" which comes *after* the denial of love, since that arrangement would have come closer to serving both his needs: *genuine* denial of his love and *feigned* abusiveness.

Whatever Booth's intentions, audiences certainly did come away convinced that Hamlet's heart was not in his denial. According to Clarke, "when he said 'I did love you—once' and when he said 'I love you *not*' the wording seemed to be secretly opposed by the feelings." The same impression was strongly conveyed also at the end of the scene. "As he turned toward Ophelia for the last time," said Calhoun, "all the bitterness, all the reckless violence seemed to die out of him; his voice was full of unspeakable love, of appealing tenderness, of irrevocable doom, as he uttered the last 'To a nunnery go, go, go' and tottered from the room as one who could not see for tears.[26] A witness to the London performance noted that "at the close there is for an instant, in the quivering lip, the agonised features, and the hysterical farewell, a sign that Hamlet did really love Ophelia. It is momentary, but it is natural" (London *Daily Telegraph*, 8 November 1880).

Audience and actor were more nearly of one mind, however, in perceiving that Hamlet is throughout the scene playing the madman for the benefit of the spies. Booth drove the point home with a variation on Macready's business during the last speech, as Clarke reports:

"I'll no more of't"; (Turns his face slowly and gazes off. . . . Partially drops his head back a little to one side, giving one a faint hint that he is actively conscious someone is listening in the gallery). "It hath made me mad." (I class Booth's delivery of these five words as one of the great points in his enactment. . . . There was a singular artificial air about them. They did not appear to rise spontaneously from the subject or the situation. They seemed to be the climax of an attempt to delude any listener, and this climax seemed to have reached up to the very limit of Hamlet's deceptive power and showed itself a trifle above that limit. It conveyed to the audience Hamlet's strong suspicion of eavesdroppers, and to some extent palliated the harshness and raillery which had preceded in his conversation with Ophelia.)

Booth was "familiar, but by no means vulgar" with the First Player; secure in his princely dignity, he was friendly, pleasant and colloquial, "his manner . . . that of one giving competent advice to another upon a matter of mutual interest, in a kindly inofficial way."

The acting and staging of the play scene sparkled with innovations, both major and minor. He tapped his forehead lightly on "I must be idle" (III.ii.91), indicating to both Horatio and the audience that he was about to assume his antic disposition. He wore it lightly, though, departing from courtly behavior in carriage and tone just enough to suggest mental aberration. He did not openly insult Polonius, for instance, but made an inoffensive aside of "It was a brute part of him to kill so capital a calf there" (III.ii.105–6). The conversation with Ophelia went directly from "Lady, shall I lie in your lap?"—spoken with "a grave, sad, yet polite air"—to "You are merry, my lord," thus leaping over all the bawdry. He lay down at Ophelia's feet to observe the springing of his trap, but except for that detail his arrangement of the scene was wholly new. Instead of locating the stage for the players up center, he put it down left, placed the royal spectators opposite it and claimed upstage center for himself, his head toward the dais. With the visual focus thus shifted to Hamlet himself, Booth was able to make the most of his caustic commentary on the unfolding action. As the New York *Sunday Times* (9 January 1870) noted, "The counter-workings of the features of both Claudius and Hamlet are not only brought into more direct antithesis, but are also more plainly put in sight of the audience." He looked steadily at Gertrude during the Player King's "Faith, I must leave, love," and on the Player Queen's vow to die a widow he gestured ever so slightly toward her real-life counterpart. On "Wormwood, wormwood" he looked at his mother again, "with a smile of bitter gratification on lips that seem to be tightly closed yet admit of the expression."

Booth did not crawl toward his prey as the climax neared, but "expectation, anxiety and confirmed suspicion" showed in face and body.

Sitting bolt upright, he stared at Claudius as he explained the poisoning of Gonzago, pointing over his shoulder to the stage.[27] As the King and the court rushed out in wild disarray, Booth leapt up "with glistening eyes, an open mouth, and an exultant smile" and ran down the stage to Horatio, collapsing into his arms "in a spasm of bewildered emotion." It was at this moment that Booth seemed to demonstrate most tellingly his view that the obligation to seek revenge was a burden too heavy for Hamlet's feeble constitution to bear. Clarke wrote:

His feelings were a medley: there was some disappointment at the confirmation of his suspicions, since it threw his duty more pressingly upon his shoulders; there was a fitful gratification at the success of his scheme; there was regret, a sense of weakness, a desire for vengeance, a pitiful giving way of the will before the perceptive mind; and all these flared out in an incoherent laugh that was full of pain and intelligence; but there was no fury of intention, no instantaneous conception of a plan for the King's death, no desire for immediate revenge or clear design of retribution in the future.

As usual, there is an admirable reserve in Clarke's analysis which inspires confidence, but it may be that a less sober account, prompted by an 1865 performance, conveys a truer picture of the full impact of the moment:

He represents the revolt of Hamlet's overtasked will in a protracted hysteria, more real, shocking and overpowering than was perhaps ever before carried into the domains of imitation; a delineating upon which we have seen, in other cities, a whole audience hang in positive terror, only half pleased, and not masters of their lungs until it was over. But the necessity for such extreme passion is only apparent to the few. Claudius, in the moment of his utmost danger, has escaped, because Hamlet has nearly died. (New York *Evening Post*, 22 March 1865)

His manner with Rosencrantz and Guildenstern showed that "he could be efficient and stable in minor matters." His rebuke of them "contained no insolence and no threat, but it did contain a warning, and its thorough earnestness disabled the wits of the two courtiers." He was a bit more obviously eccentric with Polonius, but still very subdued, downplaying his mockery as much as the lines allowed. In London, one critic thought that "the fierce gloom of his banter . . . [was] quite beside the mark" (*Observer*, 7 November 1880), but another explained that this was merely "the quiet, unconscious, method of American humour. Hamlet bantered Polonius and the courtiers without a smile, as Bret Harte in a lecture makes jokes with a grave face" (London *Times* 8 November 1880).

Early in his career, Booth restored the King's bout with his conscience and Hamlet's accompanying rumination, "Now might I do it pat" (III.iii.73–96). In 1860 the New York *Times* critic noted that the scene had been "a stranger to the stage since the time of Garrick" and insisted that it should remain so, for the same reasons that had brought about its original excision: "It offends the sense of propriety of many people, and does not add anything to the grand features of the play" (27 November 1860). Booth must have been aware that the ferocity of thought contained in the "hire and salary" speech might seem out of character for the gentle Hamlet of his conception, but he apparently thought it worth the risk if it could also illustrate Hamlet's alleged incapacity for violent, decisive action. Perhaps he hoped to give stage life to Hazlitt's view that Hamlet does not really desire his enemy's eternal damnation but only says so to excuse his inability to play the executioner. Clarke says the scene was a superb exhibition of Hamlet as Booth conceived him: "a man of first class intellect but second class will." Still it was a very close thing as Booth staged it. On catching sight of the recently "convicted" assassin, he rushed forward, sword at the ready, only to be drawn up short on "And so he goes to heaven" (74). Having reached the very brink, he quickly retreated, to rehearse at some distance his reasons for postponing the execution. Nor did his reflections on Claudius' eventual punishment sound like mere rationalizing as Booth delivered them. He raised his right hand with fingers clenched on "that his heels may kick at heaven" and shut his teeth "exultantly, with a look of gross triumph," then consigned him to hell with a vigorous downward stroke.

In the closet scene he was characteristically chivalrous toward Gertrude, severe but not brutal, critical but also compassionate. He began with such an air of calm composure that some thought it rendered Gertrude's frightened call for help "scarcely explicable." But "it is the terrible, intense quiet of his tone and manner which frightens her," Calhoun pointed out, "more than violence would have done." He rushed toward the voice behind the arras much as he had rushed at Claudius a moment earlier, his face aglow with "inflamed purpose rather than with a wholesome incitement of the will." He has resolved, Clarke says, "to punish the Queen by slaying the King before her eyes." He cut through the tapestry "without stopping to make a deliberate thrust," and though the change was generally admired, a London critic thought the blow so gentle that it "could not possibly have injured any one behind it, unless it had frightened the hidden person to death" (London *Standard*, 8 November 1880). Booth was so shaken by the deed that he could not at first speak, but stood vibrating convulsively before making an "impetuous demand" for the identity of his victim.

Booth went back to miniatures for the illustration of "Look here upon this picture, and on this" (III.iv.53) and used a picture of his own father to represent Hamlet Sr. He kissed it reverently before holding it up to Gertrude's gaze and again after drawing its counterpart from her bosom. Throughout his remonstrations he maintained an air of "dainty loftiness," keeping his denunciation at a level of "spirituality and elevation above a merely vulgar view of her crime." Surprisingly though, he restored "Nay, but to live / In the rank sweat of an enseamed bed" (III.iv.91–92) and spoke it in a "tone of disgust . . . frowning with lip curling in contempt."

At the Ghost's entrance he fell back in surpise and fear, pulling Gertrude to her feet as he did so and stationing her between himself and the apparition. Clarke thought he heard in his anxious questioning about the reason for the Ghost's reappearance the hope that he has not come to harm Gertrude, together with dread of punishment for his inactivity and "a shadow of self-reproach." When he put his hand to his forehead in consternation at the Queen's inability to see and hear, the Ghost moved around unseen behind him, so that Hamlet was indeed bending his eye on vacancy when he looked up again and pointed, on "Why, look you there!" That brought another gasp and a start backward, his hand flying to his forehead, whereupon, turning slightly, he gasped at finding the Ghost in his new position. As the Ghost drifted out through the portal, Booth fell prostrate and lay motionless, his face hidden in his hands. Clarke thought the move a "slight breach of propriety, and a superfluity," and the author of a letter to the New York *Leader* (8 January 1870) called it "too violent to warrant his immediately succeeding remark that his pulse 'temperately kept time.' " Perhaps the latter criticism, which was voiced also in the New York *Sunday News* (6 February 1870) was triggered by the way Booth emphasized the reference to Hamlet's circulation: he put his fingers on his wrist and then invited Gertrude to check his pulse-rate for herself.

He was kneeling when his mother extended her hands in the traditional benediction. "He raises his head sadly and sees them; he starts, and draws in a breath audibly, reaches up and pushes her hands away with the manner of one who is interrupting a sacrilege." But they ended the scene in a tableau of loving reconciliation, she in his arms with her head on his breast, he dropping his cheek sorrowfully against her head as he says, "Mother, good night." Clarke considered the scene Booth's best, so powerful in the complexity of its effects that he despaired of describing it adequately: "My comprehension is yet too cramped, my understanding too vague, and my observation too dull and inaccurate." The New York *World* (6 January 1870) also called it

probably the best scene and certainly the one which received the most hearty and spontaneous applause. . . . The supernatural awe which invests this scene, the terror of the mother and son, and the admirable conduct of the Ghost, relieved it of the improbable, and oftentimes grotesque, character which inheres in the scene itself. . . . To make the action of this episode as effective now as it was in the superstitious age for which it was written is . . . a triumph of histrionic art . . . impulsively recognized by the audience.

Booth was next seen answering the King's summons, the scene with the two royal "sponges" having been eliminated. He entered boldly, with his arms folded, and presented himself before his interrogator with an air of defiance. He spoke only the first line of the discourse on worms, his tone "ironical, yet cold, formal and decorous." He was "sarcastic but grave" in telling the King where he could go to find Polonius and, stepping to his side, pointed the direction. He pointed to and "saw" the cherub (Iv.iii.48) above the King's head in the 1870 production, but later tried peering intently into the King's eyes, to suggest that Hamlet sees his own reflection there and is thus himself the cherub. It is not surprising that most observers found the business irritatingly incomprehensible. More intelligible was his original treatment of the next line, "Farewell, dear mother!" Other Hamlets, Booth says in his Notebook, had always given the line abstractedly, addressing it to the absent Gertrude. He chose instead to deliver it to Claudius, designating him for the moment as his mother's honored deputy. He knelt before Claudius, spoke the line with tender, tremulous sorrow, and taking his hands, bowed lovingly over them. On Claudius' response, "Thy loving father, Hamlet," he leapt to his feet and backed quickly away, "as one might from a reptile, not with bold detestation but as from something that had shocked him and that was repugnant." "My mother, sir" (Booth added the "sir") was given in "a tone of denial as if protesting with a stranger." He then spoke more warmly, treating the King once again as the representative of his mother.

Nowhere in the scene, Clarke thought, did he show any sign of wanting to kill the King. The mission to England seemed to make him "a trifle jubilant . . . as if . . . he looked forward to such a recuperation of moral force as could empower him to execute his purpose upon his return."

That return had already been effected when Booth's Hamlet next appeared, the Fortinbras scene (Iv.iv) and "How all occasions" having once more been denied a place. He took no joy in the mischievous humor of the Clown or in his own countersallies. His wit came out from mere habit, as it were, and was not used to lighten the scene. "He is ruled," says Clarke, "by a reflective mood and there is a great sorrowful memory within his mind." He smiled only once, on "One that was a woman" (V.i.135), and that was "by no means the ripple of a buoyant spirit." "With losing his wits" provoked only annoyance, and he continued his questioning with obvious weariness. The loving reminiscence over the skull of Yorick (V.i.184–95), which still bore the decaying remnant of a jester's cap, moved Clarke to declare that "it would have erected a monument to Yorick in my memory, if I had never heard of the personage through anyone but him." In later years, Booth sometimes used Macready's business of wiping his fingers after handing the relic back.

Like Forrest, he leaned on Horatio for comfort and support on hearing of the death of Ophelia, but his outcry was not so much a lament for a lost love as "a simple, heartfelt understanding of the event and a cry of pain because of it." "When I heard Booth say ['What, the fair Ophelia!']," Clarke remarks, "I felt that some part of his spirit had broken suddenly." Barely able to stand, Hamlet was lead by Horatio to the steps of a nearby tomb, where he sat with his back to the funeral, his head buried in the arms of Horatio, who knelt before him. He rose on hearing Laertes revile him ("Oh treble woe / Fall ten times . . . " [V.i.246]), and moved toward the grave, then allowed Horatio to draw him off to one side. He advanced again on "What is he . . . ?" and delivered the rest of the speech standing in a shaft of moonlight. Laertes grappled with him there. He looked into the grave, joined his hands, and extended his arms downward toward Ophelia as he declared his former love for her. "I'll rant as well as thou" was given in a low tone expressing "defiance and partly a sneer." At the end, he shook his clenched hand in the air "in a random, distracted way" and rushed off, like a "moody child running from someone who has displeased it, yet with something more of dignity, earnestness and desperation."

Booth restored Hamlet's account of his shipboard activities (V.ii.1–80), evidently because it was needed to cover a scene shift. Clarke judged the episode undramatic, "of little interest save to literary people, or precisians," and made no comment on Booth's performance of it. Booth behaved toward Osric with characteristic beneficence, masking his dislike of him with such finesse (while revealing it to the audience) that Osric "leaves as friendly as when he came." He spoke the full speech on providence (V.ii.219–24) and ended it by repeating "let be" three times, in imitation of Hamlet's earlier verbal triptychs. E. C. Stedman, editor of the *Atlantic*, writing during the Hundred Nights run, thought that Booth nowhere more perfectly represented the tender-souled Prince of Goethe's imagination: "Philosophy hovers around her gallant child, and the sweet, wise voice utters her teachings for the last time" (May 1866). According to Clarke: "His voice was for a minute troubled and semi-prophetic. It was only the mention of a presentiment, but it was so distinctly a hint of some sombre inward foresight that it left its mark on the memory and was thought of as soon as the final catastrophe took place."

The first bout of the fencing match was an unusually showy affair. In the course of parrying a thrust, Booth whirled around and presented his back to Laertes, then scored a touch by thrusting backward under his own arm. The dispatching of Laertes was comparatively straightforward. After being wounded in the breast, Hamlet drove furiously against his opponent, closed with him, wrenched the unbated weapon from his grasp and thrust it home. With both foils still in his hands, he staggered over to lean on Horatio. On "O villainy" he held the foils horizontally aloft and turned them two or three times, examining them. After hearing Laertes' dying confession, kneeling at his side, he abandoned his own weapon in favor of the lethal one. Eluding Horatio, he raced toward Claudius, seated on the throne, fought past the blades of several defending courtiers, grasped Claudius by the throat and plunged his sword twice into his neck, then threw him into the arms of his attendants.

He died simply and quietly. After taking the poisoned cup from Horatio, he sank to his knees, Horatio supporting him, and smiled "with friendly approval." Continuing his farewell in low, weak tones, he rose a little on "Oh, I die" and, turning, fell backward into Horatio's arms, his head toward the audience. When his head drooped in death, Horatio lowered him slowly to the ground and spoke the parting blessing. The curtain fell as the survivors turned their attention to the sound of approaching troops.

Booth went on playing Hamlet in every corner of the land for twenty years after the 1870 production.[28] To the very end he remained preeminent in the role among American actors, no youthful native genius having come forward to dislodge him, as he had once dislodged Forrest. Meanwhile, London had found a successor to Macready.

NOTES

1. For complete details of this and other aspects of Booth's association with the role, see Charles Shattuck's exhaustive study, *The Hamlet of Edwin Booth* (Urbana: University of Illinois Press, 1969).

2. Adam Badeau, "American Art," in *The Vagabond* (New York: Rudd & Carleton, 1859), p. 120.

3. Adam Badeau, "Edwin Booth," in ibid., p. 288 and passim.

4. Ferdinand Cartwright Ewer, 26 April 1853, quoted in Charles Shattuck, "Edwin Booth's First Critic," *Theatre Survey* 7 (May 1966): 9, 10. See also Shattuck, *The Hamlet of Edwin Booth*, pp. 6–7. Booth's debut performance was on 25 April 1853.

5. Ewer, 27 April 1853, quoted in Shattuck, "Edwin Booth's First Critic," p. 11.

6. Shattuck, *The Hamlet of Edwin Booth*, p. 22.

7. In *The Complete Works of William Hazlitt*, ed. P. P. Howe (London: J. M. Dent, 1930), 4:233–34.

8. Johann Wolfgang von Goethe, *Wilhelm Meister's Apprenticeship*, trans. Thomas Carlyle (1824; reprint, New York: Limited Editions Club, 1959), pp. 206, 234.

9. Shattuck, *The Hamlet of Edwin Booth*, p. 36.

10. George William Curtis, "Editor's Easy Chair," *Harper's*, April 1861,

p. 702. See also E. C. Stedman, "Edwin Booth," *Atlantic Monthly*, May 1866, pp. 586–87.

11. Edwin Milton Royle, "Edwin Booth as I Knew Him," *Harper's*, May 1916, p. 845.

12. Part of the appeal of the production was undoubtedly that it was the first time *Hamlet* had been staged in the United States with new, "historically accurate" scenery of the type popularized by Charles Kean (1811–1868) in London a decade earlier. For press reaction to the innovation, see Shattuck, *The Hamlet of Edwin Booth*, pp. 57–59.

13. Lucia Gilbert Calhoun in *The Galaxy*, January 1869, p. 82. See also the New York *Tribune*, 28 November 1864.

14. The settings were freshly executed, but with minor changes they followed the designs used in 1864, the actual scenery from the earlier production having been destroyed by fire in 1866. The designs are reproduced in Shattuck, *The Hamlet of Edwin Booth*, following p. 84.

15. *Between Actor and Critic: Selected Letters of Edwin Booth and William Winter*, ed. Daniel J. Watermeier (Princeton, N.J.: Princeton University Press, 1971), p. 203; letter dated 10 February 1882.

16. Quoted in Shattuck, *The Hamlet of Edwin Booth*, p. 32.

17. Shattuck (ibid., pp. 115–281) provides a complete transcription. The quotations given here are taken from the manuscript, now in the Folger Shakespeare Library in Washington, D.C. (*HAM*, 86); unless otherwise indicated, my descriptions of Booth's business and line readings are also based on Clarke's account.

Fifteen other promptbooks survive, dealing with Booth's portrayal at various stages of his long career. Six are at The Players in New York City, four in the Harvard Theater Collection, and two at the Folger; the Boston Athenaeum, the New York Public Library, and the University of Pennsylvania Library in Philadelphia each have one. For descriptions, see Charles Shattuck, *The Shakespeare Promptbooks* (Urbana: University of Illinois Press, 1965) (*HAM*, 75, 76, 87, 101–33), and *The Hamlet of Edwin Booth*, pp. 102–14.

18. Booth made his belated London debut in the role on 6 November 1880, at the Princess's Theatre.

19. Sometime after his retirement, Booth made over two hundred marginal notations in his copy of the Booth-Winter edition of the play (1878). Now in the Walter Hampden Memorial Library at The Players, it will be cited hereafter as the Notebook (*HAM*, 109).

20. In general, Booth's 1870 text, as given by Clarke (*HAM* 86), preserved the traditional cuts, sometimes altered by a few lines. Like Forrest, he restored Polonius' advice to Laertes and cut the scene between Horatio and the sailors (IV.vi).

21. Badeau, "Edwin Booth," p. 288.

22. Booth believed he was the first to adopt this practice and complained in the Notebook that he had never been given credit for it by the critics. But according to Arthur Colby Sprague (*Shakespeare and the Actors* [Cambridge, Mass.: Harvard University Press, 1944], p. 145), Charles Mayne Young originated the business in 1807.

23. In London, Henry Nicholls had sat throughout this soliloquy as early as 1854 (ibid., p. 385). But Booth was the first actor in the United States to sit during a soliloquy, having adopted the practice in the early 1860s at the suggestion of a friend (Asia Booth Clarke, *The Elder and the Younger Booth* [Boston: J. R. Osgood, 1882], p. 154). It was one of Booth's few concessions to everyday naturalness, and when he appeared in London, in 1880, it was still considered an impropriety by dyed-in-the-wool formalists; said the London *Daily News*, "He frequently departs from the old fashion of standing in stately attitudes, and sits in an easy posture, which, we fear, would have been painful to the feelings of the admirers of John Kemble as sadly beneath the dignity of The Tragic Muse" (8 November 1880).

24. In London, however, he accompanied the line with "a movement of the hands, descriptive of the act of encompassing his victim as though with a net" (London *Morning Post*, 8 November 1880).

25. Strictly speaking, even a pretense of badgering is ungentlemanly, since Ophelia cannot know that it is pretense and must therefore find it as painful as the real thing.

26. Calhoun is describing the 1864 performance (in *The Galaxy*, January 1869); if Booth also added the two repetitions of "go" in 1870, Clarke failed to note it.

27. He did creep in the 1864 performance, according to Calhoun, *The Galaxy*, January 1869, p. 81.

28. Booth retired from the stage with a performance of Hamlet at the Brooklyn Academy of Music on 4 April 1891. Though it was known that he had for some time been physically incapable of giving more than a faint suggestion of the Hamlet of his prime, 3,000 persons turned out to witness the end of a legend. For the full story of Booth's Hamlet portrayals after 1870, see Shattuck, *The Hamlet of Edwin Booth*, pp. 285–309.

9

HENRY IRVING

Henry Irving (1838–1905) first played Hamlet before a London audience on 31 October 1874; the production achieved an unprecedented run of two hundred consecutive performances and established Irving as the foremost Shakespearean actor of his day. Four years later, as if in grateful acknowledgment of what the role had done for him, he chose Hamlet to inaugurate his managership of the Lyceum, on 30 December 1878. Again he scored a triumph. Alfred Tennyson is reported to have declared on that occasion, "I did not think Irving could have improved upon his [earlier] Hamlet; he has done so—he has lifted it to heaven." [1]

Irving's apotheosis in the role of the Prince of Denmark must rank as one of the more prodigious feats in the annals of the stage; few actors can have reached the summit after such fumbling beginnings. "Henry Irving at first had everything against him as an actor," Ellen Terry writes. "He could not speak, he could not walk, he could not *look*. He wanted to do things in a part, and he could not do them. His amazing power was imprisoned, and only after long and weary years did he succeed in setting it free." [2] There were those who claimed that he was still more frog than Prince when he first undertook Hamlet. William Archer granted him a good face; it could appear "absolutely beautiful" at times, and though he looked ten years too old for Hamlet, his countenance had a "careworn melancholy" that perfectly suited the character. But his walk was so jerky and spasmodic that he resembled a "napkin-ring when suddenly shot out from under the forefinger." Shylock might be allowed Irving's habitual hobbling, but "Hamlet's port should be erect and free." [3]

Irving's portrayal offered offense not only to the eye but to the ear as well. Henry Arthur Jones, who for the most part greatly admired him in the role, observed sadly that many passages of Shakespeare's verse "were indeed neither more nor less than murdered by Irving; . . .

[He] couldn't sing; . . . He had not as much music in him as a street accordion.''[4] To his natural vocal deficiencies Irving added a trick of warped and wayward pronunciation, turning once familiar lines into something "that might be Choctaw, or pentameters with a Zulu click in each accent.''[5] "I should be particularly obliged,'' cried one exasperated auditor, "if he would tell me why, when he has to say 'O God!' he cries, 'O Gut!' '' (*Referee*, 5 January 1879). Throughout his tenure of the role he sounded such sour notes as " 'By heaven, I'll mek a gost of him that lats me!' ''[6] and " 'dug must have his da-eh' '' (*Vanity Fair*, 9 March 1885). In the opinion of most observers, Irving eventually succeeded in eradicating, or at least toning down, most of these splotches on his performance. Even Archer admitted that his diction was much improved upon his return from the United States in 1883.[7] By 1885 no less an aesthete than Oscar Wilde could write:

A few years ago it seemed to many, and perhaps rightly, that the personality overshadowed the art. No such criticism would be fair now. The somewhat harsh angularity of movement and faulty pronunciation have been replaced by exquisite grace of gesture and by clear precision of word. . . . Hamlet seems to me essentially a good acting part, and in Mr. Irving's performance of it there is that combination of poetic grace with absolute reality which is so eternally delightful.[8]

But in 1874, and to a somewhat lesser extent in 1878, when Irving achieved his near-fabulous celebrity in the role, audiences had to take him in the raw state in which his maker had sent him into the world. How they were able to do so remains an intriguing question. Many, it seems, simply turned his defects into virtues. E. R. Russell, who wrote a detailed and highly complimentary account of the 1874 performance, admitted that Irving moved on the stage like "a fretful man trying to get very quickly over a ploughed field," but argued that there was no reason why Hamlet himself should not have had this peculiarity; it gave the characterization "a stamp of personal individuality."[9] Archer, not surprisingly, rejected that highly specious argument, pointing out the obvious fact that the actor's idiosyncrasies of movement and vocalization could lend individuality only to the first character in which one happened to see him. "In all others they mar the individuality, making Hamlet, Eugene Aram, Claude Melnotte, Romeo, and Benedick mere phases of Irving, and nothing but Irving. If Mr. Irving now wishes to individualize any one of his parts, he should carefully refrain from plodding across ploughed fields in it.''[10]

Archer preferred to think that Irving succeeded *despite* his idiosyncrasies, not because of them, and in this analysis he was probably nearer the mark. Irving seems to have brought to his work qualities that more than compensated for his technical shortcomings. Chief among these Archer listed intelligence: "By intellect he makes us forget his negative failings and forgive his positive faults. By intellect, he forces us to respect where we cannot admire him. By intellect he dominates the stage."[11] Archer is here talking about all Irving's characterizations, but the analysis is peculiarly appropriate to his portrayal of Hamlet. As the mass of reviews from both 1874 and 1878 make clear, Irving was widely perceived as having given the stage its most cerebral Hamlet. "It is not an actor's view of Hamlet but the scholar's," wrote the critic for *Era*, "and still the actor has splendidly triumphed with the scholar's view. It is the picturesque acting forth of the *mind* of Hamlet, not the mere exhibition of his actions. We see Hamlet think. We do not merely hear him speak, we positively and actually watch his mind" (3 November 1874).

There is a strong echo of William Hazlitt in these remarks, and other critics mention Hazlitt by name as the source of Irving's intellectual characterization.[12] Irving also alludes to him in his published reflections on his approach to the role, though only in general terms.[13] More to the point, perhaps, Irving had played Laertes to Booth's Hamlet in Manchester in 1861 and was apparently first attracted to Hazlitt's conception of the character as "scholar and gentleman" in that indirect way. Laurence Irving says of his grandfather that "if during the months of study [for his debut in the role] the reading of any contemporary actor had influenced his own, it was the American's philosophical approach to Hamlet's character which had illuminated his reflections."[14] But despite the influence of Hazlitt on both actors, their characterizations were far from identical. Booth was clearly more gentleman than scholar, more poet than thinker, while with Irving it was decidedly the other way around.

Related to this difference was a pronounced difference in style. Irving was natural, to a degree totally at odds with Booth's conservative notions of tragic decorum.[15] In fact, naturalness was the most arresting feature of his portrayal. For this quality he undoubtedly owed a heavy debt to another actor, Charles Fechter (1824–1879), to whom he had also played Laertes in the days of his apprenticeship. In 1861 Fechter had electrified London with an iconoclastically natural Hamlet, and Irving seems to have followed quite deliberately in his footsteps.[16] At the time of Irving's first appearance in the role a number of critics had either forgotten or chauvinistically chose to ignore the pioneering work of Fechter, who was an expatriate Frenchman, but Joseph Knight kept a clear-eyed historical perspective: "[Mr. Irving's] performance [is] noteworthy as marking a stage in the history of theatrical art, since it shows the final abandonment of old traditions of acting and of conventions of declamation; . . . [It is] revolutionary and . . . would have appeared more so but for the previous experiment of Mr. Fechter."[17]

That the natural style was still revolutionary, despite the Fechter precedent, can be seen in the negative reactions it provoked in some quarters. The *Sporting Times* (7 November 1874) offered a ringing denunciation:

That the Prince of Denmark should bear very considerable resemblance to a lackadaisical lachrymose "swell" of the present day, could surely not have been the intention of the Bard; yet the moody Dane, as enacted at the Lyceum, irresistibly reminds us of the effeminate loungers whom we are prone to encounter in the drawing-rooms of London. It is asserted by the actor's admirers that his rendering is wonderfully natural. Yes, but not natural to the play.

Others spoke with disdain of his "bourgeois cordiality" and "colloquial familiarity" (London *Daily News*, 2 November 1874; *Figaro*, 7 November 1874).

Such reactions were relatively rare, but petulant and unrepresentative as they are they tell us something about the quality of Irving's naturalness. Like Fechter before him, Irving sought to abandon the traditional representation of the Prince of Denmark as "a creature of the imagination—utterly impossible as a living human being."[18] Irving sought, as he later said, "to disentangle the character from traditions which are apt to overlay with artifice one of the most vividly real of all the conceptions in art, to leave upon [my] generation the impression of Hamlet as a man, not as a piece of acting."[19] The result was a thoroughgoing commitment to the particular, the familiar, the idiosyncratic in human behavior—a commitment to whatever would aid him in the representation of Hamlet as "a living human being." Russell put the whole matter clearly and succintly in saying that under the new dispensation the actor asked "not how a character *should* sit, [the ideal], but how he *would* sit, [the real]." [20]

If some spectators could see in this only a disgusting vulgarization of their ideal Prince, most hailed it as a great advance in the art of acting. The critic for *Entr'acte* offered one of the most apposite analyses of the change: "The picture, as a whole, is singularly free from conventionalism and that stiltedness which have been instrumental in keeping Shakespeare in somewhat an artificial position. With a certain amount of majestic elaborateness, many actors of Hamlet have made their audience wonder. Mr. Irving makes them *feel*, and feel acutely too" (14 November 1874). The reviewer for *Theatre* (9 February 1879) saw Irving's innovations in much the same way:

The performance, so far from being a mere succession of points, is a consistent and intelligible whole, and abounds in flashes of contagious inspiration. Free from the bonds of tradition, Mr. Irving presents us with a *human* Hamlet, and the realism he imparts to his acting rather intensifies than diminishes the halo of poetry which surrounds the character.

The impression he created of a real human being thinking aloud was undoubtedly the chief source of Irving's phenomenal appeal in the role, but his characterization was also studded with other distinctive touches that excited the keen admiration of his contemporaries.

For all his commitment to naturalism, Irving by no means eschewed theatrical effect, as is evident from the manner of his first entrance. As Ellen Terry reports, the entrance was "very much 'worked up.' "

He was always a tremendous believer in processions. . . . At [the tail of the procession], when the excitement was at fever heat, came the solitary figure of Hamlet, looking extraordinarily tall and thin. The lights were turned down another stage trick—to help the effect that the figure was spirit rather than man. He was weary. His cloak trailed on the ground. [21]

Contributing also to the initial effect were striking innovations in costume, representing a radical departure from practices in more-or-less constant use since the days of John Philip Kemble. As Clement Scott put it, "No imitation of the portrait of Sir Thomas Lawrence, no funereal velvet, no elaborate trappings, no order of the Danish Ele-

Henry Irving. Photogravure, from the painting by Edwin Long. Lyceum Theatre, London, 1874. Harvard Theatre Collection.

phant, . . . no bugles, no stilted conventionality. We see before us a man and a prince, in thick-ribbed silk and a jacket or paletot edged with fur . . . relieved only by a heavy chain of gold'' (London *Daily Telegraph*, 2 November 1874).

The exchanges with Claudius and Gertrude in the early moments of the court scene seem to have been unremarkable, the nature and extent of Irving's originality first becoming apparent in his rendering of the soliloquy (I.ii.129–59). In keeping with his naturalistic bent, Irving elected to sit for the opening lines of the speech, an occurrence which reviewers found noteworthy despite Fechter's having done the same. But the naturalism lay not so much in the actor's physical deportment as in his delivery; the critic for the London *Standard* (31 December 1878) found this and the other soliloquies

wonderful in their reality, as unconscious utterances of thought, totally different from set speeches, and nothing is more remarkable about them than the
manner in which the Hamlet glides into them, as it were, in place of deliberately beginning a recitative as most actors are accustomed to begin soliloquies.
We see the thought in Hamlet's face before his lips give it articulation, and
the occasional pauses, as that for instance in the lines "But no more like my
father than I to—Hercules,'' is admirably natural and expressive.

Though admiration of this sort was the order of the day, some found Irving occasionally too far gone in naturalism. Even Russell, though full of praise for the actor's ''realistic genius,'' thought he delivered the last line of the soliloquy, ''But break my heart, for I must hold by tongue'' (I.ii.159), ''needlessly and wrongly, without point'' and bade him remember that ''Shakespeare was an actor, and wrote the pet passages of Hamlet as speeches, which ought to be made effective as such.''[22]

Irving's delivery of the first soliloquy revealed not just the style his performance would exhibit but something also of its interpretive substance. One observer heard in it ''the vehement expostulation of one by no means sure of his own sanity already'' and concluded, ''Ham-
let, according to [Irving's] view, is distraught from the first'' (*Pall Mall Gazette*, 1 January 1879). Most others found him ''distraught'' only a little later, after the encounter with the Ghost, but there was wide-
spread agreement that Irving saw Hamlet as at least partially mad. In his published commentary on the role, Irving seemed to lend some

confirmation to this view, speaking of his desire to bring out "the high-strung ecstasy . . . of the man." [23] Scott linked the interpretation with the views of Hippolyte Taine, who had written of the "ethical disturbance of Hamlet's mind, which, 'as a door whose hinges are twisted, swings and bangs with every wind with a mad haste and a discordant noise.' " [24] William Winter avowed that "no actor was ever truer or finer than [Irving] in denotement of the blending of assumed madness with involuntary derangement—the forlorn state of a wild, unsettled mind, protecting itself by simulated wildness." [25]

First faintly limned in the Act I soliloquy, Hamlet's "ecstasy" would become more pronounced as the action progressed, taking its place with intellectuality and naturalness as one of the distinguishing marks of Irving's characterization. It was present immediately following the soliloquy in the interview with Horatio and the sentinels. Ellen Terry saw it as a strain of "extravagance . . . bizzarrerie," which went far to establish Hamlet as a sort of "visionary," one fully capable of seeing the Ghost. [26] But Irving sounded other notes here as well. In the way he spoke the two names "Horatio? Marcellus!" he let the audience see that in Hamlet's "mind there is some sense of the difference in rank as well as the more obvious difference in intimacy" (*Academy*, 7 November 1874). In his dealings with both he avoided the "back-slapping, rib-poking sort of familiarity of Mr. Fechter" but achieved a "friendly intimacy . . . [which] was preeminently princely." [27] The line "In my mind's eye, Horatio" (I.ii.185) he played "as though he were actually surveying a picture painted upon the imagination as vividly as upon canvas" (London *Morning Post*, 2 November 1874), thus preparing the way for a similar effect to be used later, in the closet scene. Beginning with that line, he lapsed into a reverie which made him so unconscious of his surroundings that he did not at first take in Horatio's stunning revelation: "My lord, I think I saw him yester-night" (I.ii.189). When the light dawned, he became "sharp as a needle. . . . [His] face, as he listened to Horatio's tale, blazed with intelligence. He cross-examined the men with keenness and authority." [28]

In all this, as in all that was to follow, Irving displayed an unflagging attention to detail which contributed heavily to his success. Again and again one encounters in the existing testimony praise for this facet of his artistic work. It is clear that his Hamlet was recognized and admired not merely as a dramatic character possessed of "blazing intelligence'' but as the *product* of that very quality, a creation born of the prodigious thought and study of the actor himself. As Archer said, ''Mr. Irving reads [Shakespeare] by the student's midnight oil. He is great in new glosses and daring in conjectural emendations. The stalls are startled by his critical acumen, the boxes thrilled by his archeological scholarship.''[29]

But Irving could also be conventional when he chose. He began the scene on the platform with the time-honored business, rather sneeringly described by the *Pall Mall Gazette* (3 November 1874):

Hamlet still paces the bleak platform of the castle while clad in pumps and the thinnest of black-silk stockings and divests himself, in the old artificial way, of his hat and cloak immediately on the appearance of the ghost, with a prescience that the warm work before him will counteract the ''nipping and eager air of night,'' his abandoned clothes being with ludicrous zeal collected and carried after him.

Irving delivered the line beginning ''I'll call thee Hamlet'' in Booth's way, making a full stop after ''Father'' and linking ''Royal Dane'' with ''O, answer me!'' (I.iv.44–45).[30] He spoke throughout with ''extreme and plaintive beseechingness''[31] and after freeing himself from his companions ''advanced crouching, as if drawn onwards in terror and against his will by a mesmeric spell'' (London *Examiner*, 7 November 1874). His speech upon the exit of the Ghost was, according to Russell, ''an outburst hardly distinguishable from hysteria,'' a clear manifestation of ''that tendency of Hamlet to indulged frenzy and exaltation which Irving has been . . . the first to represent with fidelity to nature.'' As a means of further emphasizing the tendency, Irving restored Hamlet's ''tables'' and wrote on them feverishly. He also restored all the irreverent responses to the Ghost in the cellarage, thus presenting his startled friends, and the audience, with an image of ''subsiding half-lunacy.''[32]

In the scenes of badinage with Polonius and with Rosencrantz and Guildenstern in Act II, Irving appeared unduly acerbic to some. A writer for *MacMillan's Magazine*, finding him guilty of ''absolute rudeness'' toward the old counselor and of ''wholly uncalled-for insolence'' toward the young courtiers, pronounced him ''totally incompetent to deal with the lighter side of the character.''[33] Irving responded to such criticism by greatly softening this aspect of his characterization in later years.[34] In the guying of Polonius he followed Kean's practice of *reading* the line "For if the sun breed maggots . . . " (II.ii.181–82), but added to it by having Polonius approach "as if to overlook his book" and then shutting it on "Have you a daughter?"[35] In the early part of his conversation with Rosencrantz and Guildenstern he restored seventeen lines in which Hamlet calls Denmark a prison, Rosencrantz introduces the sensitive topic of ambition and Hamlet replies with "O God, I could be bounded in a nutshell . . . " (II.ii.240–56).

The soliloquy following the interview with the players (II.ii.550–605) was as free of point-making as the first soliloquy had been. "He is not acting," said Scott, "he is not splitting the ears of the groundlings; he is an artist concealing his art, he is talking to himself, he is thinking aloud" (London *Daily Telegraph*, 2 November 1874). Russell was equally enthusiastic about the interpretation: " 'Now I am alone'—exclaims Hamlet . . . and the freedom, the simplicity, the abandonment, the expansiveness, the almost unhinged and yet consistently ordered excitement of his solitude—these are the phenomena, freshly seen and truly scanned, upon which Irving has founded the interpretation he has developed." At the end of the soliloquy, Irving sought to externalize further the character's feverish state by introducing a variation on a bit of business he had employed earlier; as the curtain fell, he rushed to a pillar in a "quasi-hysterical" state and, placing his notebook against it, began to scribble notes for the speech he has asked the First Player to insert in "The Murder of Gonzago."[36] Irving also introduced two new line readings in his delivery of the soliloquy, both of which were greeted with understandable suspicion by the writer for *Academy* (1 January 1879):

[The actor] dwells heavily on the word "am" [i.e., in the phrase "am pigeon-livered," II.ii.577] as if he were quoting the observation of some impertinent person which had long been rankling in his mind, and in uttering the line . . . "He would drown the stage with tears," he dwells heavily on the word "drown" as if tears might but for this thoughtful precaution be supposed to burn.

If these two examples are any indication, Irving's diligent study of the text sometimes led him into mere eccentricity.

But he scored far more hits than misses, and by the end of the second act of the opening-night performance Irving had begun to win the

audience over. Hardly more than polite at the end of Act I, applause
at the close of Act II revealed a widening and deepening enthusiasm.
By the end of Act III it had swollen to flood tide. As Joseph Knight
said, the audience "slowly and reluctantly came under the spell of the
conception, and at the close of the third act it was riveted in a way
such as we read of in records of past performances, but scarcely, so
far as English acting is concerned, can recall."[37] Irving achieved the
total captivation of the audience in this act by exhibiting in the crucial
scenes bold strokes of arresting originality. The "To be or not to be"
soliloquy early in the act occasioned surprisingly little comment, except of the sort applied to the soliloquies generally; like the others it
was praised for being delivered as "the unwitting utterance of thought."
It was rather in his playing of the nunnery scene and the play scene
(and to a lesser extent the closet scene) that Irving electrified the assembly and won its unbounded approbation.

In the nunnery scene, he entranced all but the most recalcitrant by
"presenting Hamlet as under the influence of an overmastering love
for Ophelia."[38] To some extent Fechter had anticipated him in this,
as in so many other particulars, but Irving broke fresh ground of his
own in representing the Prince's love as a powerful emotion forcefully
"*suppressed*"—to use the term and the emphasis employed by more
than one reviewer.[39] Thus, while Fechter had simply substituted tenderness for the "brutality and coarseness" traditional in the playing of
the scene, Irving kept the rough treatment which the lines seem to demand, but made the audience see through it to an underlying love, as
David Garrick and Edmund Kean had done but to a much greater extent. As the writer for the London *World* put it, "With subtle art he
suggests the presence of an extreme tenderness beneath the veil of all
his bitterness and vehemence" (8 January 1879). In an essay on this
scene, written between the 1874 and 1878 performances, Irving revealed something of the characteristic close study on which he based
his readings and in the process preserved details about his playing of
the scene. In the beginning Hamlet is allowed to reveal his love more-
or-less openly; thus "Nymph, in thy orisons / Be all my sins remembered" (III.i.88–89) is delivered as "a plaintive reminiscence of the
tender past." But having permitted himself that brief indulgence, he is
immediately on his guard against a greater, perhaps uncheckable rush
of feeling:

The voice of Ophelia recalls the past. He shrinks from the revival of the influence its tender tones once had upon him. No doubt the words of his vow recur to his mind. He is pledged from his memory to wipe away "all trivial fond records." His, "Well, well, well" is a nervous, hurried reply, with a quick glance around as if for exit or relief. But there is none. The hour he would most have avoided has come. His choking words uttered, we may suppose him hurrying from the scene, when Ophelia's next words arrest him and compel his attention. . . . In the imbecility of helplessness, rather than with any resort to his previously assumed manner, he replies, "No, not I; I never gave you aught."

Ophelia persists in the redelivery of his remembrances, following which, in Irving's analysis, "the scene takes its sudden and violent transition" at the line "Ha! ha! are you honest?" (III.i.102). How, Irving asks, "may we . . . form a rational explanation of the swiftness with which this exclamation was conceived?" His answer, as intelligent an explication as may be found of this notoriously difficult scene, deserves to be quoted at length:

Perhaps the action of Hamlet's mind was somewhat after this manner: He feels the woe of Ophelia and his own. He writhes under the stigma of heartlessness which he cannot but incur. How remove it? How wipe away the stain? It is impossible. Cursed then be the cause. His whole nature surges up against it— the incestuousness of this King; the havoc of illicit passion, which has killed his noble father, wrecked his fairest hopes, stolen from him his mother's love— nay, robbed him even of the maternal ideal. . . . His (Hamlet's) mother was once fair and honest, honest as Ophelia now. *Is* Ophelia honest? Impossible to think otherwise. But it were a mad quip to ask her, and let the after dialogue take its own course. Take what course it will, it must dwell on the one subject which will harden Hamlet's heart, and give rigour to his nature.

Hamlet thus proceeds through the insulting discourse on "beauty and honesty" until "he utters the words that may most sharply end all—'I loved you not.' This is the surgeon's knife . . . [but] he uses it more in frenzy than in judgment, in an agony of pain, amid a thousand fond remembrances, but dominated by the one conviction that he must break with Ophelia, cost what it may."[40] This fine tension between the emotion verbalized and the emotion felt reached its climax in Irving's playing of Hamlet's final speech. Taking a leaf from Kean's book, he moved back to Ophelia after being on the point of leaving, but instead of kissing her hand he made as if to embrace her, and then "with a painful effort he refrained.''[41] Ending the scene on the same note with which he had begun it, Irving delivered the final line, ''To a nunnery, go'' ''not . . . in a tone of brutal cynicism, but with an ironical and mournful expression, indicative of the intense passion and suffering gnawing at his heart'' (*Reynold's*, 1 January 1879). ''The scene with Ophelia turns the scale,'' Scott wrote of the 1874 performance, ''and the success is from this instant complete'' (London *Daily Telegraph*, 2 November 1874).

Having grappled his auditors to him with a brilliant display of psychological complexity in the nunnery scene, Irving went on to hold them fast by fresh handling of the speech to the players (III.ii.1–45). In keeping with his inclination toward the relaxed and informal, he gave ''Speak the speech, I pray you'' to a single member of the company, ''button-holed'' for the purpose; the speech thus bore ''less the air of an address to the actors on important topics than that of a few 'good things' . . . carelessly dropped into the ears of one of them'' (*Academy*, 4 January 1879). ''But with all this there was a princely air, a kindly courtesy, and an exquisite expression of refinement which astonished the house as much from its daring as its truth'' (London *Daily Telegraph*, 2 November 1874).

Stunningly effective as such strokes were, his acting of the ensuing play scene was the most admired part of his performance, not only in 1874 but throughout his career in the role. He began with a concession to tradition, sprawling in the canonical manner at the feet of Ophelia and observing Claudius from behind her fan.[42] But there was something of his own in it too, and as events moved toward their furious climax he would make it entirely his own. There was an unaccustomed intensity in the ''basilisk gaze'' he fixed on the guilty king, ''a serpent-like fascination of look and manner'' (London *Morning Post*, 2 November 1874). To make more palpable the frenzy of anticipation Hamlet feels here on the threshold of conviction, Irving devised business which sounds absurdly grotesque in the description but which audiences found wonderfully apt: ''In his nervous excitement he destroys with his teeth the feathered fan with which he has been toying, biting it convulsively as his scheme for securing conviction progresses'' (*Era*, 5 January 1879).[43]

Returning to time-honored practice, Irving began a slow crawl toward the King during the speech of Lucianus, but added a touch of naturalistic credibility to that baldly theatrical maneuver by executing

it as if Hamlet is "unawares in his excitement," locked in a state of
total absorption, which absorption Irving helped convey by speaking
the lines of the poisoner with him, *sotto voce*, while advancing in a
"snaky crawl" toward his prey. Still prone, he "hissed out like an
accusation" (*Academy*, 7 November 1874) his own following speech
" 'A poisons him in the garden for his estate" (III.ii.261), and when
that and the cunning of the scene produced its intended effect, driving
the usurper from his seat and from the room, Irving sprang the theatrical trap he had been preparing through the whole of his preceding
characterization. In what proved to be the resounding *coup de théâtre*
of his performance, he leaped to his feet "in momentary wildness,"
let out a shriek of triumph at the success of his enterprise, hurled
"frighted with false fire" as a taunt after the retreating Claudius and
then threw himself on the vacant throne, suggesting in that act a re-
possession of the realm by its rightful owner.[44] So stunned was the
audience that it at first "forgot to cheer," but after a moment's silence
"it rose to its feet and fairly satisfied itself at last with a great roar in
recognition of [the actor's] power" (*Academy*, 7 November 1874). The
ovation all but drowned out the "stricken deer" quatrain, recited from
the throne with the actor "swaying from side to side in irrepressible
excitement."[45] But the tumult had subsided when Irving put the fan
to use again a moment later. Reciting the doggerel verse ("For thou
dost know, O Damon dear") Hamlet gropes for a concluding metaphor: "A very, very—" (III.ii.281–84). Irving had his glance fall at
that moment on the peacock-feathered fan—or what was left of it—
and then ended with "A very, very—peacock." *Bell's* thought the new
business "a palpable hit" (7 November 1874).

In the ensuing colloquies with Polonius and with Rosencrantz and
Guildenstern Irving exhibited more of that ferocity he had unleashed
on them earlier. He became so outraged at the attempt of his old
schoolfellows to play upon him that he broke the recorder with brutal
violence and tossed the pieces from him, on " 'Sblood, do you think
I am easier to be played on than a pipe?" (369–70).[46] One observer
found it out of keeping with "the easy superiority which the young
Prince not only exercises, but knows well that he exercises, over all
the courtiers and hangers-on of the palace" (London *Daily News*, 2
November 1874). Even when, in later years, he attempted to soften his
treatment of the courtiers, he retained this business; he was still being
censured for it in 1885. At the conclusion of the recorder speech, after

"Call me what instrument you will, though you fret me, yet you cannot play upon me" (III.ii.370–72), Irving inserted Hamlet's later characterization of Rosencrantz as a "sponge . . . that soaks up the King's countenance . . . " (IV.ii.12–24). At the end of the scene, before the concluding soliloquy, he inserted "Good night, Horatio" and spoke it "very tenderly tho' rather absently and wearily—extending his hand which Horatio kisses."[47]

Parts of Claudius' soliloquy, "O, my offence is rank," were restored (III.iii.36–50, 65–72), and also Hamlet's murderous meditation "Now might I do it pat," a speech which some still found "rather revolting."[48] As he spoke, Hamlet held a torch with which he had equipped himself at the close of the preceding scene, prudently, it was said, since the passageways of the castle were sure to be dark. Others objected that to stand over Claudius with the thing blazing away was to warn him, absurdly, of his peril, "as a danger-signal warns a coming train of a possible accident." After depositing the torch in a wall bracket at the rear of Gertrude's closet, Irving next "involved himself with the chamber-candle-sticks." "It may be thought, perhaps, that the scene thus becomes more real," wrote the critic for the London *World*, "but these details tend to vulgarise poetic tragedy, which should occupy ground removed from the trivialities and the homeliness of ordinary life" (8 January 1879). For the most part, however, Irving's fondness for the paraphernalia of realism won warm favor with the Victorian audience. In other ways as well Irving brought a new level of verisimilitude to the scene. Shunning point-making on "Is it the King?" (III.iv.26), he simply "threw the line away," to the consternation of old-school playgoers. More strikingly heterodox was his handling of "The counterfeit presentment of two brothers" (III.iv.54ff.). As already suggested, he did not "handle" them at all, but simply located them out in space, in the "mind's eye." The innovation irritated about as many as it pleased, and in the 1880s Irving abandoned it in favor of the conventional miniatures.[49]

Upon the arrival of the apparition, Irving again showed how he could play on audience sensibilities by giving to familiar lines a new reading, produced by subtle variation in timing and emphasis: "Pointing to the Ghost he asks the Queen 'Do you see nothing?' and then, after a pause, adds, almost in a whisper, the word 'There?'; few among the spectators could have failed to feel the influence of suggested wonderment and terror" (*Graphic*, 4 January 1874). There were raised eyebrows at the end of the scene when Irving restored the Folio business, long since omitted from stage presentation, and exited "tugging in Polonius." "Very doubtful taste," wrote the critic for *Reynold's* (8 November 1874), and the man from *News of the World* objected that it "destroys the dignity of the scene" (8 November 1874).

Irving omitted entirely the first four scenes of Act IV and was thus seen next in the graveyard scene. He was admired there chiefly on three counts: (1) for delivering the address to the skull in the manner of a soliloquy, "apart from the rest, and in a softened tone, the actor stroking the remnant of humanity gently with his hand" (London *Daily Chronicle*, 31 December 1878); (2) for eliminating the leap into the grave—though he was not, as some thought, the first to do so; and (3) for the fervor of his declaration of love for the dead Ophelia, made over her grave with his back to the audience, following which he threw himself into his mother's arms. In short, the scene gave fresh evidence of his predominantly natural approach.

The final scene also provoked commentary chiefly on three topics: the management of the duel, the killing of Claudius and the death of the Prince. "The fencing scene—" one admiring observer wrote, "which till now has seemed almost predestined to be bungled . . . was . . . full of spirit and vigour . . . and the poisoned and 'bated' foils were exchanged with a rapidity, and with an appearance of reality about the accident which we do not remember to have witnessed before" (*Graphic*, 4 November 1874). Further light is shed on how it was done by a report in *Saturday Review*: "Hamlet gets possession of his adversary's foil, and then throws his own foil to the adversary—by mistake, as we must suppose—and he neatly catches it" (7 November 1874).

Similarly, the dispatching of the unmasked King won praise because it showed a considerable gain in the "appearance of reality." Irving expunged "the somewhat clumsy process of forcing the contents of the poisoned goblet down the King's throat, as if he were an animal being dosed," and though he was lauded for thus "being content . . . to kill his enemy once," it was argued, surely with good reason, that the line "drink off this potion" should also have been cut (*Saturday Review*, 7 November 1874). The climactic moment also acquired added naturalistic force by the way in which the actual execution was conducted: "The death of the king is managed far more effectively than usual," runs one report. "He is dragged off his throne and run through by Hamlet instead of being dispatched where he sits" (*News of the*

World, 8 November 1874). The London *Daily News* reporter said, "There was . . . a certain grandeur in the contemptuous brutality with which, having pierced the King, he cast his body to the ground" (2 November 1874).

This same reviewer had very different feelings about Hamlet's last earthly act, Irving's last gesture as his impersonator: "[Hamlet's death] would have been better without the accompanying pointing upward with the finger, apparently intended as a corrective to the suggested materialism of 'The rest is silence,' a piece of pretty resignation which should be left to the print-shop windows." Another reviewer called it "a puerile innovation . . . unworthy of the serious notice of the critic" (*Sporting Times*, 7 November 1874).

Pretty though his dying moment may have been, it was a predominantly unpretty Hamlet which Irving revealed. Partly out of a necessity imposed by his own nature, partly as a matter of conviction, Irving brought Hamlet down off the pedestal of the ideal and made him a credible, if not merely ordinary, human being, dealing with life in a way that had in it more rough authenticity than grandeur or nobility. His Hamlet was not man as he ought to be but man as he is, not better than ourselves but like ourselves, not beautiful but true. Despite relentless prodding by Shaw, Irving never associated himself with the plays of Henrik Ibsen and his English imitators, but to a remarkable degree he acted Shakespeare as though it were Ibsen. In that respect, his Hamlet portrayal exactly suited the taste of his contemporaries. It is clear from the press response to other Hamlets of the 1880s and 1890s that as long as Irving's characterization remained before the public or was remembered by them, a new impersonator could expect to win acclaim only by adopting Irving's main line of approach, whatever excellence of an original sort he might also bring to bear. In 1897 such a claimant appeared in the person of Johnston Forbes-Robertson.

NOTES

1. Alfred Tennyson, quoted in Laurence Irving, *Henry Irving: The Actor and His World* (New York: Macmillan, 1952), p. 316.

2. Ellen Terry, *Memoirs*, ed. Edith Craig and Christopher St. John (1932; reprint, New York: B. Blom, 1969), p. 61.

3. William Archer, *Henry Irving, Actor and Manager: A Critical Study* (1883; reprint, St. Clair Shores, Mich.: Scholarly Press, 1970), pp. 63–64.

4. Henry Arthur Jones, *The Shadow of Henry Irving* (1931; reprint, New York: B. Blom, 1969), p. 49.

5. Archer, *Actor and Manager*, p. 67.

6. Ibid., p. 69.

7. Ibid., p. 68.

8. Oscar Wilde, in *Dramatic Review*, 9 May 1885. For a remarkably similar opinion, see George Bernard Shaw, *Our Theatre in the Nineties* (1932; reprint, London: Constable, 1954), 1:271.

9. E. R. Russell, *Irving as Hamlet* (London: H. S. King, 1875), p. 4.

10. Archer, *Actor and Manager*, pp. 75–76.

11. Ibid., p. 92.

12. London *Daily Telegraph*, 2 November 1874; London *Examiner*, 7 November 1874. Goethe and Coleridge are also mentioned frequently.

13. "If Hazlitt could have had his way," Henry Irving writes, "and if *Hamlet* had been forbidden to the stage as 'hardly capable of being acted,' some of the purest pleasure actors have ever known would have been denied to them" ("My Four Favorite Parts," *The Forum* 16 [1893], p. 34).

14. Laurence Irving, *Henry Irving: The Actor and His World*, p. 242.

15. Booth thus suffered by comparison when he played London in 1880. Clement Scott called him "cold and classical" (London *Daily Telegraph*, 8 November 1880). "It was the Hamlet of the stage," said *Vanity Fair*, "correct and passionless" (13 November 1880). "His chief aim is theatrical effectiveness of the old-fashioned sort" (London *World*, 16 November 1880).

16. For an account of Fechter's performance, see my article "The Modesty of Nature: Charles Fechter's *Hamlet*," *Theatre Survey* 15 (1974): 59–78.

17. Joseph Knight, *Theatrical Notes* (London: Lawrence & Bullen, 1893), p. 6 (a reprint of Knight's *Athenaeum* review of 7 November 1874).

18. Arthur à Beckett, *Green Room Recollections* (Bristol: J. W. Arrowsmith, 1896), p. 23.

19. Henry Irving, "Four Favorite Parts," p. 34.

20. Russell, *Irving as Hamlet*, p. 8.

21. Terry, *Memoirs*, p. 103.

22. Russell, *Irving as Hamlet*, p. 24.

23. Henry Irving, "Four Favorite Parts," p. 35.

24. Clement Scott, in London *Daily Telegraph*, 2 November 1874. Scott is quoting, a trifle inaccurately, from Taine's *History of English Literature*, trans. Henri van Laun (Edinburgh: Edmonston & Douglas, 1873), 2:409.

25. William Winter, quoted in Austin Brereton, *The Life of Henry Irving* (London: Longmans, Green, 1908), 2:62.

26. Terry, *Memoirs*, p. 106.

27. Russell, *Irving as Hamlet*, p. 25.

28. Terry, *Memoirs*, p. 106.

29. Archer, *Actor and Manager*, p. 89.

30. Promptbook in the Shakespeare Centre Library, Stratford-upon-Avon (*HAM*, 93). Irving made all the traditional cuts, plus a few others of note: II.i.71–116 (Ophelia's report of Hamlet's visit to her closet); II.ii.19–36 (the King and Queen's exchange of courtesies with Rosencrantz and Guildenstern); 86–105 (Polonius' declension of Hamlet's madness); III.i.171–75, 176–80 (Claudius and Polonius on Hamlet's madness); IV.v.201–20 (Claudius and Laertes on the death of Polonius); IV.vi (Horatio and the sailors); IV.vii.36–70 (Hamlet's letter to Claudius and the inception of Claudius' plan to deal with him); V.i.6–13, 23–40 (parts of the Clowns' discussion of Ophelia's death and funeral); V.ii.267–74 ("Set me the stoops of wine . . . "). Cuts and restorations involving Hamlet will be discussed in the text.

31. Russell, *Irving as Hamlet*, p. 28.

32. Ibid., pp. 29–30.

33. A. Templar, "The New Hamlet and His Critics," *Macmillan's Magazine* 31 (1875): 239.

34. Thus, in 1878, the writer for the London *Daily News* reported with satisfaction that "he does not now . . . launch his sarcasms at poor old Polonius with so needless an expenditure of bitterness" (31 December 1878). Henry Arthur Jones thought that the "sardonic tone of lofty banter" which Irving eventually brought to these scenes was "a very distinctive note of his rendering" (Jones, *The Shadow of Henry Irving*, p. 63).

35. *HAM*, 93. This is the only piece of significant business assigned to Hamlet in this promptbook. The other existing books are equally uninformative on that score. They are *HAM*, 90, in the Harvard Theatre Collection, and *HAM*, 92 and 94, at the Folger. Irving's studybook (*HAM*, 91), in the Harvard Theatre Collection, is marked by him with numerous interpretive notes.

36. Russell, *Irving as Hamlet*, p. 35.

37. Knight, *Theatrical Notes*, p. 3.

38. Ibid., p. 246 (a reprint of his *Athenaeum* review of 4 January 1879).

39. See, for example, *Reynold's*, 8 November 1874, and *Figaro*, 4 January 1879.

40. "An Actor's Notes on Shakespeare, No. 2: Hamlet and Ophelia, Act II, sc. 1," *The Nineteenth Century* 1 (1877): 526–28. As for the eavesdroppers, Irving says (p. 524) that the early entrance given to Hamlet in Q1 and Q2 (*before* Polonius says "let's withdraw, my Lord") means that he sees them go behind the arras at that point, but, owing to the "gravity of his mood," he remains only half-conscious of the significance of their action until he is reminded of it by catching sight of them later. Irving did not, however, use the early entrance, and detected their presence only at "Where's your father?" (*HAM*, 93).

41. Alfred Darbyshire, *The Art of the Victorian Stage* (1907; reprint, New York: B. Blom, 1969), p. 98.

42. As usual, no language unfit for the ears of a maiden escaped Hamlet's lips here, nor did he later make indelicate references to Gertrude's lovemaking, in the closet scene. Irving did, however, restore "incestuous sheets" (*HAM*, 93).

43. According to the London *Post* (31 December 1878), the business was new in 1878.

44. The critic for *Entr'Acte* wrote: "For an actor to arouse excitement equal to that which is displayed nightly at the Lyceum in a scene which is familiar to everybody, and where no surprises are anticipated is, we contend, a tribute to his exceptional power" (14 November 1874).

45. Russell, *Irving as Hamlet*, p. 46. The speech was cut for the 1878 performance.

46. Ellen Terry's rehearsal book (*HAM*, 95), now at the Ellen Terry Memorial Museum, Smallhythe, near Tenterden, Kent, England. The notes on Irving's business in the play scene are in an unknown hand.

47. Ibid.

48. *Echo*, 2 November 1874. The speech does not appear in the promptbook (*HAM*, 93), the text for which is Irving's 1878 edition of the play, but comments in the reviews make it clear that he used it both in 1874 and 1878. It is also excluded from Irving's revised edition of 1879.

49. Irving may have gotten the idea for "air-drawn" portraits from Charles Dillon (1819–1881), who did the scene that way in Montreal in 1866; the event was reported by a correspondent to *Era*, the theatrical trade-paper, on 14 October 1866. Irving acted with him in Edinburgh in 1859, but Dillon was probably not using the business at that time; there is no mention of it in the reviews of his London debut as Hamlet two years earlier, in March 1857. Irving defended his own usage in "An Actor's Notes on Shakespeare, No. 3: 'Look Here, Upon This Picture, and on This,' " *The Nineteenth Century*, 3 (1879): 260–63.

10

JOHNSTON FORBES-ROBERTSON

In an act of graceful abdication rare in stage annals, Henry Irving himself thrust his successor to the fore and rejoiced in his triumph. It was Irving who urged Johnston Forbes-Robertson (1853–1937) to undertake the role and offered him the Lyceum stage and Hamlet scenery for the purpose. Robertson opened on 11 September 1897.[1] The next morning, having read the highly favorable reviews, Irving sent for his protégé and declared, "Well, you've done it! Yes, you've done it, and now you must go and play Hamlet all over the world."[2]

Irving was not alone in seeing that Robertson had the potential for a great Hamlet portrayal. One observer wrote, "The refined and dreamy melancholy of his habitual expression, the graceful suppleness of his form, the delicate romanticism of his whole character and being, had long established him in the public mind as a favourite candidate for the reversion of Hamlet's inky cloak and customary suits of solemn black" (*Clarion*, 18 September 1897). Another saw somewhat different qualities but was no less admiring: "The pale intellectual face, the almost ascetic appearance, the nervous apprehensive look, constitute an ideal realization of the popular impression of the moody Dane" (*St. James's Gazette*, 13 September 1897). Not since Kemble had an actor so perfectly looked the part.

In addition, he possessed a voice which seemed ideally suited to the role. Its "unparalleled music" sent critics in search of worthy analogues; one likened it to a " 'cello, giving under the hands of a master the melody of some great musician" (*Westminster Gazette*, 13 September 1897). George Bernard Shaw, only recently diverted in his critical rounds from concert hall to playhouse, wrote that "to the musician it suggests a clarionet in A, played in the chalumeau register; but then the chalumeau sympathetically sounded, has a richly melancholy and noble effect."[3] To this natural endowment Robertson joined superb technical accomplishment. Tutored early and expertly by Samuel Phelps (1804–1878), and possessed of wide experience in Shakespearean roles, he was virtually without peer as a speaker of blank verse.

In all this Robertson presented a striking contrast to Irving, but in other, more crucial respects the two were cast in the same mold. It was his ability to fuse the most highly valued elements of Irving's impersonation with precious metals of his own which gave Robertson's Hamlet its compelling appeal. Most conspicuously, he followed Irving in further advancing the artistic revolution that had been gathering head for some thirty-five years; Clement Scott summed it up:

> The effort since Fechter first stood on the English stage as Hamlet [1861] . . . has been to free the play of "Hamlet" from its conventionality, tediousness, and staginess. . . . The three recognized intellectual forces who have advocated the natural as opposed to the conventional Hamlet—the Hamlet of the scholar and student as against the Hamlet of the stage and the actor—have been Fechter, Henry Irving and Forbes Robertson. (London *Daily Telegraph*, 13 September 1897).

Robertson was uniquely qualified to win a great victory in this cause, having been trained as a young man not only in the old-school methods of Samuel Phelps but also in the newly-popular cup-and-saucer school of naturalistic restraint. He was thus able to strike a balance between the psychologically true sense of the character and the musical sound of the verse. Even while paying close attention to meter, he managed to convey the impression of animated human discourse. As Shaw said, "We get light, freedom, naturalness, credibility, and Shakespeare" (*Saturday Review*, 22 October 1897).

As might be expected, a number of critics found the new style simply rather tame and expressed a certain nostalgia for the excitement of the old school. He was said to be "uninspired" and to lack "emotional power" and "vivid coloring." According to a typical account of this sort:

> You cannot make omelettes without breaking eggs, and you cannot rouse the keenest kind of excitement if you are determined never to be excited yourself. Thus Mr. Forbes Robertson fails to make one's flesh creep over the interview with the Ghost, to sound the deepest note of pathos in the farewell to Ophelia,

or to touch the highest passion in the reproach of the guilty Queen. He is always interesting and often impressive; but he never carries us with him as in a whirlwind, or electrifies us with a flash of lightning. (*Illustrated Sporting and Dramatic News*, 18 September 1897)

But having thus paid homage to the memory of Edmund Kean, even this critic concludes on a note that marks the inevitable ascendancy of the modern mode; "Apart from this, which may hardly seem a drawback to those who dread any hint of melodrama in tragedy, the embodiment could . . . hardly be bettered; and as it is it is perfect in taste and feeling, in consistency and in musical expression."

Robertson also greatly resembled Irving in modeling his Hamlet on the philosophic, scholarly Prince described by William Hazlitt. His press notices often sound virtually interchangeable with many of Irving's in their praise for his intellectuality and their citation of the great Romantic critic as authority for that interpretation.[4]

But there the similarity ends. Robertson was widely perceived to have embodied another quality described by Hazlitt but scarcely touched on in Irving's portrayal. Hazlitt had called the Prince "the most amiable of misanthropes," and whether by natural inclination or conscious artistic choice, Robertson made amiability the most original and arresting feature of his characterization. So much stress did the actor lay on that part of Hamlet's personality that some wondered whether he had gone too far. The *Illustrated London News* reported, "He is not content with being 'the most amiable of misanthropes'—he is positively genial" (18 September 1897), and the London *Theatre* declared that he had "made of the character a misanthrope amiable almost to the verge of affability" (1 October 1897). The critic for the London *Clarion* was sure that it was all a terrible mistake: "Can this dark-curled, fire-eyed, supple, mobile, elegantly affable, self-possessed, mocking Florentine courtier be the same phlegmatic, dubious, morbid, wildly whirling Northman that Shakespeare drew?" (18 September 1897). Scott admitted that he was too carefree in some scenes but thought his "constant waves of brightness and sunshine" made the performance so enjoyable that the audience could easily have "sat it out from end to end all over again" (London *Daily Telegraph*, 13 September 1897).

Shaw had no reservations at all. Never one to deal lightly with actors, especially Shakespearean actors, he clearly saw in Robertson's realization of the mind and soul of Hamlet the nearest approach to perfection possible. Many actors, he said, had succeeded in the role by emphasizing the commonplace emotions of love, grief and vindictive hatred. But only Robertson was able to show "the characteristic side of Hamlet, the side that differentiates him from Fortinbras." He urged his readers to

go and watch Mr. Forbes Robertson's Hamlet seizing every opportunity for a bit of philosophic discussion or artistic recreation to escape from the "cursed spite" of revenge and love and other common troubles. . . . See that, and you have seen a true classical Hamlet. Nothing half so charming has been seen by this generation. It will bear seeing again and again. (*Saturday Review*, 2 October 1897)

A key factor in the creation of this essentially amiable Hamlet was Robertson's omission of any suggestion of mental imbalance. "He is sane always," said the London *Times*, "—perhaps the sanest of all the Hamlets who have ever trod the boards" (13 September 1897). By eliminating theatrical displays of maniacal behavior, he put the character on a common footing with the audience and thus won from them an unqualified and unhesitant sympathy. He was "overwrought, no doubt, but eminently human and lovable" (*Academy*, 18 September 1897). Even Hamlet's assumed madness Robertson wore with a difference. In the lobby scene his simulation was so slight, so close to "mere irony," that it was difficult to see how Polonius could be taken in by it (*Referee*, 12 September 1897).

The fresh, relatively untheatrical approach to the role that all these generalizations describe was in large part signalized for spectators in the visual image Robertson presented on his entry to the Danish court. He wore his own hair—a touch of modernity which the conservative *Illustrated Sporting and Dramatic News* found out of keeping "with the tone of his surroundings" (18 September 1897). His costume was a "suit of rusty black," so "unadorned and unrelieved' that Scott thought he looked "a little dowdy" (London *Daily Telegraph*, 13 September 1897). As for age, he made Hamlet appear on the young side of twenty-five and cast Gertrude and Claudius as a couple in their early forties.[5]

His delivery of Hamlet's first line also did much to point the direction to be followed throughout. "A little more than kin and less than kind" was spoken "not apparently in any spirit of bitterness but rather of sorrow. . . . A Hamlet more gentle or less truculent it would, indeed, be difficult to conceive" (*St. James's Gazette*, 13 September 1897). Something of Hamlet's sweetness of disposition may have been suggested by action on his part even before his first utterance. According to the promptbook, on Claudius' parting words to Laertes, "Time be thine, / And thy graces spend it at thy will" (I.ii.62–63), "Laertes rises, Hamlet crosses to him and he kisses Hamlet's hand and x's back to R by Polonius."[6] Though the business is certainly curious and capable of more than one interpretation, it was probably designed as a gesture of respect from Laertes to the heir apparent; but Hamlet's moving to him seems to denote a degree of princely condescension very much in keeping with Robertson's conception of the character.

The first soliloquy (I.ii.129–59) revealed his talent for combining old and new, art and nature. "Every sentence, every word," wrote the *Referee* critic, "receives its proper intonation; but it is acting, as well as elocution, that makes us feel that Hamlet, in delivering his soliloquies is not merely reciting, but is thinking aloud. There is no excess of gesture, no noisy outburst, and even in his most passionate moments the actor is restrained" (12 September 1897). He spoke the first two lines of the soliloquy with "a shuddering terror in his voice, a half-acknowledged fear of the future" (London *Morning Leader*, 13 September 1897). In a wholly uncharacteristic lapse of intelligence, Robertson gave the line "But two months dead—nay, not so much, not two" (I.ii.138) as if Hamlet "were going through a mental calculation, and were suddenly struck by the fact that he had made a mistake in his reckoning. That was a grave blunder," said the London *Standard*, "but it stood well nigh alone" (13 September 1897). The provision of background music for the speech—a common Victorian practice—provoked a scornful comment from reform-minded Shaw: "The sooner Mr. Hamilton Clark's romantic Irving music is stopped, the better. Its effect in this Shakespearean version of the play is absurd" (*Saturday Review*, 2 October 1897).

Further indication that amiability was to be the leitmotif of his characterization emerged from Robertson's manner of greeting Horatio. He said "We'll teach you to drink deep ere you depart" (I.ii.175) "not in sarcastic allusion to the King's debaucheries" but as if he really looked forward to convivial evenings with his newly arrived friend (*Illustrated London News*, 18 September 1897). In his reaction to the sentinels' report of the Ghost's sighting there was nothing of Irving's tone of incipient "ecstasy"; he "put his questions in a grave and earnest fashion, but with no token of involuntary impulses" (*Graphic*, 18 September 1897).

Robertson was similarly controlled in the Ghost's presence, addressing it "with loving gentleness and in a tone of mingled awe and reverence." He made a "heartrending, almost sobbing entreaty" of the words "I'll call thee Hamlet, / King, father, royal Dane: O answer me!" (I.iv.44–45), reverting to the older punctuation of the line but putting special stress on "father." Like Irving, he got free of his friends' attempted restraint without drawing his sword against them, but he followed the beckoning spirit "with arms extended, his whole body bent in entreaty, and trembling with emotion," rather than in the attitude of mesmerized terror which Irving had adopted. Upon the Ghost's departure he fell "prostrate to the ground as one half dead with nervous dread at the horror of the situation" (*Stage*, 16 September 1897). He remained there, "exhausted and supine . . . looking up at the stars, in order fitly to cry 'O all you host of heaven' " (*Manchester Guardian*, 23 May 1898).

He quickly recovered himself, however, and played the rest of the scene with great self-possession. Thus, he kept the newly popular business with the tables, but wrote on them "as naturally as a business man making a memorandum" (London *Times*, 13 September 1897). James Agate recalled many years later that Robertson was "marvellously effective after the Ghost had gone, because he had done nothing before," having had the stage darkened during the interview "so as to be himself almost invisible."[7] Agate was especially impressed with his rendering of "For every man hath business and desire" (I.iv.130). In saying it, "his Hamlet realized that whereas business and desire may be sorry things, it is his unhappiness that he must abstain from both."[8] Robertson restored some of the wild and whirling words, but underplayed them, according to Archer:

Such a phrase . . . as "Aha, boy, art thou there!" [*sic*] . . . he speaks with respectful melancholy, instead of the feverish freakishness which is surely the keynote of this scene. I cannot but hope that Mr. Robertson will reconsider these scenes, which are certainly well within his compass. Artistic self-restraint is a very good thing, but in this case it verges on timidity.[9]

If any doubts remained after these scenes that this was to be a remarkably easy-tempered Hamlet, they were swept away by the gentle forbearance with which Robertson treated Polonius and Rosencrantz and Guildenstern. Scott described it with great relish:

Where other Hamlets scowl or snarl, Forbes Robertson only smiles; not a cynical, cruel or sarcastic smile, but a smile that lights up his mobile face and seems to say to Rosencrantz and Guildenstern, "My dear fellows, you are both humbugs and fawning toadies, but I am too well-bred, too much of the Prince to snap at you"; or to Polonius, "I should uncommonly like you to know that you are boring me to tears; but still, you are an officer of the Court, a far older man than I am, so I must show my contempt for you with a smile instead of a sneer." There are frequent evidences of this buoyancy of nature united to a supreme courtesy of manner. (London *Daily Telegraph*, 13 September 1897)

There was a suggestion of lightheartedness even in the "paragon of animals" speech (II.ii.295–310). The beginning lines, revealing Hamlet's loss of all his mirth, were given with "full pathos," but Robertson went on to show that Hamlet could "throw off melancholy, forget his mission, and even find some enjoyment in the philosophic contemplation of life" (*Illustrated London News*, 18 September 1897). The same capacity for resilience showed itself in Hamlet's interview with the players. He seemed to have forgotten the Ghost's mandate and to be looking forward to their performance "with something akin to cheerfulness" (London *Globe*, 13 September 1897). But Robertson was not all buoyancy even here. When the First Player ended his recitation, Hamlet unobtrusively brushed a tear from his cheek (*Stage*, 16 September 1897).

Even those who had reservations about Robertson's general approach to the character found themselves deeply affected by his rendering of the soliloquy which follows the exit of the players (II.ii.550–605). William Archer wrote that he had "never heard any similar passage of Shakespeare better delivered" (London *World*, 15 September 1897). Part of the powerful impact of the speech was due to the new business which accompanied it. After saying "Now I am alone," Robertson began to study the text of "The Murder of Gonzago," placed in his hands by the departing First Player. As he read, his thoughts were carried back to the exhibition of mimic passion he had just witnessed. Then he spoke; according to the London *Daily News* (13 September 1897) account:

> Limpid and musical as water from a spring flow the words of the exquisite speech, . . . but beautiful with a new beauty of utter naturalness. And when this tide of passion is at the full and the wonderful voice rings out "The play, the play's the thing" [*sic*] it is again over the leaves in his hand that he bends, excitedly turning the pages as the curtain falls.

Shaw looked at Robertson's reading in somewhat more depth, seeing in it a clear and forceful revelation of Hamlet's characteristic sophistication:

> The great soliloquy—no, I do NOT mean "To be or not to be"; I mean the dramatic one, "O what a rogue and peasant slave am I!"—is as passionate in its scorn of brute passion as the most bull-necked affirmation or sentimental dilution of it could be. It comes out so without violence: Mr. Forbes Robertson takes the part quite easily and spontaneously. (*Saturday Review*, 20 October 1897)

Few would have agreed with Shaw that "To be or not to be" is, in itself, less "great" than the earlier soliloquy, but many found Robertson's *playing* of it inferior. His manner was said to be too "set and formal"—though he spoke it while resting in a chair—and "directed too much to the audience."[10] Archer declared it "not quite so happy" as the treatment of "O, what a rogue and peasant slave," but his dissatisfaction centered more on interpretation than on style:

> His face seems to light up at the phrase "To sleep—perchance to dream!"—whereas the thought should clearly overcloud the momentary serenity with which Hamlet has been contemplating the "consummation devoutly to be wished." On the whole, however, Mr. Robertson's handling of the meditative passages could scarcely have been improved. (London *World*, 15 September 1897)

In Robertson's playing of the nunnery scene it was evident that Hamlet's love for Ophelia was "a very secondary emotion of his life" (*Morning Leader*, 13 September 1897). Abandoning the tradition which had begun with Kean and reached its finest expression with Irving, Robertson behaved toward Ophelia "less as a lover than as one who has lost interest in woman" (*Advertiser*, 13 September 1897). For Shaw,

Robertson's omission of the marks of forcibly suppressed love showed more than mere "loss of interest"; for him it was further evidence of Hamlet's alienation from "common sentiments" and, as such, precisely right: "Even his instinctive sexual impulses offend his intellect; so that when he meets the woman who excites them he invites her to join him in a bitter and scornful criticism of their joint absurdity . . . , all of which is so completely beyond the poor girl that she naturally thinks him mad" (*Saturday Review*, 2 October 1897).

Robertson also eliminated the standard practice of having Hamlet catch a glimpse of the "lawful espials," Polonius and Claudius. Instead, his question "Where's your father?" (III.i.129) was put impulsively, and he read the answer in Ophelia's face. The London *Times* judged it "less effective, because less intelligible, than the customary 'business.' Hamlet is in a position to read the truth in Ophelia's eyes, but the public are not" (13 September 1897). The *Stage*, among others, approved the change, arguing, "It cannot be imagined that the Prince, refined and sensitive, should be guilty of thus airing his thoughts so as to reach one in hiding; to think so is to make Hamlet somewhat of a sneak and a coward" (16 September 1897). Robertson was praised for making his exit without recourse to Kean's farewell kiss; as the *Advertiser* explained, "For the moment his feelings have been too outraged to indulge in any such sentimentality, and the yearning look which Mr. Robertson cast behind him expressed in all its fulness the poet's meaning" (13 September 1897).

Along with the Kean kiss, Robertson also jettisoned the Kean crawl in the play scene; with implied disdain for the many who had followed the practice, the London *Times* reported that "he does not wriggle across the floor on his stomach in his eagerness to watch the King, but retains a rational degree of composure" (13 September 1897). There was rational composure also in his response to the play's tell-tale effect on Claudius. Without mentioning the older actor by name, critics noted, usually with approval, how strikingly Robertson differed from Irving in this respect. "Mr. Robertson ends the scene," said the London *Daily News*, "not in a whirl of ferocious glee, but in the almost playful vein of satirical exultation which is more consistent with the text" (13 September 1897).

A similar coloring of playfulness, tinged with a most subtle sarcasm, suffused the scenes with the King's two "sponges" and with Polonius. This was not a Hamlet to break recorders or humiliate a faithful minister. As Scott said, "In the memorable sentences about the camel and the weasel and 'very like a whale,' the new Hamlet does not show the slightest sign of irritability or contempt. His nature is too sweet to offend any one, however much a toady or a bore, and he is too well-mannered to condescend to snappishness with his inferiors" (London *Daily Telegraph*, 13 September 1897).

Hamlet's long expunged "Now might I do it pat" speech (III.iii.73–96) had been restored by some recent Hamlets, but Robertson chose to follow the older custom of omitting it. So much had taste changed that he was criticized for doing so, though it was widely acknowledged that for Robertson excision was a virtual necessity, since "the speech exhibits a brutal aspect of Hamlet's meditated revenge not in keeping with his own gracious portrait of the man." [11]

Few Hamlets can ever have responded to Gertrude's summons with quite the nonchalance that Robertson brought to it. The *Referee* declared that the "easy indifference with which he said 'Now, mother, what's the matter?' . . . almost bordered on the grotesque." [12] Throughout the scene he showed much the same self-possession he had used with Ophelia, a fact which troubled Scott: "It will not do to stretch the point of courtesy so far as to suggest that Hamlet was not really in love with Ophelia, or angry with his mother. . . . These thoughts certainly do occur to the mind in following the new Hamlet, with all its variety, beauty, and charm" (London *Daily Telegraph*, 13 September 1897). Toward the end he rested his mother's head on his breast and kissed her tenderly. "Rarely, if ever," said the *Stage*, have the lines—"O, throw away the worser part of it, and live the purer with the other half" been more expressively given, with the tears in the voice as if rending the heart of the speaker. This scene will long remain in the memory, for it is full of tenderness and pity" (16 September 1897).

For the speech comparing Hamlet's father with his "uncle-father," Robertson employed neither Irving's imaginary portraits nor the traditional miniatures which they had briefly supplanted, but went back instead to full-length portraits. One or two commentators argued that mental pictures would have been more suitable for such a scholarly Prince, but the change otherwise attracted no notice.

The chat with the Clown, carried on with Hamlet leaning over the churchyard wall, revealed more of his characteristic cheerfulness and delight in philosophic speculation. His protestation of love for Ophelia was "a wail that goes straight to the heart" and seemed to make amends

Johnston Forbes-Robertson. The Play Scene (III.ii). Lyceum Theatre, London, 1897. Harvard Theatre Collection.

for his previous coldness toward her (*Stage*, 16 September 1897). Robertson was faulted for delivering the difficult speech immediately following (" 'Swounds, show me what thou't do" [V.i.274–84] as "merely a sarcastic counterblast to the vauntings of Laertes, and not the fierce outpourings of a distracted mind" (*St. James's Gazette*, 13 September 1897). But Shaw thought it wholly natural that "the shock of Ophelia's death relieves itself in the fiercest intellectual contempt for Laertes" (*Saturday Review*, 2 October 1897).

The scene with Osric gave Robertson another opportunity to show Hamlet's irrepressible delight in repartee. "No gloomy encounter this," said the *Stage*, "for Mr. Robertson keeps his Hamlet well in hand, and shows him, as ever, one well able to hold his own with his fellows despite his great object in view" (16 September 1897). Hamlet's "the readiness is all" speech (V.ii.219–24)—only recently restored to the stage in its entirety—Robertson delivered "earnestly and confidentially and with that winning smile and the pure mind 'half-way to heaven already' as much as to say, 'Oh, dear friend, we all ought to think of those things.' " Scott heard in it the actor's "exquisite appreciation of Hamlet's philosophic pondering on the inevitable" (London *Daily Telegraph*, 13 September 1897).

The soul of graciousness to the very end, Robertson responded to Laertes' confession of treachery with an embrace "gallantly and comradely" bestowed; Scott complained that this and his many other courtesies made it appear that "on the whole, he loved Laertes better than Horatio" (London *Daily Telegraph*, 13 September 1897).

Hamlet's death was staged in a way never before seen. Instead of falling into Horatio's arms, Robertson staggered to the throne and sat down. In a display of technique reminiscent of Thomas Betterton's blanching before the Ghost, Robertson's face took on a "fatal pallor" as death approached; he delivered the final words in a "quiet, exhausted voice," then let his hands fall to the side, as his countenance became "composed and fixed" (*Stage*, 16 September 1897). Horatio then took the crown from a table and placed it between his knees. The London *Daily Chronicle* disapproved, arguing that the crown, "considering the duties its possession imposed, was probably the very last thing [Hamlet] would have really desired" (13 September 1897). But the new arrangement was generally pronounced strikingly effective: "It would be difficult to indicate with greater point," said the *St. James's*

Gazette, "the regality of the man or to emphasize more forcibly the remorseless irony of fate" (13 September 1897).

There was something else new in the way Robertson's Hamlet spent his last moments on earth. The play did not end with "The rest is silence." Instead, Fortinbras was at last given an entrance, after nearly two centuries of waiting in the wings. After a brief exchange with Horatio, he gave orders for the military funeral Shakespeare designed, and the play ended with the rites in progress: placed on a shield in a half-sitting, half-reclining position, Hamlet was borne out shoulder-high "through a large central arch, through which, as also through two smaller adjacent arches, [might] be seen a throng of warriors bearing lighted torches."[13] The majority of critics dubbed the resurrected Shakespearean ending an "anti-climax"—the very objection which had led to its excision in the first place. It was at best, they held, "picturesque," the occasion for "an exceedingly impressive tableau."[14] Archer, while admitting its pictorial effectiveness, declared flatly that it was "of no literary value" (London *World*, 15 September 1897). But Fortinbras had his champions, chief among them being Shaw, who had, in fact, persuaded Robertson to make the restoration.[15] In reviewing the production he remained silent about his part in it, but could not resist pillorying the long line of actor-managers who thought they knew better than "the poor foolish old Swan"; Robertson, he wrote, "bowled them all out by being clever enough to be simple" (*Saturday Review*, 2 October 1897).

In the spring of 1904, having in the meantime toured Europe extensively, Robertson brought his Hamlet to the United States, where it was received with great enthusiasm. Since Booth's retirement in 1891, American audiences had seen few Hamlets of any sort and none of the first rank. That remained the case for some twenty years longer. When at last John Barrymore restored the nation's honor with his acclaimed portrayal, it was of Robertson's Hamlet that the older members of the audience were chiefly reminded.

NOTES

1. Press accounts of the performance give the actor's name without hyphenation, or omit "Forbes" altogether; I employ the latter style through the

remainder of this chapter. Robertson was knighted in the year of his retirement, 1913.

2. Sir Johnston Forbes-Robertson, *A Player Under Three Reigns* (Boston: Little, Brown, 1925), p. 184. See also Laurence Irving, *Henry Irving: The Actor and His World* (New York: Macmillan, 1952), p. 610. In an interview given to the New York *Times* (13 March 1904), Robertson said that while Irving was the first to suggest that he play Hamlet, it was Ellen Terry who finally persuaded him: "She argued that a pianist never hesitated to play a Beethoven sonata, that it was considered a pious and not an arrogant ambition."

3. George Bernard Shaw, review of *King Arthur* in *Saturday Review*, 18 January 1895.

4. Among those naming Hazlitt were *St. James's Gazette* (London) 13 September 1897; *Illustrated London News*, 18 September 1897; London *Daily Telegraph*, 13 September 1897.

5. London *Times*, 13 September 1897. Inconsistently, however, he left the Ghost "a venerable gray-bearded figure" (ibid.). Robertson was forty-four years old.

6. *HAM*, 126. Now in the Huntington Library, Pasadena, California, this is a lightly marked copy of Robertson's acting text, published in 1897. No other promptbook exists. Except as will be noted, Robertson made the traditional cuts.

7. In a review of a Hamlet performance by John Gielgud, London *Sunday Times*, 2 July 1939.

8. Gielgud review, London *Sunday Times*, 18 November 1934.

9. London *World*, 15 September 1897. In addition to the line quoted, Robertson spoke the next response to the Ghost, beginning *"Hic et ubique"* (I.v.156), but omitted the third and most irreverent, beginning "Well said, old mole" (I.v.162).

10. *Stage*, 16 September 1897; *Daily Chronicle*, 13 September 1897; *Pall Mall Gazette*, 13 September 1897.

11. *Illustrated London News*, 18 September 1897. The *Theatre* (1 October 1897) made the same point. The *Sketch* critic was among those who thought the omission made for "a serious loss of light as to Hamlet's character," but he showed some sympathy with the older critical view in describing the speech as "the well-known repulsive soliloquy showing [Hamlet's] alleged reasons for not killing Claudius when at his prayers" (15 September 1897). It is curious that the speech appears in Robertson's published acting version. He may have added it to his performance after opening night and prior to publication.

12. *Referee*, 12 September 1897. A photograph from his silent film version of the play shows Robertson entering the closet holding his sword casually across his shoulders with both hands; see *Hamlet, the Story of the Play Concisely Told. With fifty-five illustrations taken from the cinematograph film*

showing Sir Johnston Forbes-Robertson and Miss Gertrude Elliott, etc., vol. 1 of *The Cinema Books* (London: Stanley Paul, 1913). I have found no evidence that he ever used the business on stage.

13. *HAM*, 126.

14. *Sketch*, 15 September 1897; *Modern Society*, 18 September 1897; *Referee*, 12 September 1897.

15. See William A. Armstrong, "Bernard Shaw and Forbes-Robertson's Hamlet," *Shakespeare Quarterly* 15 (1964): 28–29.

11

JOHN BARRYMORE

During the first two decades of the twentieth century, E. H. Sothern (1859–1933) and Walter Hampden (1879–1955) used their modest talents to keep alive, in an age increasingly less sympathetic to it, the style of refined ideality which had reached its zenith with Edwin Booth's Hamlet. In a society that felt itself changed utterly by the Great War, such homage to the past no longer satisfied. What was wanted was a Hamlet who could mark a new beginning, a Hamlet for the new age. When John Barrymore (1882–1942) appeared in the role in the early 1920s, he seemed the very thing. He opened in New York at the Sam H. Harris Theatre on 16 November 1922, in a production directed by Arthur Hopkins. Two years later, on 19 January 1925, he moved to the stage of London's Haymarket Theatre, and there too he was viewed as having caught the temper of the times.[1] "It is the realest Hamlet we have known," said Alexander Woollcott (New York *Herald*, 17 November 1922). The reviews from both theatrical capitals are full of similar remarks, but no one described the emphatic originality and historic significance of Barrymore's performance with quite the eloquence of Ludwig Lewisohn, writing in *The Nation*: "His bearing and gestures have the restrained but intense expressiveness of the bearing of modern men who live with their nerves and woes in narrow rooms. Yet they seem utterly right—right in an un-sought for and unhoped-for measure" (13 December 1922). "This generation," said Kenneth MacGowan, "has found its Hamlet" (New York *Globe*, 17 November 1922).

But the performance was not a total break with the past. In a letter to the New York *Times*, playwright Rachel Crothers stressed that, for all its originality, Barrymore's characterization rested firmly on the foundations laid down by Johnston Forbes-Robertson eighteen years earlier. Both actors played the part "from an absolutely human standpoint," and while Barrymore's manner was "necessarily still more simple and natural" than Robertson's had been, "because of that it loses nothing in classic dignity and nobility—and I'll wager Sir Johnston would say so himself" (24 December 1922). "Still more simple and natural" and therefore, so the argument ran, a Hamlet for the times. As befitted an age which prided itself on being undemonstrative, Barrymore's delivery was subdued, relatively expressionless, more conversation than recitation. Lewisohn likened it to "the key of modern poetry, of the finest modern fiction." William Poel thought Barrymore superior to both Henry Irving and Robertson for the way he "talked his part all the way through and got the other actors to do the same." [2]

As in the case of all the other new and "natural" Hamlets since David Garrick, conservative opinion held that something essential and precious, namely, poetry, had been wrongly cast down. This was more the case in London than in New York, but even in London the new wave of natural speaking was no more to be resisted than the earlier ones. Christopher St. John countered criticism of Barrymore's lack of poetic fervor with the modernist shibboleth that truth counted for more than beauty: "I am not inclined to rebuke Mr. Barrymore . . . for sins against the iambic pentameter. . . . What does it profit us to hear Shakespeare beautifully spoken if the speakers do not bring his characters to life?" (*Time and Tide*, 27 February 1925).

Barrymore brought Hamlet to life and made him easily and pleasantly accessible to contemporary audiences not merely by bringing on to the stage the vocal and physical manner of a twentieth-century gentleman, but also by eliminating from the character everything that was likely to mystify, antagonize or otherwise alienate. This was not so much a conscious strategem, calculated to win the widest possible popular favor, as the result of genuine conviction about the nature of the character. In his rambling, anecdotal autobiography, published just one year after he closed the play in London, Barrymore recalled that his study of the play had led him to the conclusion that there was nothing either complicated or mysterious in Hamlet's makeup: "I was amazed to find how simple Hamlet seemed to be, and I was no little bewildered that any thing of such infinite beauty and simplicity should have acquired centuries of comment. It seems to me that all the explanation, all the comment that is necessary upon Hamlet Goethe wrote in *Wilhelm Meister*." [3] He then quoted the famous "costly vase" passage, which he had seen quoted in the Temple edition he was using as a study book. Barrymore evidently took from Goethe only the idea that Hamlet could be "simply" understood and played as a man temperamentally incapable of action. On the question of *why* he was incapable of action he went his own way, vigorously rejecting the idea that the cause was "delicacy." Barrymore had such an abhorrence of appearing in any way epicene that it was all he could do to bring himself to wear tights.[4] He told Arthur Hopkins that he wanted his Hamlet "to be so male that when I come out on the stage they can hear my balls clank."[5] Only Lewisohn, of the score or more of critics who described the performance, identified it closely with the Hamlet of *Wilhelm Meister*, and even he stressed elements other than delicacy:

Hamlet is what Goethe used to call a "problematic nature. . . . "Other actors can act Hamlet; [Barrymore] *is* Hamlet, the "problematic nature," the eternal concrete symbol in literature of the introvert, of him whose sensibilities are too delicate for the rough uses of the world, of him who, thinking too curiously and feeling too intensely, cannot act.

Almost to a man other observers focused on "thinking too curiously" as the shaping element, the defining factor in the characterization. Barrymore made Hamlet an inveterate analyzer, an earnest rationalist, a man sealed off from the world in a nearly impregnable fortress of thought. He could be made to feel only briefly and superficially. Each encounter, with ally and antagonist alike, for the most part provided only further grist for the mill of steady cerebration.

The result was a characterization that was at once disappointing in its narrowness and compelling in its shimmering intellectual clarity. "It is difficult for us to conceive of [a Hamlet] more intelligent," wrote Heywood Broun, "but from our point of view he does not quite sustain all the emotional values of the play" (New York *World*, 17 November 1922).[6] Herbert Farjeon was prepared to accept a thinking Hamlet, but he argued that Barrymore had diminished the character by making him "a persevering rather than an inspired thinker, a two-and-two-make-four soliloquiser, a man who attacked problems instead of a man whom problems were always attacking. The result of this was that the character came out, somehow, too small, lacked fire, elasticity, flow" (*Sphere*, 7 March 1925).

Just about every critic, English and American, who analyzed the performance in any depth, admitted that Barrymore's undeviatingly cerebral prince was a more monolithic figure than the one Shakespeare created, but for most of them it was no very serious matter. James Agate, critic for the London *Sunday Times*, noted that at many points Barrymore's "debating method does not carry us away," but these failures obviously did not weigh heavily against the actor in Agate's estimation. "To sum up," he wrote, "this was a great though not an overwhelming performance. The magnanimity of genius was not present, and at times mere conscientiousness threatened her pale wing. But all that intellect could do was done" (22 February 1925). In the United States, Stark Young spelled out Barrymore's shortcomings with a bluntness and thoroughness unmatched even by those least sympathetic to the performance. But he then went on to describe the positive strength of the portrayal in a way that set the scale tipping sharply in the opposite direction. The characterization needed "more abundance in all the reactions, more dilation of spirit," it lacked depth and breadth, took too much for granted, left too much out, but in the process acquired an elemental, pristine power; at its best, "it achieved what primitive art can achieve: a fundamental pattern so simple and so revealing that it appeared to be mystical; and so direct and strong that it restored to the dramatic scene its primary truth and magnificence" (*New Republic*, 6 December 1922).

This impression of archetypal simplicity, so forcefully conveyed by Barrymore's style and interpretation, was greatly enhanced, for those who were receptive to it, by the scenic investiture of the production. Designed by Robert Edmond Jones in the style of the "New Stagecraft," the setting consisted of a massive flight of stairs at center, flanked by walls angling off toward the wings and topped with a towering Romanesque arch, through which the sky was visible; except for a few short scenes played on the apron in front of a silk drop-curtain, this unit functioned as background and playing area throughout. Lewisohn wrote that it "lifts the play and the action into a region of the permanent and significant without any loss of human values."[7]

Barrymore's costume was also essentially timeless in its stark simplicity: black tights and slippers and a black, loose-fitting long-sleeved doublet which reached to mid-thigh; a narrow, lightly figured cincture, buckled off-center in line with the neck opening, and a thin necklace were the only concessions to opulence. He looked nearly as much a peasant as a prince—and more like Everyman than either.

Barrymore was forty when he opened in New York, and while no one called him "boyish," he struck most observers as quite satisfactorily youthful. In London two or three critics who remembered Edwin Booth, or pretended to, thought he bore his nineteenth-century predecessor a close resemblance.[8] His hair was shorter though, barely distinguishable from contemporary fashion.

Barrymore sat throughout the first soliloquy, a display of modern informality which no longer shocked even the most reactionary.[9] It was his delivery, not his posture, which seemed to break new ground. There was no suggestion of the set piece ritually declaimed in accordance with hallowed rubrics. Instead, said Woollcott, it was "something genuine and alive, . . . just a lonely, unhappy man's thought." (New York *Herald*, 17 November 1922). It had no "power to *sweep* the listener off his feet," Agate noted, but at least it was not "gabble"; the speech was "built up of successive images which come into the mind before the word is coined to represent them" (London *Sunday Times*, 22 February 1925). As for interpretation, the soliloquy firmly established the attitude of coolheaded rationalism which was to be the dominant feature of the performance. He was "a man dispassionate, chilled with the sadness and melancholy of continued introspection" (*Adelphi*, 25 April 1925). In his studybook, Barrymore wrote "surprised" opposite "Frailty, thy name is woman," which suggests an intellectual rather than an emotional reaction.

He greeted Horatio joyously, springing up to meet him and clasping his shoulders. He was "overcome by emotion" on "take him for all in all" (I.ii.187) and had to struggle to regain control on "Saw, who?" (190). But he received the news of wondrous doings during the early morning watch with equanimity: "He became alertness and efficiency personified. There was a ghost loose? Very well; he—or it—would be looked into that very night" (London *Daily Express*, 21 February 1925). "My father's spirit in arms!" (254) is marked "light" in the studybook.

There was further evidence of a cool head and a steady hand in the actual meeting with the Ghost. Barrymore explained his approach to the scene to his friend and biographer Gene Fowler:

[The Ghost is] the sort of stupid bastard whose wife was bound to cheat on him out of sheer ennui. But in the play, Hamlet is fond of the old boy. . . . So I, as Hamlet, also must be fond of him. The play, you know, rather depends on this bond of sympathy to promote the revenge. Ergo, when the ghost of the father appears, I am a bit startled, and for the moment confused, yet I actually am glad to be with him once again. So I don't rant or scream. I listen attentively to the old man, hear his gossip, then engineer the appropriate murder.[10]

The idiom is pure Broadway, but the idea (though Barrymore does not seem to know it) is as old as Edmund Kean.

Actually, Barrymore exaggerated in this account the degree of serenity he maintained in the scene, at least as far as the initial sighting of the Ghost was concerned. Far from being only ''a little startled and confused,'' he registered, according to a number of witnesses, something close to the profound shock other actors had brought to the moment. ''You will not soon forget,'' Percy Hammond told readers of the New York *Tribune*, ''his awesome stricken look when he first sees the ghost of his father'' (7 November 1922). In London, the *Daily News* was pleased to report, ''This Hamlet, too, did not, as many do, take the appearance of his father's spirit as a matter of course. He was almost speechless with terror, and he made one feel that whether Hamlet was really mad or not it would have been very extraordinary if so great a shock left no effect on so sensitive a nature'' (20 February 1925). The promptbook says only that he stooped suddenly, ''sensing a ghost,'' and began ''Angels and ministers of grace'' in ''a high head tone.''

But whatever the precise degree of his alarm, Barrymore was thoroughly upstaged by the Ghost, which was represented by a circle of light on the silver-blue night sky of the cyclorama; when it came time for ''it'' to speak, the voice came from somewhere offstage. Reactions ranged from good-natured ridicule to outrage, and the experiment was later modified. In London the ''nebulous luminosity'' was used only up to the point where Hamlet removes with it to another part of the platform; on his return he was seen to be following the familiar armor-clad figure of tradition.

In order to convey the impression of listening with calm attention, Barrymore knelt with his back to the audience as his father told his story, and for part of it lay prostrate in deep shadow. John Corbin said, ''Where other actors have intensified the awe and passion of that moment by expressing it in face and figure, he obliterates himself" (New York *Times*, 17 December 1922). In keeping with that approach, he allowed the Ghost to speak "O, horrible, O, horrible, most horrible!" (I.v.80). He fell prostrate on "O earth! what else?" (92) and drew himself up to a sitting position on "bear me stiffly up" (95).[11] He gave "damned villain" (106) on his feet, "shrieking in rage," and ended by writing on his "tables."

He made no distinction between Horatio and Marcellus as possible confidants. Instead, rather as Kean had done with Rosencrantz and Guildenstern in a later scene, he at first made as if to answer their questions, drew them into a mock conspiratorial huddle on "But you'll be secret?" (121), dashed their hopes by giving the "arrant knave" line (124) "as though it were all a great joke and moved off in handsome profile with an airy wave of his hand."[12] During this and the subsequent swearing business he seemed to be experiencing "a wave of madness" (London *Daily Telegraph*, 20 February 1925). Hamlet's replies to the importunate underground voice were all retained and spoken in a tone of barely controlled hysteria. He knelt on "Rest, rest, perturbed spirit" and, as it were, came to rest himself. "O cursed spite" was said "boyishly" (studybook).

With Polonius he took Booth's and Robertson's line of gracious lenity. Young noted:

Most actors for the applause they get play up for all it is worth Hamlet's seemingly rude wit at the old man's expense. But Mr. Barrymore gave you only Hamlet's sense of the world grown empty and life turned to rubbish in this old counselor. And, without seeming to do so, he made you feel that Polonius stood for the kind of thing in life that had taken Ophelia from him. (*New Republic*, 6 December 1922).

Agate thought he did less than lyrical justice to the skyey metaphors in Hamlet's explanation of his altered disposition:

Certain it is that Mr. Barrymore cannot cope with such words as "This majestical roof fretted with golden fire." His Hamlet has too much of the *indoor* look, as the essayist remarked of Raphael's figures, and will find his images in his own brain. Such a one would not rack the heavens for a comparison. Sun and stars are not his concern, and the words, being perfunctory, are robbed of their just splendour. (London *Sunday Times*, 22 February 1925)

Agate also disapproved of the handling of the "Now I am alone" soliloquy (II.ii.550–605). It was too "ratiocinative"; instead of being "blasted with ecstasy," he "blasted it with pure reason." It was not, however, entirely lacking in passion, judging from other accounts. "O Vengeance" he gave "shrieking hysterically" and "stamping" up the stage. The *Spectator* found this eruption of violence effective in its place, but not enough to compensate for his overly "subdued" manner elsewhere (28 February 1925). He sat, for the first time in the speech, on "About, my brain!" put his hands to his head and rocked back and forth for a moment in silent cogitation. Christopher St. John chided him for delivering "The play's the thing . . . " as if it were "a sudden inspiration [when] it is as plain as a pikestaff . . . [that] Hamlet has been laying the 'mouse-trap' with great deliberation in the preceding lines" but nevertheless rated this "the best of his soliloquizing" (*Time and Tide*, 27 February 1925). He exited writing on his "tables" and muttering to himself. The opening night audience in London broke into "a roar of cheer" as the curtain fell. Desmond McCarthy complained that the pitch of emotion reached here made the following play scene an anticlimax: "True, 'The play's the thing, wherein I'll catch the conscience of the King' is a splendid curtain, but damn curtains" (*New Statesman*, 7 March 1925).

The "To be or not to be" soliloquy (III.i.55–87) pleased almost everyone. Even John Rankin Towse, who found most of his portrayal lacking in "anything resembling emotions of tragic intensity," allowed that here his reading was "intelligent and refined, if not princely, and in [its] abstracted quietude . . . there was original and attractive naturalism" (New York *Post*, 17 November 1922). He went on to point out, though, that "the delivery of the text, though clear, was marred in countless instances by misplaced or disregarded emphases." Towse seems to have been the only American critic to make that charge, but it cropped up in a number of English reviews. The London *Sunday Express* writer claimed that *all* the soliloquies were "ruined by wrong emphasis. He had no medium between a rather dull, though not distinct, monotone and the sudden screaming out of a single word, usually an unimportant one. . . . The last word [of 'be all my sins remembered'] was shot out fortissimo, as if it were a clarion summons to the distinguished Director of Public Prosecutions" (22 February 1925). The London *Star* critic also heard false emphases in the soliloquies, but excused them on the grounds that since these speeches "were the

true expression of inmost thought and speculation . . . some disjoint-
edness of utterance was justified" (20 February 1925).[13]

The nunnery scene Barrymore played more in anguish than in anger. He seemed cut to the quick by Ophelia's "Rich gifts wax poor
when givers prove unkind" (III.i.100), and he sobbed in declaring that
he did love her once. On "crawling between earth and heaven"
(III.i.127), he paused after "earth" and, taking Ophelia's face in his
hands, finished the line in a tone of longing tenderness which conveyed that *she* was heaven. "[This sort of thing] is traditional,"
McCarthy remarked, "but it is a bad tradition. Hamlet is no lover"
(*New Statesman*, 7 March 1925). Ivor Brown also thought there was
far too much prettiness in the scene: "The other Hamlet, tortured and
torturing, at once allured and revolted by sensuality, capable of cruelty
and mouthing terrible words, is not an early casualty in Mr. Barrymore's production: he simply never was born" (*Saturday Review*, 28
February 1925). Shaw quipped that he had turned Hamlet and Ophelia
into Romeo and Juliet.[14]

He spotted Polonius in the wings, over Ophelia's shoulder, just after
"Go thy ways to a nunnery" (III.i.129), crossed and looked off, then
turned back and very calmly asked, "Where's your father?" There was
a flash of angry resentment following her deceitful answer, but according to Horace Howard Furness, Jr., "Even with this anger his love
almost conquers him and it is only by a great effort that he restrains
himself from clasping her in his arms" (*The Drama*, March 1923).
The rest of the scene was played as a lunatic charade for the benefit of
the eavesdroppers. He did not again reveal in pantomimic action his
awareness of their presence, but the tirades were delivered, Furness
says, "as though with a backward glance at the two spies, meaning
'Do you want madness? You shall have your money's worth then!' It
was a circumscribed and understated madness though, not so much a
matter of bodily and vocal extravagance as of "intense inward febril-
ity" (New York *Times*, 17 December 1922). The final "To a nunnery,
go" was so unemphatic as to be almost ineffectual, in the opinion of
the *Spectator*: "[It] sounds upon the poor lady's perplexity almost as
a discreet recommendation to the one legal way out of a scandal. She
could hardly have believed him in earnest" (28 February 1925).

Barrymore cut nearly half the speech to the players (III.ii.1–45) and
delivered the remainder in a "matter-of-fact and business-like" manner with a hand on the shoulder of one of his listeners. The London

Times critic missed the "gracious courtesy of Forbes-Robertson in the scene" (20 February 1925).

In his conversation with Ophelia at the start of the play scene, Barrymore was as chaste as his predecessors, but the day had at last come when some students of the play were ready for a restoration of the character's original scurrility; at least this was so in London, where an occasional full-text performance had lately been seen. "We miss," said Brown, " . . . the abrupt and earthy Hamlet, the Hamlet of smutty jest and relentless sexual metaphor" (*Saturday Review*, 28 February 1925). McCarthy, too, seems to have had "country matters" in mind (as well as other passages, spoken and unspoken) when he maintained, "Where Mr. Barrymore's interpretation failed throughout was in conveying Hamlet's bitter-gay, intellectual exhilaration, which is the desperate reaction of a thinking, sensitive nature against life's humiliations and the depravity of man" (*New Statesman*, 7 February 1925).

The mimic play was performed atop the staircase, with Hamlet stretched out on the second step where he could divide his attention between the actors and the King and Queen, seated below him on opposite sides of the stage. Hammond regretted that "superstition" made it necessary for Hamlet to "sprawl a little ludicrously," but he commended Barrymore for managing the traditional pose without appearing "artificial" (New York *Tribune*, 17 November 1922). As he lay in his place, making his barbed commentary on the action, his surface calm was punctured sporadically by little burbles of involuntary laughter. As the trap snapped shut on his unsuspecting quarry, he bounded up the stairs and "gyrated" in triumph on "For some must watch . . . " (III.ii.273). The London *Times* remarked that here and elsewhere Barrymore showed "a bodily agility that would do no discredit to Mr. Douglas Fairbanks" (20 February 1925). Agate pronounced the play scene "immensely fine, its climax being a miracle of virtuosity" (London *Sunday Times* 22 February 1925).

Barrymore kept all of Hamlet's verse-making with Horatio but omitted the entire episode of his rallying of Rosencrantz and Guildenstern (III.ii.296–372), including the recorder sequence. Shaw branded the excision "a breath-bereaving extremity . . . rather like playing *King John* without little Arthur."[15] He also cut, at the end of the scene, Hamlet's rumination on how he should conduct himself with his mother (III.ii.395–99); most probably he found the lines inconsistent with the way he intended to play the closet scene.

John Barrymore. The Play Scene (III.ii). Sam H. Harris Theatre, New York, 1922. Harvard Theatre Collection.

The next scene, played downstage in front of the drop-curtain, began with Claudius' soliloquy, "O, my offense is rank" (III.iii.36ff.). He knelt at the end of it on the apron, facing the audience, and was joined by Hamlet entering through the curtain. Young thought the austerity of the *mise-en-scène* perfectly complemented Barrymore's "primitive" rendering of the character and story:

One man is here, one is there. Here are the uplifted hands, there the sword drawn. Here, sick conscience, power, and tormented ambition; there, the torture of conflicting thoughts, the irony, the resolution. Two bodies and their relation to each other, the words, the essential drama, the eternal content of the scene. No tricks, no plausible business, no palace chapel. And no tradition. (*New Republic*, 6 December 1922)

Hamlet's description of Claudius plunging headlong into hellfire (III.iii.73–95) no longer shocked anyone to the point of wishing to see the speech expunged, but there were still those who insisted, with William Hazlitt, that Hamlet is not to be taken at his word when he plots his enemy's eternal damnation. Thus, the *Stage* critic faulted Barrymore for reading the lines "with a quiet deliberation, as well as a directness of application that misses the subtle intention underlying the speech. . . . In this aside Hamlet less means what he says than unpacks his mind of these words as a sort of salve to his conscience for his inaction in killing Claudius" (26 February 1925).[16] McCarthy, evidently pleased to find Barrymore at last showing something of Hamlet's darker side, thought the speech had probably never been done better and never would be (*New Statesman*, 7 February 1925).

There was an air of *sangfroid* also in Barrymore's manner of dispatching the intruder behind the arras. According to Hammond, he made it "a graceful, deliberate homicide" (New York *Tribune*, 17 November 1922). He inquired after the identity of his victim with a "tameness" which Towse condemned as "indicative of an astonishing imperception" (New York *Post*, 17 November 1922).

For the comparison of the two kings, he took one locket from his doublet and referred to another worn by Gertrude. He spoke quietly, calmly, without a hint of vituperation, his head against his mother's breast or resting in her lap, his hands now and again stealing over her in soft caresses. "It was really comic," Christopher St. John asserted, "to watch Hamlet and the Queen looking 'on this picture and on that' for all the world as if they were having a pleasant evening over the family album'' (*Time and Tide*, 27 February 1925).

A few observers, however, detected more in this intimacy than innocent filial affection. Heywood Broun credited Barrymore with putting to use here the newly popular doctrines of Viennese psychology:

Barrymore's most original contribution to the role probably lies in his amplification of the subconscious motives of the Prince. He plays the closet episode with the Queen exactly as if it were a love scene. Nor did this seem fantastic to us. Shakespeare was a better Freudian than almost any of the moderns because he did not know the lingo. He merely set down the facts. After seeing Barrymore's interpretation we are convinced that he added nothing, but merely grasped suggestions which were already there. (*World*, 17 November 1922)

McCarthy also detected mental abnormality in Barrymore's playing of the scene but judged it spurious: "Hamlet's neurotic condition—another note in the complicated chord of his character—he did strike. Indeed, in Hamlet's relation to his mother he struck it too hard, so that the scene between Hamlet and his mother took on a Freudian significance. This is a mistake and artistically uninteresting'' (*New Statesman*, 7 March 1925). Shaw also took him to task for appearing to give Hamlet an Oedipus complex, but the scene was not generally or even widely interpreted in Freudian terms.[17] Nor is it at all clear that Barrymore meant it to be. When Fowler questioned him on the general subject of subliminal motivation, Barrymore said he thought Hamlet subconsciously both loathed and was jealous of Claudius' sexual intimacy with his mother, but said nothing about wanting to hint at repressed incestuous longings in the closet scene.[18] When he discussed the scene with Lark Taylor, he revealed only that he disliked Hamlet's lacerating accusations of his mother and sought to take the sting out of them. This was the reason, he explained to Taylor, for his unusual treatment of the lines beginning "Nay, but to live in the rank sweat of an enseamed bed'' and continuing through "A king of shreds and patches'' (III.iv.91–101). Just prior to that sequence, Barrymore was enveloped by the shaft of light identified earlier with the Ghost; standing with his hands rigid and his body "trembling with the tenseness,'' he spoke the lines in a voice which mimicked the hoarse tones of the Ghost's earlier speeches—the idea being that Hamlet is here possessed by his father's spirit and is speaking his father's words, not his own.

"It took the curse off the scene," he told Taylor, and made Hamlet "so much more decent."[19] Not surprisingly, this very *outré* interpretation provoked a jumble of responses. Some understood it but disapproved; others misunderstood but approved; still others both misunderstood and disapproved.[20]

At the entrance of the Ghost proper, the light went off, Barrymore gave a loud gasp and fell to his knees and gave "Save me and hover over me" in full-voiced hysteria, then continued more quietly, looking "straight out front." During the Ghost's reply he moved on his knees to his mother's arms, "weaving together the bodies of those two, who, whatever their sins might be, must belong to each other at such terrible cost" (Young, *New Republic*, 6 December 1922). He continued to clutch his mother during the Ghost's exit and thereafter, bidding her goodnight without the traditional "blessing" pantomime. The speech over the body of Polonius (III.iv.211–17) was restored, but the curtain fell before Hamlet could be seen to "lug the guts into the neighbor room."

In a follow-up article, published a month after the New York opening, Corbin denied that there was anything Freudian in Barrymore's interpretation of the scene and defined its merits in orthodox terms; it was, he said, "the most tenderly impassioned and compelling passage of emotional acting in modern memory" (New York *Times*, 17 December 1922). Agate also, without recourse to Freud, declared, "The closet scene was perfection. Much of [it] was spoken on Gertrude's breast and the pathos was overpowering" (London *Sunday Times*, 22 February 1925).

Barrymore cut completely the scenes of Hamlet's apprehension, exile and meeting with the Norwegian Captain, and there were cuts as well in the graveyard scene. He did not speculate on the identity of the skulls tossed up by the Clown, and he omitted Alexander and the beer-barrel from his reflections on the base uses of mortal clay. McCarthy thought the part of that speech he did retain, "Imperious Caesar, dead and turned to clay, / Might stop a hole to keep the wind away" (V.i.213–14), should have been spoken "wildly" instead of "ruthfully," but he considered "the measured and quaint melancholy" of the Yorick speech "perfectly" done (*New Statesman*, 7 March 1925). The staging of the scene, down center at the foot of the stairs, claimed more of the attention of some critics than Barrymore's acting. Broun wryly remarked, "Ophelia is buried in the front parlor. . . . The necessity of making a graveyard of the palace is not apparent'' (New York *World*, 18 November 1922).

Barrymore stayed out of the grave and in general played down Hamlet's chastisement of Laertes. "He is . . . plainly unwilling," said the *Spectator*, "either to 'grapple' or to 'rant' '' (28 February 1925). Young explained what was behind the subdued approach:

And what a stroke of genius it was, when by Ophelia's grave Hamlet had rushed through those mad lines, piling one wild image on another, and comes to the "Nay, and thou'lt mouth, I'll rant as well as thou" to drop on that last, on the "I'll rant as well as thou," into an aspirate tone, hoarse, broken with grief and with the consciousness of his words' excess and the excess of irony in all things! (*New Republic*, 6 December 1922)

Agate found him "half impish and half 'fey' '' during the first part of the duel (London *Sunday Times*, 22 February 1925). On discovering that Laertes had drawn blood, he attacked furiously, disarmed him by stepping on the unbated foil during a low thrust, then exchanged weapons, renewed the attack and ran him through. He did not stab the King on "Then, venom, to thy work!" (V.ii.322), but on "Follow my mother" (327), the command to "Drink off this potion" (326) having been cut. He crept toward him slowly on "Here, thou incestuous, murderous, damned Dane" (325) and then, in a maneuver which recalled Douglas Fairbanks, leapt "across ten feet of air" and "spitted the King with gusto" (New York *Globe*, 17 November 1922; London *Sunday Times*, 22 February 1925).

He made his dying speech on his feet, supported by Horatio. Before "The rest is silence," Taylor noted, "Hamlet reaches up with entire body, looks out—taking long time, perhaps 10 seconds; Horatio holds him above waist." When death came, Horatio lowered him to the floor, head toward the audience, and knelt above him. "When he lies there at Horatio's feet, little and slim and dead," Woollcott wrote in eulogy, "you wince at the pang of a good fellow forfeited, a gay, charming, immensely likeable person thwarted by a most cursed spite" (New York *Herald*, 19 November 1922). But that was not the audience's last glimpse of Hamlet. Fortinbras entered to take command, and on his orders four captains bore the body on their shoulders up the stairs and stood for a moment silhouetted against the moonlit sky. "Thus ended,'' said Woollcott, "an evening that will be memorable in the history of the American Theatre.''[21]

As the recipient of similar accolades from nearly every member of the New York critical fraternity, Barrymore could easily have stretched his run at the Harris into many months, perhaps even years. But he was temperamentally unsuited to long runs, and after some sixty performances he began to yearn for release from the nightly ordeal. When a deputation of elderly theater folk approached him with a request that he withdraw after ninety-nine performances, so as to leave inviolate the record of the great Booth, he saw a way to abandon the role with a flourish. After lecturing the suppliants on the unwisdom of living in the past, he announced, to their dismay, that he would step down after exactly one hundred and one performances. He reached that mark on 9 February 1923 and, true to his word, resigned.[22] By prior agreement with Hopkins, who had had to refund a great deal of money because of his star's premature departure, he reopened in the play at the Manhattan Opera House on 26 November 1923. After a three-week stand, the company embarked on a nine-week tour of major American cities. The London engagement, which Barrymore seems to have undertaken in response to a challenge, was originally scheduled for six weeks but was lengthened to twelve to satisfy public demand. It closed on 18 April 1925, ending forever Barrymore's association with the role. Except for a radio performance in 1937, he never played Hamlet again.[23]

Perhaps it was just as well. The very taste for naturalism which had contributed so greatly to his success made it unlikely that he could have gone on being acclaimed in the role as he moved into middle age. As recently as 1913, Robertson had been lovingly received at the age of sixty, but that was an indulgence which twentieth-century audiences were ill-disposed to repeat. Hamlet was henceforward to be a young man's role, as events quickly proved.

NOTES

1. For the London run, Barrymore employed an English cast and staged the play himself, but he did not significantly alter his characterization.

2. Quoted in Robert Speaight, *William Poel and the Elizabethan Revival* (London: Heinemann, 1954), p. 27.

3. John Barrymore, *Confessions of an Actor* (Indianapolis: Bobbs-Merrill, 1926), n.p.

4. Gene Fowler, *Good Night, Sweet Prince* (New York: Viking Press, 1944), p. 208.

5. John Kobler, *Damned in Paradise: The Life of John Barrymore* (New York: Atheneum, 1977), p. 174.

6. For a nearly identical view by a London critic, see *The Spectator*, 28 February 1925.

7. Most of the American critics disliked the setting; see Daniel Krempel and James H. Clay, " 'New Stagecraft' Forty Years After: The Hopkins-Jones *Hamlet*," *Western Speech* 24 (1965): 201–210. The setting was used also in London; Agate pronounced it the most beautiful thing he had ever seen on any stage (London *Sunday Times*, 22 February 1925), and *The Saturday Review, Observer* and *Nation and Athenaeum* bestowed similar honors; *The Spectator, Time and Tide* and *Stage* all condemned it.

8. *Referee*, 22 February 1925; London *Daily Telegraph*, 20 February 1925. The former added that, like Booth, "he speaks the English and not the American language," and the latter thought his "minutely finished style" probably owed something to a study of Booth as well.

9. For Barrymore's business, I have used the promptbook (*HAM*, 154) of the 1922 New York production, now at the Folger Shakespeare Library in Washington, D.C. It was prepared by Lark Taylor, a member of the cast. Three other promptbooks, all by Taylor, also survive. One (*HAM*, 155), now at the Joint University Libraries, Nashville, Tennessee, is a record of the production in its second New York season. Another, at the Folger (*HAM*, 156), records changes made during the American road tour, 1923–1924. A third, also at the Joint University Libraries (*HAM*, 157), brings together all the material of Taylor's other books. I have also consulted Barrymore's studybook (*HAM*, 158), now at The Players in New York City; it shows cuts and stresses and occasional interpretive notes. No promptbook survives for the London production. With few exceptions, to be noted, Barrymore used a traditional acting text.

10. Fowler, *Good Night, Sweet Prince*, pp. 210–11.

11. So says Taylor. When Arthur Corby Sprague saw him (he docs not say when), Barrymore imitated Robertson's business of falling supine on "O all you host of heaven!" so as to be able to address that line to the stars; see Arthur Colby Sprague *The Stage Business in Shakespeare's Plays: A Postscript* (1954; reprint, Folcroft, Pa.: Folcroft Press, 1969), p. 16.

12. Bernard Grebanier, *The Heart of Hamlet* (New York: Crowell, 1960), p. 144.

13. The *Referee* and *New Statesman* critics also mentioned the subject, the former calling it a "continual" irritant, the latter only an "occasional" one.

14. In a letter to Barrymore dated 22 February 1925, quoted in full in Kob-

ler, *Damned in Paradise*, pp. 197–99. Shaw attended the London opening as Barrymore's guest and as the escort of Mrs. Barrymore.

15. Ibid., p. 198. Most of Shaw's lengthy and generally negative response to the performance had to do with Barrymore's cutting of the text. "I wish you would . . . concentrate on acting," he wrote in conclusion, "rather than on authorship, at which, believe me, Shakespeare can write your head off."

16. The London *Evening News* also argued that Hamlet's stated reason for putting up his sword should have been played as "a mere excuse to avoid action, the real reason being hidden much deeper in the soul" (20 February 1925).

17. The only other critical comment on the topic I have found was Woollcott's: "[It seemed] a new play. Not that . . . the new psychologists, except perhaps in the overtones of one scene, have been permitted to read into it a swarm of writhing meanings on which its writer never dreamed" (New York *Herald*, 17 November 1922). Fowler (*Good Night, Sweet Prince*, p. 213) says that Richard Watts, Jr., was "among the first to recognize the Freudian implications of Jack's Hamlet portrayal," but this seems most unlikely. In 1922, Watts was a cub reporter for the Brooklyn *Times*; he did not become a drama critic until 1936 (see *Who's Who in the Theatre*, 10th ed., rev. [New York: Pitman, 1947], p. 473).

18. Because Barrymore's answer was peppered with obscenities, Fowler did not report this discussion in *Good Night, Sweet Prince*, but gave an unexpurgated account of it to Kobler for use in his own biography thirty years later (see Kobler, *Damned in Paradise*, pp. 179–80). Apparently some garbling occurred in the process of transmission, because Kobler quotes Fowler as saying, "Now, in like language, [Barrymore] held forth for perhaps two minutes on his own jealousy of his mother when in the arms of his hated stepfather." Surely he meant to say "his own jealousy of his hated stepfather when in the arms of his mother."

19. The conversation was recorded in a log Taylor kept during the run of the play; a typescript of the log is now in the Special Collection of the Joint University Libraries, Nashville, Tennessee.

20. McCarthy associated the "neurotic trance" with possession but thought the idea "degraded the scene" (*New Statesman*, 7 March 1925); MacGowan saw nothing more in the effect than stage lighting being used so artistically as to make the actor's "own genius a dozen times more luminous" (*Globe*, 17 November 1922); Gilbert Seldes thought it most inappropriate for Hamlet suddenly to fall victim to an "epileptic fit" (*Dial*, January 1923).

21. There were still some holdouts against the "new" ending; Hammond wrote, apparently without irony: "The tableau . . . is so well done that you

forget that the play should end with 'The rest is silence.' Still, you feel that the grandeur of the scene fades with every subsequent moment'' (New York *Tribune*, 17 November 1922).

22. Fowler, *Good Night, Sweet Prince*, p. 217.

23. Hollis Alpert, *The Barrymores* (New York: Dial Press, 1965), pp. 230, 232.

12

JOHN GIELGUD

Moth and rust had hardly had time to begin their work on Barrymore's scenery and costumes when a new London production demonstrated that *Hamlet* could be played with a degree of contemporary verisimilitude which made his approach look almost traditional. At the Kingsway on 25 August 1925, the Birmingham Repertory Theatre offered a twenty-nine-year-old Hamlet (Colin Keith-Johnston, 1896–1980) dressed in a business suit and surrounded by similarly clad figures smoking cigarettes and drinking cocktails—all of them speaking the lines at a velocity that had more to do with the age of jazz than with the age of Elizabeth.

A few pundits dismissed the whole proceeding as a tasteless stunt, but there was far more praise then censure. Ivor Brown argued that the intimate relation between dress and acting style meant that doublet-and-hose productions were always inclined to envelop the play in a mist of spurious romantic beautification which obscured the "actualities of suffering, sensuality, and despair" lying at its heart. Modern dress and a realistically youthful actor in the title role had the effect of shifting the balance: "When Hamlet is played as a modern youngster," Brown concluded, "all this beautification can be sloughed away. Mr. Colin Keith-Johnston's admirable performance of the part gave me intense satisfaction for the simple reason that it was an ugly Hamlet: it had in it just that caddishness born of despair which the romantic Hamlet dare not present" (*Saturday Review*, 29 August 1925). Beautified Hamlets would still be necessary from time to time, Brown conceded, "to keep the balance and to remind us that Shakespeare could not even spit venom at providence without doing it to music." Apparently he did not expect to see an actor who could combine Keith-Johnston's strident, rasping young cynic and rebel with the lovely, angel-voiced poet-Prince of tradition. Five years later he joyfully saluted John Gielgud (1904–   ) for having done precisely that.

The portrayal in question was first exhibited on the stage of the Old Vic on the night of 28 April 1930, and moved to the Queen's Theatre in the West End a month later.[1] Gielgud had celebrated his twenty-sixth birthday just two weeks before the opening.[2] As Brown sensed, his youth was of the essence, not so much because it lent beauty to the characterization as because it gave it sap and vigor and a marked astringency. "Mr. Gielgud's Hamlet is young and is never fixed in handsomeness," said Brown. "It has beauty when the text proclaims it, and the ugly mockery of disillusion when that is needed. It is angry, violent, and tender as the sense demands" (*Manchester Guardian*, 29 May 1930). Gielgud himself later described his first Hamlet as an "angry young man of the twenties . . . [full of] rebellion against convention," and that is just how it was perceived at the time.[3]

At the Old Vic the play was given in its entirety (or as some actors ruefully put it, "in its eternity"), and that fact no doubt helped Gielgud create a more churlish Hamlet than audiences were accustomed to seeing. But it was not a major factor. There had been other full-text portrayals which remained traditionally soft-edged. Moreover, Gielgud continued to appear uncommonly virulent even when, for the move to the Queen's Theatre, some cuts were made, including "Now might I do it pat." He was still fiery and rude, "full of amazement and disgust and indignation at the general rottenness of humanity."[4]

Because it was so unfamiliar, Gielgud's illumination of the corrosive side of Hamlet's nature claimed the lion's share of most critics' attention, but Brown was not the only one to record that the real merit of his performance lay in the skill with which he joined that long-neglected facet to what was genuinely beautiful and lovable in the character. James Agate found the fusion not quite perfect but as near to it as any reasonable person could expect, given the difficulty of the task:

Hamlet must make us cry one minute and shudder the next, and the actor who goes a little way toward fulfilling both halves of the contract is always a better Hamlet than one who fulfills one half abundantly and the other not at all. Let it be said that though Mr. Gielgud has not quite enough pathos, he knows where the occasions for pathos are, and marks the passages with the greatest sensibility. (London *Sunday Times*, 11 May 1930).

Though his interpretation was powerfully original, Gielgud's style of speaking was thoroughly traditional. "He plays the part as a young man of the present day feels it," said A. E. Baugham, "but he is not slipshod or modern in his diction" (London *Daily News*, 29 May 1930). He paid strict attention to meter and kept his vocal tone musically pure even in moments of the strongest feeling. It was a style which in later years would come to seem bloodless and mannered, compared with that of more naturalistic actors, and Agate confessed some slight impatience with it even in 1930; in general, however, critics heard in it an altogether proper balance of sense and sonority, of nature and art.

Descriptions and evaluations of Gielgud's behavior at specific moments in the performance are unfortunately far from plentiful.[5] Theatrical journalism had been shrinking rapidly since the turn of the century; fewer and fewer reporters, even in the weeklies, were being allowed the space to conduct the sort of scene-by-scene review which had been commonplace a generation earlier. Only Agate, in the columns of the magisterial London *Sunday Times*, was able even to approximate the expansive coverage of a more leisurely age, and it is from his review that most of the surviving details derive.

Hamlet's scene with the Ghost, historically a favored topic of the commentators, elicited only one notice—of a general but revealing character. "I have never seen," wrote Baugham, "a Hamlet so utterly thrown down by the discovery of his father's murder. Here and throughout the play was no actor's Hamlet but an intelligent, sensitive, emotional and manly young man born to command, but not yet certain of himself" (London *Daily News*, 29 April 1930).

Agate made the nunnery scene an exception to his charge that the performance was insufficiently pathetic: "The words 'Get thee to a nunnery' were delivered at the first time of utterance, and before Hamlet perceives the eavesdroppers, with maximum pathos as though Hamlet would draw out of that refuge its power to heal as well as mortify" (11 May 1930). He did not bully Ophelia (London *Post*, 29 May 1930), though he did present "a somewhat terrifying figure with a livid face" (*Advertiser*, 29 May 1930). The *Spectator* critic thought his reading of the scene, particularly the passage "I loved you not," was the best he had ever seen (14 June 1930).

The play scene and its aftermath were "taken at terrific speed and with the right kind of nervous energy," according to Agate. "At the words 'What, frighted with false fire!' the house was really excited, and with the genuine excitement of a crowd when a goal is scored in a Cup final'' (11 May 1930). At the Queen's Theatre, Gielgud cut the concluding soliloquy ('' 'Tis now the very witching time of night'' [III.ii.388–99] and ended the scene instead by breaking the recorder over his knee and giving Rosencrantz and Guildenstern each a piece as he said, "Leave me friends."[6]

Agate approved of his slow reading of the "How all occasions" soliloquy ("One of the finest pieces of sheer exposition I have ever heard") but thought "the rant over the grave did not quite come off, perhaps because the actor was tiring" (11 May 1930). The *Spectator* critic found in the graveyard scene evidence of a lack of "sorrow of thought." "Alas, poor Yorick" and "Alas, poor ghost" before it were given, he claimed, in so "dry" a tone that "these two dead persons seemed to be regarded as supernumerary bores" (14 June 1930).

Except for these few observations, the reviewers had nothing to say about particulars. But without citing chapter and verse, they were ready enough to assure their readers that the performance was of the highest distinction. "Mr. Gielgud is splendid," said the London *Sunday Pictorial*. "Acknowledge him. Support him. Give him his due as the best Hamlet of this generation" (1 June 1930). Agate returned for a second look when the play reopened across the river, and this time he endorsed the performance without qualification:

This actor is young, thoughtful, clever, sensitive, his performance is subtle, brilliant, vigorous, imaginative, tender, and full of the right kind of ironic humour. It has elegance of body and elevation of mind: it is conceived in the key of poetry and executed with beautiful diction. I have no hesitation whatever in saying that it is the high-water mark of English Shakespearean acting of our time. (London *Sunday Times*, 1 June 1930).

Despite such acclamation from every quarter, the play did not draw well at the Queen's and closed after only a month; the presence of two other *Hamlet* productions in the city (one of them at an adjoining theater) and the recent departure of a third no doubt had much to do with the poor attendance figures.[7]

But having won such laurels while still so young it was all but inevitable that Gielgud would return to the role later in his career. He did so on four occasions.

Gielgud's first revival, for which he acted as his own director, opened at the New Theatre on 14 November 1934.[8] Most observers found the characterization significantly altered and in general not for the better. "Something vital has gone out of his performance," Herbert Farjeon lamented. "The feeling is there, but we are not always convinced that this Hamlet would have been able to say these things if he had not learnt them by heart" (London *Sunday Pictorial*, 18 November 1934). Farjeon surmised that the falling off was due to the actor's being distracted by the duties of the director, and that seems not unlikely. Indeed, the London *Evening News* commentator concluded that as director he had deliberately and commendably "sunk the part in the play" (15 November 1934). Be that as it may, there was a general feeling of dissatisfaction.[9]

What seemed to be missing, or at any rate markedly diminished, was the molten anger of thwarted youth. This Hamlet was not the enigmatically double-souled creature that Gielgud's first Hamlet had been. Ugliness had been banished in favor of a chaste representation of the beautiful. He was all high poetry and sensitive philosophy, more like Richard of Bordeaux, whom he had recently played, than like his earlier Hamlet.[10] He seemed simply too good for this world, in it but not of it, a refugee from a better place, from Eden before the fall. He was exquisitely civilized, a perfect realization of the highest aspirations of the species, a cloud-walker, not so much disdainful of the dirt of life as oblivious to it. The characterization did not suck the audience into a maelstrom of thought and feeling. It had instead the cold, clear placidity of a mountain lake. "He seems aloof and abstracted from everyone and everything," said the *Referee*. "There is no bitterness in his disdain, no rage in his hatred, no affection in his friendship, no wildness in his melancholy" (19 November 1934). He seemed to be convinced from the start of the futility of human action and to have found serenity in that conviction. He was like a mathematician turning over and over in his mind an equation whose logical beauty so absorbs him that he has no thought to spare for the painful consequences of its practical applications. It was an austere conception, designed, as the London *Times* said, "to penetrate the soul by way of the intellect" (15 November 1934).

Further light on the sort of impression Gielgud created with his second rendering is shed by remarks made on individual scenes.[11] For the court scene, staged as a discovery, Gielgud removed himself so completely from the focus of attention that he was barely discernible among the assembled courtiers. Agate, with his customary interest in detail, questioned the appropriateness of such a beginning: "Is he a trifle too spectacularly in the shade, a thought too determined to be the unobserved of all observers? Is there too petulant a charm in the sweep of chin and throat, like Byron sitting for his portrait?" (London *Sunday Times*, 18 November 1934).

The first speech was given "pianissimo . . . as by a man in a trance" (London *Evening Standard*, 15 November 1934). Through all the talk of his protracted mourning he revealed, in Farjeon's opinion, "a Hamlet surpassing all his predecessors in adoration of his dead father" (London *Sunday Pictorial*, 18 November 1934). The same note of filial devotion was sounded in the "Take him for all in all" colloquy with Horatio a few moments later (I.ii.184–90). Agate thought it made for a considerable gain in pathos over his earlier characterization, so much so that "the spectator must have a heart of stone not to be moved by Hamlet's obvious affection for his dead father" (London *Sunday Times*, 18 November 1934).

He placed himself so that his back was turned when the Ghost appeared, and perceived what had happened by the look on Horatio's face, whereupon he turned slowly to confront it (London *Evening News*, 15 November 1934). He seems to have been the first to use this business, and he later wrote that it "came off very well" but it did not attract much notice in the press.

Although he spoke all of Hamlet's wild and whirling words after the Ghost's speech, there was no hysteria in his behavior, not even any excitement (London *Post*, 18 November 1934). Agate noted that he made "singularly little . . . of the promise to put on an antic disposition" and supposed that his flat delivery was intentional, "because, except for one subsequent hurried disarrangement of hair and garments, there is never any question . . . of the Dane being either mad or pretending to be" (18 November 1934). Some of the old anger showed up in his dealing with Polonius, and also with Rosencrantz and Guildenstern. "This is a Hamlet," said the London *Evening Standard*, "whose darting intellect sees through those heavenless twins . . . as easily as through glass, and delights to make delicious mockery of their vain blows" (15 November 1934).

Gielgud made the "Rogue and peasant slave" soliloquy (II.ii.550–

605) "the keynote of his whole performance," according to *Time and Tide*. In it he showed that Hamlet "would act, and act decisively, if any form that revenge could take had a lasting validity for a mind reflecting in its own disillusionment a spiritual world of contending forces" (24 November 1934). In contrast to this soliloquy, delivered "like the first movement of some tremendous concerto," the "To be or not to be" speech (III.i.55–87) had "the tenderness of a Mozartian slow movement" for Agate's ears, and so did the nunnery scene following:

Since Mr. Gielgud jettisons all suggestion of madness . . . we come back willy-nilly to the scene played as sheer music. Our present Hamlet, realizing that this is one of the great things in the play, tackles it for all his vocal grace and physical and mental elegance are worth, and his pathos here is again extraordinary. (18 November 1934)

The remainder of the performance was for Agate a desert of discarded opportunities dotted here and there by oases of verdant lyricism and sturdy intelligence. He charged Gielgud with throwing away the speech to the players, with underplaying most of the play scene to the point of inaudibility, with turning the recorder scene into a "dialectical exercise" and with reducing the closet scene to "a cold lecture on moderation in second marriage." Gielgud's excision of the "politic worms" scene (IV.iii) left Agate agape: "How any actor can omit this beats me utterly, since half of Hamlet is portrayed here." On the credit side of the ledger he listed only the "rapt beauty" of the speech to Horatio (III.ii.54–87) and "the almost mathematical exposition" of the "How all occasions" soliloquy (IV.iv.32–66).

"Now might I do it pat" (III.iii.73–96) was retained for this production and supplied with some new business. Traditionally, actors had either to undergo the inconvenience of wearing a sword in the play scene or to arm themselves, rather implausibly, immediately following it. Gielgud solved the problem by having Claudius lay aside *his* sword at the beginning of the prayer scene, after having checked the premises to be sure he is safe. Hamlet then took it up for the aborted assault on the kneeling King and carried it with him as he continued on his way to join Gertrude. On rising, Claudius was seen to notice "with a little start of terror" that the weapon had been taken (London *Evening News*, 15 November 1934).

The *Stage* critic joined Agate in praise of "How all occasions" but linked it to a detail from the preceding scene of which Agate most probably did not approve: "His intellectual treatment of this difficult passage is a fine example of vocal point and emphasis, while the final reference to bloody thoughts eloquently indicates a Hamlet who faint-heartedly turns away his face while blindly stabbing at Polonius through the arras" (14 November 1934).

The set-to with Laertes at graveside was also played without heat or rancor, and a similar avoidance of strong emotion persisted through the denouement. "In the end," said *Time and Tide*, "the penalties which consistent underplaying has enforced upon the play, though we have condoned them, seem to add themselves together and to make the death of Hamlet accidental, not tragic" (24 November 1934). Agate went further:

The impression we have by this time gathered is of a Hamlet who can fly into the most shattering of pets. He has accesses of grief but they do not leave him moody, there is no melancholy in him, his mind has not the madness of his words, he is not fey or marked for death, and his talk of ripeness is academic and not the ultimate philosophy of a man who feels that his course is run. To sum up, this Hamlet's specific gravity is akin to Romeo's, and when he dies we are conscious of losing no more than a gay, gallant, romantic companion; we do not feel that part of ourselves has died with him. (18 November 1934)

Fortunately for Gielgud, who in addition to being director and star was manager of the enterprise, all this adverse criticism did no more to weaken audience attendance than universal acclaim for his earlier performance had done to strengthen it. As he later remarked, "The public . . . flock[ed] to see me as Hamlet at the New Theatre. But many people told me, of course, that I had been much better in the earlier production which so few came to see." [12] The play chalked up a run of 155 performances—the longest since Henry Irving's record-setting 200 in 1874.

This experience was more or less duplicated eighteen months later when Gielgud took his Hamlet to the United States. The press gave the opening, on 8 October 1936, a tepid reception, but popular interest carried the production to a new American record of 132 performances. [13]

It was not quite the same Hamlet, however. Prompted, it may be, by the recent London complaints that he was too icily intellectual, he placed much greater stress on emotion. With the aid of a blond wig (he was growing prematurely bald), he recaptured the youthfulness of his first portrayal, but instead of the anger of early manhood it was late adolescent fragility which now emerged as the dominant trait. This was in large measure a resurrected Wilhelm Meister Hamlet, a darling bud of May shaken by the rough winds of sexual and political intrigue. "He will be remembered, I think," wrote Joseph Wood Krutch in *The Nation*, "as the only actor who ever undertook to play Hamlet 'like Niobe all tears,' as not so much the 'melancholy Dane' as the 'weepy' one. He is harassed, all but hysterical, and, I suppose I may grant, 'appealing' " (24 October 1936). When Leslie Howard (1893–1943) offered New York its second Hamlet of the season a month later, Krutch contrasted him with Gielgud in just this respect: "Mr. Howard . . . is strong precisely where Mr. Gielgud is weak, and he brings to vivid life exactly those aspects of Hamlet's character which, in his rival's performance, simply do not exist. He is above all else the intellectual and the ironist, the tender and ingenious thinker." [14]

Other critics, perhaps better acquainted with the nineteenth-century precedents for making Hamlet fatally delicate, were more sympathetic toward Gielgud's interpretation. Elinor Hughes, reviewing the New York production for the Boston *Herald*, acknowledged that the performance lacked "the profound and deeply stirring tragedy that a man of different physique and temperament can bring to the role," but proclaimed it a "remarkable experience" to see Hamlet played as "an untried youth faced with a heart-breaking duty that he must perform against seemingly insuperable obstacles" (18 October 1936).

Some months after the closing, Rosamond Gilder, drama critic for *Theatre Arts Monthly*, published a book-length study of Gielgud's performance, *John Gielgud's Hamlet*, consisting of a lengthy descriptive essay and the full acting text, accompanied by a running commentary on business and interpretation based on notes taken by her during performances. This is the only detailed account of any of Gielgud's several portrayals and is therefore of great value, but it must be read with caution. Gilder saw in the interpretation a degree of balance and variety not perceived by most other experienced observers. "Gielgud is willing to play him both nobly and angrily," she wrote, "extenuating nothing of his harshnesses but painting so clearly the picture of his outraged purity, his sorrow and his spiritual isolation that Hamlet becomes in his hands the prototype of all lost and lonely souls, as well as a prince most royal, the 'unmatch'd form and feature of blown youth.' "[15] Undoubtedly Gielgud showed the stronger side of Hamlet in some degree at some moments, but the fact remains that weakness predominated in the view of most spectators. As long as that is borne in mind, Gilder's account can be extremely illuminating. Here and there one of the more voluble reviewers adds to the record, as does Gielgud himself, both in his memoirs and in an essay contributed to Gilder's book.[16]

There was a mixture of severity and sensitivity in Gielgud's playing of the early moments, according to Gilder. " 'A little more than kin,' " she writes, "is spoken quietly, but it is a venomed dart and the curling, almost cruel lips frame it with deliberate, courteous malice" (p. 30). "Ay, madam, it is common" was spoken "with that careful control of breath which the immediate fear of bursting into tears at the sound of one's own voice makes necessary." The tears flowed unchecked during the early lines of the soliloquy but gave way to "mounting fury until with the 'incestuous sheets,' that 'nest of vipers,' he spits out all his horror" (p. 33).

Gielgud knew by heart Ellen Terry's description of Irving's playing of the interview with Horatio and Marcellus and "tried to follow him in every detail."[17] Lost in reflection during Horatio's momentous "My lord, I think I saw him yesternight" (I.ii.189), he answered distractedly, perfunctorily, on "Saw?" Then, Horatio's words having finally registered, he came alive on "Who?" and pursued the questioning vigorously.

The scenes on the platform also contained a number of borrowings from predecessors. He paced the stage in nervous expectation, sank to one knee on "father," used the sword hilt as a protective cross, held up his arm as if the words of his father's tale were blows that must be deflected, accompanied "sweep to my revenge" with a violent descriptive gesture, took for his own "O, horrible, O, horrible, most horrible!" and threw himself sobbing to the ground on the Ghost's departure. There were two noteworthy innovations. He repeated his London business of inferring the Ghost's arrival from the expression on Horatio's face. For the "tables" speech he dispensed with actual writing materials and instead struck his forehead at the conclusion on "So, uncle, there you are" (I.v.110), to indicate that Hamlet has inscribed his memorandum on the table of his mind.

He turned to precedent again in making Marcellus trigger Hamlet's evasive conclusion to "There's never a villain dwelling in all Denmark," but he seems to have added a highly original coloration to that familiar reading. According to Bernard Grebanier, "he suddenly ceased, looked in dazed bewilderment at both men, clapped a hand over his mouth to dam the current, and staggered away almost drunkenly, while muttering 'But he's an arrant knave!' Words—anything to finish the sentence which he has nearly terminated by a revelation that could have proved fatal to his cause."[18] The scene closed with another borrowing, this one from H. B. Irving (1870–1919). Having lost his cloak in the earlier scuffle, Gielgud's Hamlet shivered with cold as he knelt alone at center for "O cursed spite. . . ." Seeing this, Horatio returned and put his own cloak around him. Hamlet accepted it unconsciously and started out, then, taking thought of Horatio's exposure, returned to share the garment with his friend.

Acting on a suggestion from Dover Wilson, Gielgud made an early entrance to the lobby scene, in time to overhear Polonius say "I'll loose my daughter to him" (II.ii.162), then withdrew unseen.[19] On his reappearance at the usual cue, his antic disposition was evident both in his disordered dress and in his "subtly stagey" walk. His hand rested absurdly on the top of his head. He circled the old man lugubriously, wagging a finger in "sardonic solemnity" on "Conception is a blessing" (184), then broke away to rummage wildly among some books and papers on a nearby table during Polonius' aside. Gilder found him "sharp and hard" (pp. 53–54) on some of his replies, but according to the *Literary Digest* he was "bored with the prating Polonius rather than angered by him" (24 October 1936). "Into my grave" was "quick, almost flat . . . addressed to space . . . without emphasis, a leaden reality, startling after the innuendo, the malice, the double-edged wit of what has gone before" (Gilder, pp. 53–54).

Hearing the approach of Guildenstern and Rosencrantz, he framed himself in the doorway in a madcap pose, but dropped his act immediately on seeing who it was. He was cordial and casual at first, but he grew increasingly suspicious and slammed a book shut in anger when Guildenstern hesitated before finally admitting, "My lord, we were sent for" (292). He sat, scarcely moving, for the "paragon of animals" speech, but leapt to his feet in a fresh outburst of anger at their smiling. Drawing on the past again, he seized Rosencrantz's miniature and threw it contemptuously to one side on " 'Sblood, there is something in this more than natural . . . " (366–67).

The plan for determining the King's guilt or innocence was born in the mind of Gielgud's Hamlet during the First Player's recital of Aeneas' tale to Dido. "At the description of Hecuba," wrote Gilder, "he gives a sudden, harsh cry, overcome by the picture summoned to his imagination and by the shock of an idea, apprehended vaguely a few moments before but suddenly crystal clear in his mind. His hand covers his face, as though to protect his thought from the prying eyes around him until he has made it his own, hidden it deep within" (p. 62).

In the "Rogue and peasant slave" soliloquy (II.ii.550–605), he lashed himself into a frenzy of murderous resolve climaxing at "O Vengeance," drew his dagger and with arm raised to strike hurtled himself against the chamber door, whereupon the passion suddenly drained out of him, the avenging hand dropped, letting fall the dagger, and he slumped to a dispirited crouch. He planned the play trap in "a hoarse, whispered voice" (p. 65) but exploded in a fresh paroxysm of excitement on the concluding line "The play's the thing . . . ," then seized paper and pen and scribbled frantically. Christopher Morley, in the *Saturday Review of Literature*, advised that instead of this "frenzy of gasping and hysteria" Gielgud should have been showing "coldest, calculating malice, steely and stealthy" (24 October 1936).

Of the "To be or not to be" soliloquy (III.i.55–87) Krutch wrote that "the famous soliloquy has so little relation to the character Mr. Gielgud is portraying that he can only treat it as a set piece which tradition unfortunately compels him to interrupt his part to speak" (*Nation*, 24 October 1936). That accusation must have been especially painful to Gielgud, if he read it, because he had consciously worked to avoid the impression of a set speech and so had "slipped in the opening words, trying to make not too long a pause before them and to get underway before the audience was quite sure it really was the big speech."[20] He pantomimed the "bare bodkin" with a simple gesture of his left hand. With "puzzles the will," Gilder wrote, "his tone becomes anxious, a note of bafflement creeps into his voice and he begins pacing restlessly across the stage . . . as the exasperation of his own inaction, his sense of frustration and block grows upon him" (p. 69). Gilbert Seldes admired another detail: "It is easy to know what Shakespeare meant by 'sicklied o'er with the pale cast of thought,' but when Mr. Gielgud passed his arm across his face in a gesture of weariness and dislike, one suddenly understood what those words meant to Hamlet himself" (*Scribner's*, December 1936).

As Ophelia approached, Gielgud reminded the audience of Hamlet's earlier discovery of the spying plot by giving a quick look around, then making as if to go. Thinking better of thus foiling his enemies' plans, he stopped and returned to face her. When she gave back his love tokens, a string of pearls, he laughed at her in bitter rebuke for allowing herself to be used and seized her roughly as he challenged her honesty. The declaration of love was given sincerely, but "with the finality of a thing past" (Gilder, p. 69). The first "Get thee to a nunnery" was given "in a whisper, almost tenderly"; Gielgud described his approach to the rest of that speech: "The lines in which Hamlet accuses himself seem to me most poignant if they are spoken as if pleading with Ophelia to admit that she is not telling the truth. He is giving her every chance to speak out by showing her that he has just the same weaknesses as she."[21] When Ophelia failed to respond and turned away, he pursued, offering her one last chance on "Where's your father?" then flared up in fury at her lying answer, threw the pearls at her feet and played the remainder of the scene at white heat. After a peremptory attempt to locate his persecutors, the threat to Claudius ("all but one") was "thrown against the listening walls." Then he crumbled in weariness, drained by the effort. Catching sight of Ophelia's face, he raised his hand, "palms out, as though pushing the vision away—denying the last faint shadow of hope" (p. 70). Scarcely able to speak the parting line, he groped blindly to the exit.

Reactions were mixed. John Mason Brown complained that there were no indications of love and expressed a preference, on that account, for Barrymore's treatment (New York *Post*, 9 October 1936). Douglas Gilbert thought it an admirable example of Gielgud's generally "lucid" approach: " 'Get thee to a nunnery!'—and Hamlet means precisely what he says. The base passion of his mother that has made her virtually an accessory to the crime has soured him upon all women. This simple, silly girl thus is an affront to him and he dismisses her with purposed anger" (New York *World-Telegram*, 9 October 1936). Apparently neither of these critics made any connection between the playing of the scene and the overhearing of the spying plans.[22] But Elinor Hughes did: "It is but the opening of a door and the noiseless appearance of Hamlet while the others are deep in converse, but it provides a perfect clue to Hamlet's subsequent harshness to Ophelia. . . . He knows they are there and, torn between anger and pity for the submissive girl, he can give the listeners a run for their money" (Boston *Herald*, 18 October 1936).

He instructed the players with a copy of the script in his hand, borrowed from one of the company as he began to speak. Brown wondered why the speech was delivered "with a professional's interest in its admonitions and no remembrance of the scheme to trap the King which underlies that interest" (New York *Post*, 9 October 1936). Gilder detected, in addition to authority and interest, a "note of gaiety, of pleasure in things of the intellect" (p. 72).

Prompted by Harley Granville-Barker's analysis of the play scene, Gielgud attempted to show that at certain moments Hamlet remembers "his mission of vengeance and is shocked to find how easily he has been forgetting it," but he wondered afterward whether his byplay was not lost on spectators, with so much else going on in the scene to command their attention.[23] He kept "country matters" (but not "a fair thought to lie between maids' legs"), delivering it, along with his mad chatter about a father "died within's two hours," while standing between Ophelia and Gertrude, who were seated with Claudius on a platform overlooking the mimic playing area. As the Prologue ended, he moved down to a vantage point halfway between the real King and Queen and their stage impersonators, pausing en route to drop "As woman's love" into his mother's ear. As he crouched on the stage watching, now and again urging the actors on by beating time to their lines, the manuscript in his hand crackled under the pressure of his grip. Having moved up between the thrones to ask his mother's opinion of the play, he was in a position to speak "poison in jest" directly into the ear of Claudius. With a bow on "we that have free souls," he moved off again as Lucianus entered. At the King's rising, he leapt into his path, then onto the throne, waved the manuscript triumphantly on high as he recited his exuberant jingle, then tore the pages, scattered the pieces, sent Horatio off for some music and collapsed onto the throne, "shaken, his breath coming in gasps, his whole body quivering" (Gilder, p. 78).

He behaved with transparent hatred toward Rosencrantz and Guildenstern, accompanying "pickers and stealers" with a gesture suggesting a barely suppressed desire to strangle. "I lack advancement" was an unequivocal "proclamation of his thwarted right to power" (Gilder, pp. 78–79). He turned the recorder into a telescope on "Methinks it is like a weasel" and, as at the Queen's Theatre, ended the scene by breaking it over his knee and handing the pieces to his two tormentors.

He made off with Claudius' sword as in London, but wielded it against Polonius with considerably more relish of the deed than he had shown there. On hearing the interloper's cry for help, he leapt onto the bed and delivered a double thrust through the concealing drapery;[24] as he turned from his work with the weapon flashing over his head,[25] he looked to Gilder like a "towering figure of revenge and atonement on the couch which the terrified and moaning woman below him has defiled" (p. 82–83).

He spoke daggers to the Queen about her choice of bedfellows but used no props to make his point, preferring instead Henry Irving's imaginary likenesses. Brown called the method "strangely disappointing." He kept himself between his mother and the Ghost, and when instructed to speak to her he did so "in a somnambulist's voice," his hand reaching back toward her, his eyes still riveted on the apparition. He pursued the departing figure to the doorway and leaned against it moaning until recalled by Gertrude's voice. He treated her more lovingly now, allowing and returning an occasional embrace, but he gave the "bloat king" speech with the same snarling disgust he had earlier poured into picturing her second marriage-bed as a "nasty sty." He spoke of England, of blowing his enemies to the moon and of lugging out the remains of his recent victim in tones of defiance, but his mood altered abruptly at the sight of his mother leaving the room: "As she disappears through the doorway his braggadoccio drops from him like the false mask that it is. He sways against the wall, his head and shoulders sink. For a moment he looks after her and then, with repressed anguish, the one word 'Mother'—the cry of a child left in the dark—the hopeless, lost cry of a creature torn from its one safe anchorage" (Gilder, pp. 87–88).

The scenes preceding the departure for England were retained in this production and included some highly expressive pieces of fresh business. A green scarf taken from the body of Polonius did service as a sponge and was squeezed out and tossed aside at the appropriate moment. On "your fat king and your lean beggar," Hamlet pointed "with malicious joy" first to Claudius, then to his lieutenants. On hearing Claudius' lying protestation of concern for his safety, he covered his face in "mock shame." "Farewell, dear mother" he "flung full in the King's face, both hands blowing a mocking kiss" (Gilder, p. 90).

Gielgud's reading of the "How all occasions" soliloquy (IV.iv.32–66) showed a Hamlet "already on the way to becoming captain of his soul." "He is as merciless as ever in his judgment of himself," Gilder wrote, "yet he can think of his shortcomings without the hysterical despair of his Hecuba musings" (pp. 91–92). Brown also detected a newfound control in the "tremendous austerity" with which the speech was delivered.

By the time of his return from England the transformation was more marked, though not so much as to obliterate all signs of his former self. As Gilder saw it:

Gielgud shows . . . that though Hamlet's conflict has been resolved and his way to action discovered, his personality is untouched. He flares into a rage at Laertes, throws an enigmatic taunt at the King, indulges in fantastic quibbles with Osric, talks philosophy with Horatio as of old. But through all this he walks forward, his eyes open on a foreseen and calamitous end. In every gesture, every intonation, every quiet word and relaxed pose, this Hamlet is a contrast to the tense, tormented creature of the first scenes. Emotion and will are at last fused. . . . He is sure of his strength, because he is healed within. (Gilder, p. 10)

He was relaxed enough to sit and take snuff while conversing with the Clown and smiled good-naturedly over his impertinent jesting. But he was reduced to sobs after grappling with Laertes at the graveside. Recovering, he paused in his exit speech to look down into the grave, then gave the closing couplet as "a final fling at the curs who snarl at his heels" (Gilder, p. 100). He was more amused than irritated by Osric's verbal and sartorial affectations. The "augury" speech (V.ii.219–24) was given slowly, with pauses after each sentence, without movement "or any rise in inflection or any marked emphasis on a particular word or phrase" (Gilder, p. 102).

Gielgud used rapier and dagger for the fencing match and affected the exchange of weapons by disarming his opponent, both men having previously discarded their daggers. But as he considered himself an indifferent swordsman and was in any case too exhausted by the performance for a protracted contest, he restricted the duel to what was "absolutely necessary." [26] The practice may have contributed something to Elinor Hughes' protest concerning "the terrific speed with which the final scene is played, robbing Hamlet's death of all tragic feeling. Of course, the mass slaughter is melodramatic, but it need not be played with a stop watch in one hand and a starting gun in the other" (Boston *Herald*, 18 October 1936). He did, however, take the time to force the poisoned cup on Claudius after running him through. For Gilder, the killing of Claudius was the act of an avenging hero who has at last found the way to action. But Krutch could see in the Hamlet of this moment "merely a dejected young man who finally works himself to a hysterical blood-letting" (*Nation*, 24 October 1936).

Gielgud died on his feet, a suggestion from his director which he rebelled against at first but in time came to see the virtue of: "It proved an admirable departure from tradition, for there are three recumbent figures on the stage already, and Hamlet in Horatio's arms is always faintly reminiscent of 'Kiss me, Hardy' at the death of Nelson." [27] As he felt the approach of death, he gave "a look of faint surprise, then of complete acceptance" (Gilder, p. 107). Horatio caught him in his arms when he collapsed, laid him gently down and crossed his hands on his breast. Fortinbras' captains raised him to their shoulders on command and stood in tableau as the lights went to black.

Gielgud's next revival came in the summer of 1939, when he was asked to direct and star in the play for presentation at Elsinore in the courtyard of Kronborg Castle. As it happened, the Lyceum theater was at the time scheduled for demolition—a fate it subsequently escaped—and it was decided that a week's run of the new production, prior to the move to Denmark, would make an ideal farewell tribute to the venerable house. Thus it was that the London critics got their third look at Gielgud in the role, commencing on the night of 28 June 1939. [28]

In an interview in the *Observer*, published three days before the opening, Gielgud confessed that he had at first been filled with revulsion at the thought of playing Hamlet again but had rekindled his interest by reading Harley Granville-Barker's *Preface to Hamlet* (1937). [29] Any improvements he might make on his last performance, he said, would be due to Barker's influence as well as to the fact that he had with the passage of years grown more mature, more perceptive (25 June 1939).

Improvement there was, in full measure. Agate proclaimed it "an immense advance upon the performance of five years ago." He seemed to have recovered and amplified the asperity he had had in the beginning. Ivor Brown thought it "a stronger, fuller, more passionate performance than either of his earlier renderings." He had gained in "earthy vigour" and was now clearly "not only a prince with a vein of poetry [but a] cynic railler, coarse jester, and potentially loose-liver" (*Observer*, 2 July 1939). He was still essentially high-minded and thin-skinned, by no means a rough-neck. The harsher notes he now sounded humanized his portrayal, rescued it from preciosity and exquisiteness, but did not take it off in a fundamentally new direction. Gielgud offered just enough earthiness to enchant a generation eager to respond to refined ideality but a little uncomfortable with it in its purest form. W. A. Darlington, voicing the general view, declared him "the best English Hamlet of his time" and predicted that he would be even better when he grew more at ease with his newfound strength (*Daily Telegraph*, 29 June 1939).

The opportunity to make good on Darlington's prediction came five years later, on 13 October 1944, when at the age of forty Gielgud played his fourth and final Hamlet.[30] Darlington was no longer writing for the London press, but Agate was still at his old post, and to him it seemed that Gielgud had indeed completed at last the conquest of the role begun so auspiciously in 1930. He was "now completely and authoritatively master of this tremendous part," as much at home with raillery and mordancy as with pathos. "He imposes on us this play's questing feverishness. The middle act gives us ninety minutes of high excitement and assured virtuosity; Forbes-Robertson was not more bedazzling in the 'O what a rogue and peasant slave' soliloquy. In short, I hold that this is, and is likely to remain, the best Hamlet of our time" (London *Sunday Times*, 22 October 1944). The review bore the terse caption "A Great Hamlet." Most of the other critics cast similar votes; Gielgud was now numbered among the immortals.[31]

But the winds of change were blowing again in the English theater. An old pattern was about to be repeated. At the very moment of his triumph, Gielgud's preeminence was challenged by the exponents of a new style. Throughout his career, on both sides of the Atlantic, Gielgud had been generally lauded, whatever one thought of his interpretation, for employing a style of speech and movement which seemed to suspend nature and art in a near-perfect equipoise. Moreover, to those few who could see no such balance, his style seemed more natural than otherwise.[32] Now, for the first time, there were rumblings of dissatisfaction. The London *Times* critic (14 October 1944) wrote at length of a "new artificiality," and though he thought the performance nevertheless "brilliantly accomplished, and immensely stimulating," others did not. James Redfern, in the *Spectator*, characterized the delivery as "mere eloquence, admirable academic eloquence" and the movement

John Gielgud. Soliloquy, the Nunnery Scene (III.i). Lyceum Theatre, London, 1939. Angus McBean Photograph. Harvard Theatre Collection.

as "either too studied or too self-conscious." True, it was all very skilled, "to the point of sheer virtuosity," but "there is nothing so boring as virtuosity which is nothing more than virtuosity." For that reason he could not join his colleagues in "their .* . . extravagant praise of this Hamlet. If, as they maintain, it is perfect, it is a dead and chilling perfection" (27 October 1944). To some extent, no doubt, Gielgud *was* by this time employing a more overtly artful, less spontaneous approach than had been his custom earlier.[33] But there was something else at work as well. In recent years, Laurence Olivier had been building a distinguished reputation with a succession of Shakespearean portrayals acted in a style which made Gielgud's manner appear artificial by comparison.

NOTES

1. The production was staged "in the Elizabethan manner" by Harcourt Williams, a disciple of William Poel and Harley Granville-Barker. He gives a brief account of his directorial approach in *Old Vic Saga* (London: Winchester, 1949), pp. 88–91.

2. Gielgud was born on 14 April 1907. He was knighted in 1953.

3. John Gielgud, *Stage Directions* (London: Heinemann, 1963), p. 57.

4. Gilbert Wakefield, *Saturday Review*, 14 June. For similar views, see London *Sunday Dispatch*, 1 June 1930; *Spectator*, 14 June 1930; *Graphic*, 7 June 1930; London *Daily Mail*, 29 May 1930.

5. According to Charles Shattuck (*The Shakespeare Promptbooks* [Urbana: University of Illinois Press, 1965], p. 26), the promptbook, like those of other prewar productions at the Old Vic, was destroyed by enemy action.

6. John Gielgud, "The Hamlet Tradition: Some Notes on Costume, Scenery and Stage Business," in *John Gielgud's Hamlet*, by Rosamond Gilder (London: Methuen, 1937), p. 151.

7. Esmé Percy (1887–1957) had been at the Court in February. Henry Ainley (1879–1945) was at the head of an all-star cast presenting a limited series of matinees at the Haymarket, in aid of theatrical charities and in honor of Shakespeare's birthday (they opened on 22 April 1930). Alexander Moissi (1880–1935) brought his German-language production to the Globe, next door to the Queen's, on 2 June 1930, for a one-week stay.

8. The costumes, by Motley, were of the Dürer period (1471–1528). The setting, also by Motley, was a revolving unit comprised of slopes and levels, with variable fittings. See John Gielgud, *Early Stages*, rev. ed. (London: Falcon Press, 1948), p. 191.

9. See, for example, London *Daily Telegraph*, 15 November 1934; *Illus-*

trated Sporting and Dramatic News, 23 November 1934; *Saturday Review*, 24 November 1934; London *Sunday Times*, 18 November 1934.

10. Gielgud had scored a great success with Gordon Daviot's *Richard of Bordeaux* at the same theater ten months earlier; it opened on 2 February 1934 and closed on 24 March 1934.

11. No promptbook survives.

12. Gielgud, *Early Stages*, p. 136.

13. Directed by Guthrie McClintic, the production opened at the Empire and moved to the St. James on 21 December 1936. The costumes, by Jo Mielziner, were based on Van Dyck. Mielziner's set was made up of unlocalized steps and platforms surmounted by two towers.

14. *Nation*, 21 November 1936. Howard opened at the Imperial Theatre on 10 November 1936. Krutch had little company in preferring him to Gielgud. John Mason Brown quipped "Compared to Mr. Howard's Prince, Mr. Gielgud is Hyperion to a Satyr" (New York *Post*, 14 November 1936). Grenville Vernon, of *Commonweal*, declared, "The bitterness, the passion, the tortured despair of the Prince is beyond Mr. Howard's compass" (27 November 1936).

15. Gilder, *John Gielgud's Hamlet*, p. 12.

16. Unless otherwise indicated, all information given here concerning Gielgud's business and line readings is taken from Gilder's *John Gielgud's Hamlet*. Direct quotations from Gilder are documented parenthetically in the main text.

The promptbook (*HAM*, 165), now in the New York Public Library contains only a few markings.

A number of traditional cuts were made in Hamlet's part, totaling some 250 lines; the major omissions were: I.iv.19–38 (following "they clepe us drunkards"); II.ii.336–63 (on the "aery of children"); III.ii.274–86 ("cry of players" and "O Damon dear"); 388–99 (the "witching time of night" soliloquy); III.iv.71–81 ("Sense sure you have . . . "); V.i.79–116 (on the identity of the skulls); V.ii: forty-one lines on Hamlet's shipboard activities; twenty-eight lines of banter with Osric; ten lines (230–40) of the apology to Laertes. No scene was entirely omitted; the Reynaldo-Polonius colloquy was trimmed to eight lines; Voltimand and Cornelius were eliminated; IV.i and IV.ii were run together; and the Lord (V.ii) was eliminated and one of his speeches (206–8) given to Osric.

17. Gielgud, "The Hamlet Tradition." p. 39. Gielgud also wrote that this scene "has always been my favourite in the whole play, and I knew every word of it by heart long before I ever dreamt I should have the chance of playing the part."

18. Bernard Grebanier, *The Heart of Hamlet* (New York: Crowell, 1960), pp. 143–44.

19. Gielgud, "The Hamlet Tradition," p. 51. Dover Wilson first proposed the change in his *Hamlet* edition (Cambridge, Eng.: Cambridge University Press,

1934), p. vi., and developed the idea at greater length in his *What Happens in Hamlet* (Cambridge, Eng.: Cambridge University Press, 1935), pp. 103–10.

20. Gielgud, "The Hamlet Tradition," p. 55.

21. Ibid., p. 56.

22. Of his experience with the early entrance in two productions, Gielgud afterward wrote: "One or two people have noticed this treatment, but on the whole I do not think it clarified the meaning sufficiently to warrant the trouble we took with it at rehearsals. I was also afraid that the audience might mistake my meaning or wonder what was happening (whether one had made a mistake and come on too early) and, while they were speculating thus, miss what followed" (ibid., p. 51).

23. Ibid., p. 52.

24. Gielgud had long thought the scene should have a bed in place of the usual chair, and after including a suggestion of one in his London production he introduced a real one in New York. This made it necessary for Gertrude to sit on it and, as someone pointed out, that was a mistake: "A Queen would never sit on a bed—it makes her look like a housemaid!" (ibid., p. 64).

25. Gielgud put his sword over his head, in imitation of Sarah Bernhardt (1845–1923), who, he had read, used it to form "her whole figure into a great interrogation mark" (ibid., p. 63). Bernhardt opened in *Hamlet* at the Adelphi Theatre in London on 12 June 1899.

26. Ibid., p. 70.

27. Ibid., p. 71. Gielgud was apparently unaware of the John Barrymore precedent.

28. The costumes, by Motley, were again "Düreresque." McCarthy described the setting as an "Elizabethan compromise," with an "inner and outer stage, but . . . no projecting fore-stage" (*New Statesman*, 8 July 1939).

29. Granville-Barker watched a run-through of the play in rehearsal and afterward conferred at length with Gielgud about his characterization. According to Ronald Hayman (*John Gielgud* [New York: Random House, 1971], p. 117), Barker advised him "to be stronger and more deliberate at the beginning of the Closet Scene and then—in contrast—wilder, more disturbed and despairing after killing Polonius." Hayman also says (ibid., p. 118) that it was this study session which led Gielgud to trim away much of his accustomed business, including breaking the recorder and filching Claudius' sword.

30. The theater was the Haymarket; the director was George Rylands, a Cambridge don. The setting, by Ruth Keating, was modified Elizabethan: a cleared stage with simple architectural background. For the first time, Gielgud wore tights, with a fur-trimmed doublet.

31. See also London *Stage*, 19 October 1944; *Time and Tide*, 21 October 1944; *Observer*, 15 October 1944; London *Evening News*, 14 October 1944.

32. Elinor Hughes, for instance, wrote, "The stately magnificence, the beautiful cadenced speech of Mr. [Walter] Hampden's prince is not the same as the electrical sympathetic modernism of Mr. Gielgud" (Boston *Herald*, 18 October 1936).

33. In his 1939 interview in the *Observer*, Gielgud said that he "should like to have ten days with the cast just sitting round a table speaking the verse. Nothing else. We are in danger of losing the purely vocal music of Shakespeare in our concern with the psychological problems" (25 June 1939).

13

LAURENCE OLIVIER

Laurence Olivier (1907–) was first seen as Hamlet at the Old Vic on 5 January 1937. The contrast with John Gielgud could hardly have been more marked. Olivier spoke the verse as prose, raced through some of the long speeches with colloquial offhandedness and seemed to care little for sonority. "Mr. Olivier does not speak poetry badly," said James Agate. "He does not speak it at all" (London *Sunday Times*, 10 January 1937).

As for interpretation, Olivier was stunningly virile. The word appeared in practically every review, and more than one commentator suggested that this Hamlet must have been the mainstay of the Wittenberg athletic program before being called home. A youthful twenty-nine, muscular and handsome, Olivier seemed the perfect embodiment of a dashing and gallant Renaissance courtier, a man more at home with action than with contemplation. In his hands the play became something not easily distinguishable from blood-and-thunder melodrama.[1] It was all tremendously exciting and refreshing, but was it Hamlet? Opinion varied widely. The *Sphere* critic preferred it to Gielgud's "precious and lackadaisical" approach (16 January 1937), and Raymond Mortimer declared that by comparison "most Hamlets, whatever their merits, look a little like governesses." Here was a Hamlet "as elegant and vivid as a Botticelli portrait," and Mortimer found himself "riveted" to attention by the new image (*New Statesman and Nation*, 16 January 1937). Agate was the chief spokesman for the conservative view. He admitted that Olivier's "pulsating vitality" was at some moments splendidly appropriate, but he held that there was far too much of it. He wrote off the characterization with a quip which has enjoyed a certain fame in theatrical circles ever since: "Mr. Olivier's Hamlet is the best performance of Hotspur this generation has seen" (London *Sunday Times*, 10 January 1937).

The problem with so forceful a Hamlet, as even Olivier's admirers acknowledged, was that there seemed no reason why such a man would not kill Claudius forthwith. Some were content to accept the discrepancy. "No one Hamlet can be all Hamlets," wrote Ivor Brown, and a Prince without a discernible cue for inaction, a Prince with "more of thistle and sword-grass than of sensitive plant in his composition," ought to be enjoyed as such, however one-sided the characterization (*Observer*, 10 January 1937). The London *Daily Telegraph* critic argued that the discrepancy is inherent in the text; Shakespeare leaves unanswered the question of why this bold and bloody resolute does not obey the Ghost's command:

Shakespeare insists again and again that Hamlet, in ordinary life, was a virile man of action. Mr. Olivier suggests with certainty and brilliance such a man held back from his obvious duty by a strange streak of inertia for which he cannot account. This interpretation of the part is all of a piece and—to my mind—completely satisfying. (6 January 1937)

That analysis came very close to uncovering Olivier's actual intention in playing the role, but it did not go far enough. Prompted by his director, Tyrone Guthrie, Olivier had read Ernest Jones' psychoanalytic interpretation of Hamlet's delay and adopted it as the basis of his characterization.[2] The hidden cause of that "strange streak of inertia," Olivier believed, was an Oedipus complex. Though normally as hardy as the Nemean lion, Hamlet cannot strike at Claudius because beneath the threshold of consciousness lies the guilty knowledge that he has himself longed to do what Claudius has done: destroy King Hamlet and take his place in Gertrude's bed.

Even though Olivier descended into the Freudian labyrinth with more firmness of purpose and a clearer sense of direction than John Barrymore seems to have had, the result was roughly the same: hardly anyone noticed. A week after the opening, Marjorie Rowland used a good part of her *Era* review (13 January 1937) to accuse her colleagues of obtuseness. By using the Jones interpretation, Olivier had, she protested, "solved the greatest problem in all dramatic literature," and yet "not one of the major critics appears to have noticed anything unusual in it." She acknowledged that one might legitimately reject the Freudian reading—she did not herself subscribe to it—but she thought it ought to be said that "according to the chosen interpretation, this is a very good performance of Mr. Olivier's, full of sound and fury that signifies a great deal.'' Thus primed, two other critics alluded to the Jones influence in later reviews. One of them did so in order to deny not the validity of the interpretation but its very presence. ''Mr. Olivier's interpretation,'' said Herbert Farjeon, ''seemed no more psycho-analytical than George Howe's excellent performance as Polonius, or Alec Guinness's brilliant little sketch of Osric. . . . If D'Artagnan (no friend of Freud) had played Hamlet, he might have given a performance not unlike Mr. Olivier's'' (*The Bystander*, 27 January 1937). Mortimer diagnosed a ''mother-fixation'' and praised it as ''one of the peaks'' of the performance, but he did not make it the cornerstone of Olivier's interpretation, the explanation of Hamlet's delay in exacting revenge.

The real ''secret'' of Hamlet's character, Mortimer argued, is not that he has an Oedipus complex but that he is ''multiple and unintegrated,'' and Olivier was thus, whatever his conscious intention, ''wiser than all the scholars and critics'' in making him ''quizzical, protean, mercurial, leaping in and out of every mood, alternating even in the same sentence between depression and manic amusement, playing a new part every minute with himself for the audience.'' It is not inertia but volatility itself which paradoxically holds Hamlet back so long from his appointed task, and Olivier had managed to convey this with his vibrant activism. It was a wholly new concept, and one which Mortimer considered superior to the conventional wisdom:

Coleridge's view that Hamlet suffered from an aversion to action consequent upon ''an almost enormous intellectual activity,'' though it throws light on one *persona* in him, appears to me far less generally illuminating than Mr. Olivier's performance, which makes him the victim not of too much cerebration but of too rapid emotion, each impulse living only long enough to beget its opposite—in his own words—''Passion's slave''– the slave not of one ruling passion, but of every conflicting passion, so that he is not so much one man as a whole troupe of players—hero, villain, lover, wiseacre and clown. (*New Statesman and Nation*, 16 January 1937)

No one else saw the performance in quite that way, but the analysis is clearly the product of a supple and informed critical intelligence, and there is nothing inherently improbable in it. Nor is there anything in the other commentaries, taken either singly or collectively, which argues strongly against it. At the very least we may conclude that Oli-

vier's characterization had some measure of the quality Mortimer assigned to it, for those who were perceptive, and receptive, enough to
apprehend it.

Only a few details survive. In the first soliloquy he used the Q2
reading, "sallied" (emended to "sullied"), and as he spoke it wiped
his mother's parting kiss from his face as though defiled by it. If this
was meant as a first step in the revelation of an Oedipus complex, it
apparently failed of its intended effect. The reporter for the *Sphere*,
the only one to comment on it, was simply mystified: "How did Hamlet's flesh become 'sullied'? Who did the sullying, and when, and
where?" he demanded (16 January 1937).

The scenes on the platform were charged with that bustling vitality
which was to be the keynote of the performance. He took "I will go
pray" (I.v.132) at "immense speed" and "skated over" the "antic
disposition" passage (London *Sunday Times*, 10 January 1937).

He arrived at the lobby in time to overhear the plan to "loose"
Ophelia. It was an "ingenious notion," said Brown, but "I doubt
whether it is theatrically effective." On the other hand, the banter with
Polonius was "admirably taken, springing quick from a quick mind"
(*Observer*, 10 January 1937). There was little sign of feigned distraction. "Like almost all modern Hamlets," said Mortimer, he did not
ape madness "with the gusto so histrionic a nature would bring to this
ruse" (*New Statesman and Nation*, 16 January 1937).

He was openly abusive to Ophelia and Gertrude in the play scene,
delivering the sexual innuendos loudly enough for the whole court to
hear and "positively shouting" the line "for look you how cheerfully
my mother looks, and my father died within's two hours" (III.ii.126–
27) (*Manchester Guardian*, 6 January 1937). His athleticism was given
full play at the climax. "Hamlet acts literally all over the stage," said
James Agate, "his 'Why, let the stricken deer go weep' being accompanied by a tremendous leap from the perched-up throne onto the mimic
stage below, and thence down to the footlights in an access of high
hysteria." At the end, "Now could I drink hot blood" (III.ii.390) was
"rattled out . . . as though it were casual information" (London *Sunday Times*, 10 January 1937).

According to Mortimer, Olivier played the "Now might I do it pat"
speech (III.iii.73–96) as "an obvious excuse: Hamlet cannot bring
himself in cold blood to stab a man in the back." Mortimer explained

the reading as simply an understandable concession to the feelings of a modern audience, but it may be that it was meant to suggest that the true motive for postponing execution lay elsewhere, in Hamlet's subconscious.

If the closet scene was played with signs of suppressed desire, as the commitment to Freud would presumably have dictated, the fact went unreported. Rowland found the critics' silence on that point "particularly curious," but even she revealed only that Hamlet's manner with Gertrude, here and elsewhere, was "marked—startling" (*Era*, 13 January 1937).

Characteristically, Olivier made a great show of soldierly skill and daring on "Hide fox, and all after" (IV.ii.30–31). "It is not a usual experience," the *Stage* reported, "to see a Hamlet placed practically under arrest and scattering his guards like ninepins before he departs for England" (7 January 1937).

For the rest, there is only Agate's unsympathetic testimony. The "How all occasions" soliloquy (IV.iv.32ff.) was done "incomparably well," but it was a case of too little, too late: "The lines 'I do not know why yet I live to say, etc.' are trumpet-moaned as though it has at last broken in on the young man that indecision is his bane. Up to that time Hamlet has been the one person in all Denmark likeliest to get his own way about anything from pitch-and-toss to slaughter." There was not enough "reflective emotion" in the graveyard. The fencing was done with "real virtuosity," but the final moment confirmed the actor's incompatibility with the character; he was simply too much the heroic avenger to die pathetically (London *Sunday Times*, 10 January 1937).

The production ran for only six weeks, and except for a brief revival at Kronborg Castle the following summer, Olivier never again played the part on the stage. A decade later, however, he directed and starred in a film version of the play and in that medium created a Hamlet which has undoubtedly been seen by more people than any other in the history of the role. It opened at the Odeon in London on 6 May 1948, with the King and Queen in attendance, the performance being a benefit for King George's Pension Fund for Actors and Actresses. The New York opening was at the Park Theatre on 29 September 1948.

In his second portrayal Olivier exhibited in more marked degree the features that had defined his first Hamlet. Maturity had, if anything, made him look even more powerfully athletic. With his hair dyed blond and worn short and his cheekbones and jawline emphasized by makeup, he was the image of vigorous Nordic manhood. He moved and gestured very little; this time he was more discus-thrower in repose than acrobat. It was strength taken for granted, not insisted on, and somehow more palpable for being so. Vocally also he seemed a man confident of his power, the sort of man accustomed "to say to one, 'Go,' and he goes, and to another, 'Come,' and he comes." He could be soft-spoken as well as stentorian, but the ring of authority was unmistakable in either case.

The impression of ready resourcefulness and of easy mastery which Olivier conveyed by his mere physical presence in the role was greatly amplified by cuts in the text.[3] The problem he had encountered earlier of making audiences believe that so obviously strong and able a man would ever have delayed Olivier very nearly eliminated on this occasion by the simple and drastic expedient of eliminating the delay, or most of it. He cut not only Hamlet's *talk* of procrastination, by excising the "O what a rogue and peasant slave" (II.ii.550–605) and "How all occasions do inform against me" (IV.iv.32–66) soliloquies, but much of the *evidence* of it. By radical curtailment of the action itself, he greatly shortened the distance between Hamlet's receipt of the Ghost's charge and his confirmation of Claudius' guilt, and Hamlet thus seemed to be tending to business much more promptly than is usually the case. Rosencrantz and Guildenstern did not appear, and the omission not only speeded up the action but meant that Hamlet had no one to whom he could report his strange lethargy: "I have of late—but wherefore I know not—lost all my mirth . . . " (II.ii.295–310). The players thus arrived sooner, announced by Polonius, and were hustled off to supper without Hamlet's having asked their leader to recite for him Aeneas' tale to Dido. He did take time to ask for the insertion of some lines of his own in the play to be performed on the morrow, but that proved superfluous; in the event, only the dumb-show was presented.

Despite these and other cuts, *some* delay was still evident and this Olivier attempted to account for the way he had at the Old Vic—by giving Hamlet an Oedipus complex. Everybody noticed it this time;[4] through symbol and business it was made so obvious that even those who could not have put a name to it must have seen that there was something abnormal in Hamlet's relationship with his mother. The Freudian explanation of Hamlet's delay was also prepared for by a

Laurence Olivier. The Closet Scene (III.iv). The J. Arthur Rank film, 1948. Harvard Theatre Collection.

prologue, in which Olivier's voice was heard on the soundtrack speaking a shortened version of the "vicious mole of nature" passage (I.iv.23–36). Apparently audiences were expected to connect this preliminary reference to "the stamp of one defect" with subsequent telltale signs of psychic disorder in Hamlet's behavior. Immediately following the quotation, Olivier added the statement "This is the tragedy of a man who could not make up his mind," by which he apparently meant to suggest that Hamlet is indecisive because of "a particular fault," namely, his subconscious Oedipal longings.[5] Occasional exposure of Hamlet's unconscious did little to rescue the characterization from psychological shallowness. Seeing Hamlet kiss his mother full on the mouth—for that was the chief method of revealing the complex—could not compensate for the loss of the two soliloquies and the "quintessence of dust" passage. This was a Hamlet barely conversant with spiritual anguish, a Hamlet little inclined to scrutinize in pain and anger the terms of the human contract with the gods.

And yet he was not all extrovert either. "O, that this too too solid flesh" and "To be or not to be" were still there to indicate a troubled soul-life. Not everything was sacrificed to clarity and excitement. "He finds time," said the London *Times*, "to turn away from his dramatic leaps and runs . . . to commune with his own conscience and his secret self. Not much time, to be sure. . . . " There was unquestionably "some pandering to melodrama," but the character was not completely turned to pasteboard, and it was in any case "melodrama magnificently managed" (5 May 1948). This assessment accords very well with Olivier's own modest claims for the film. He asked that it be viewed not as a representation of the "true" Hamlet but merely as an "essay in Hamlet," a "treatment," which used some of Shakespeare's materials, rearranged here and there, while deliberately excluding others, so as to appeal to the average movie patron.[6] Judged in that light, the film was an honorable and laudatory accomplishment. Speaking, as it were, for the scholarly establishment, James McManaway wrote, "Much of the complexity and subtlety of Hamlet's character has been edited out of the script, along with much of the richness and complexity of the story. What remains is magnificent action and splendid poetry, but this is not all of Shakespeare's *Hamlet*."[7]

For all its limitations, Olivier's film portrayal abounds in imaginative and provocative strokes of interpretation.[8] Hamlet is not seen until addressed by Claudius, and he does not reply to him, either aside or directly.[9] He sits a little apart from the council table and faced away from it, shrouded in melancholy. His response to Gertrude is without satiric edge; mourning has left no place for other feelings. She kisses him on the mouth in parting, but there is no lust in it, for either of them. It is merely an old habit, the subterranean "meaning" of which is unknown to them, though guessed at, it may be, by Claudius, who stands scowling in the background.

The soliloquy (I.ii.129–59), like others to come, is not spoken but "thought"; that is, the words come from the soundtrack, as a voice-over, while Hamlet sits brooding with lips closed. The mood from start to finish is one of utter dejection. His mother's incestuous frailty provokes neither tears nor anger. He seems a man so depressed in spirit as to be incapable of emotion.

He speaks "I am glad to see you well" (I.ii.160) mechanically, while moving away, cutting dead an unwelcome intruder, then realizes it is Horatio and greets him courteously. But he remains low in spirits. "Thrift, thrift, Horatio" contains only the slightest hint of sarcasm. "Saw who?" is given as two separate questions with precisely the same inflection. He takes in their intelligence with cool self-possession, analyzes it, weighs it, and decides on a course of action. One has the impression of a well-trained mind, adept at problem-solving. The closing soliloquy is a voice-over down to "foul deeds will rise"; the rest is spoken, in a whisper. It is calm, firm, purposeful, with no touch of awe or bravado.

On the platform he has the air of a man very much at home with danger and mystery, at ease and unthreatened. He speaks of the native drinking custom and its effect on Denmark's reputation in the tone of a naturally reflective man puzzling over an intriguing phenomenon. At the Ghost's appearance he grows excited but not frightened. His first words are made to mean something near to "Whatever you are, I mean to stand my ground." On "I'll call thee Hamlet . . ." he grows progressively more anxious lest the Spirit vanish without communicating with him. "O, answer me!" is half plea and half demand. He breaks from his friends with a fine show of valor in both body and voice. On "My fate cries out . . ." (I.iv.81–86), he is as spirited and game as Henry V at the walls of Harfleur.[10]

"Alas, poor Ghost" and "O God" are subdued, contained, involuntary vocalizations of private thoughts. "Murder!" is made a surprised question. There is a mixture of grief and anger on "Haste me to know it.'' He bites his knuckle to hold back tears at the mention of the ''most seeming-virtuous queen.'' As the Ghost describes the poisoning, the picture dissolves to a reenactment of the scene.

Hamlet falls supine when left alone, then rolls over, struggles to raise himself and falls prone. The first few lines are tearful, but tight-lipped determination and seething anger soon supplant grief. He is on his feet, sword in hand, fully heroic on ''I'll wipe away all trivial fond records.'' By ''unmixed with baser matter'' he is in a snarling rage; on ''Yes, by heaven!'' he points the sword heavenward, then hurls it from him. The reference to ''tables'' is cut. After ''So uncle, there you are,'' he recovers the sword and holds it as a cross for ''I have sworn't.''

He is guarded from the first with Horatio and Marcellus, making no distinction between them. ''There's never a villain dwelling in all Denmark'' is given as a simple statement of fact. Then, after a very long pause, ''But he's an arrant knave'' is added, as something newly discovered and most surprising. The rest of the scene is taken at great speed, but there is no sense of hysteria, either real or feigned. He seems preoccupied, impatient for action. ''O cursed spite'' is a manful shouldering of a heavy but by no means insupportable burden.

Hamlet is *seen* visiting Ophelia's closet, as she describes the scene to Polonius. He plays it as a somnambulant—vacant-eyed, absent, with no hint that his behavior is anything but genuine.

He does not merely chance to overhear the plan to bait a trap with Ophelia but is shown deliberately eavesdropping, starting at Polonius' line ''Take this from this . . . '' (II.ii.156). Before making himself seen by the conspirators, he prepares himself, actor-fashion, and then makes an entrance with a consciously assumed air of deep absorption in his book. Once in view, he supports himself against a pillar with his elbow and puts his hand to his eyes, as if pondering over what he has been reading. The colloquy with Polonius is all subtle, light, and deft play-acting. Hamlet seems completely relaxed and assured, skillfully executing a plan and enjoying himself in the process. There is neither anger nor pain behind the mask of eccentricity. It is all calculated foolery, as when he looks around for a third party on ''Between who?'' With a casual glance he applies ''most weak hams'' to Polonius, but there is no cutting edge to his voice. Even ''except my life, except my life, except my life,'' tossed over his shoulder as he drifts off, is entirely for Polonius' benefit, a cryptic statement revealing nothing of the inner man.

The nunnery scene follows immediately. Moving to another part of
the castle he sees Ophelia at her prie-dieu and without speaking the
"To be or not to be" soliloquy (reserved for later) says "Soft you
now . . ." and approaches.[11] He runs his hand lightly over the arras
located at some distance behind her, gives a look around the room,
tosses his book over his shoulder and goes up to her. "Nymph, in thy
orisons / Be all my sins remembered" is a mild command. He glances
around repeatedly as she speaks of returning his remembrances, and
his mind is clearly occupied with locating the spies when he replies,
"No, not I, / I never gave you aught." After her protest, he asks "Are
you honest?" and, following her reply, goes directly to "I did love
you once," leaving out "Are you fair?" and the subsequent disquisi-
tion on honesty and beauty (III.i.110–14). Down through the end of
the first nunnery speech he is disappointed with her and himself and
saddened by the course their relationship seems to be taking. The lines
are whispered, confidential, meant for her ears alone. He looks at the
arras again on "Where's your father?" and makes the line neither a
trap nor an accusation but a genuine request for information. Her answer touches off a sustained display of irascibility. It is not pretense
but a true expression of bitter resentment, toward Polonius and Claudius for daring to lay a trap for him and toward Ophelia for making
herself a party to the scheme. He throws her to the floor when she tries
to embrace him, and after vilifying her points to the arras on "all but
one." Then he softens toward her, apparently repenting his outburst
so far as it concerned her, kneels and kisses a lock of her hair as she
lies weeping, whispers "To a nunnery, go" and hurries out.

After a musical bridge and a shot of waves crashing against rocks
at the foot of the castle, Hamlet is seen perched on a wall high above
the sea. "To be or not to be" is given as "thought," the next few
lines as speech. He takes out his dagger, absently, on "end them" and
pointing it toward his throat, still absently, lapses into thought again,
his eyes closed. He awakes with a start on "Perchance to dream,"
reverting to speech, and continues in that mode to the end. He looks
around at the castle on "law's delay" and stares vacantly at the dagger
on "his own quietus make." The dagger slips from his hand on "we
know not of," and he watches it fall to the water below. His tone
throughout is hushed, meditative, solemn; at the end he walks off into
a bank of fog.

The next shot is of Hamlet seated in a chair in a darkened room, his hand to his brow. His reverie is broken by the entrance of Polonius announcing the arrival of the players. He beams with pleasure at the sight of the troupe, springs up to meet them and addresses them with easy joviality. "I am glad to see thee well" is bestowed on a puppy that has barked in greeting. After conferring with the First Player and sending him off, he glances around at a raised portion of the floor some distance away, runs to it, does a pirouette in the circle of light falling on it and shouts "The play's the thing / Wherein I'll catch the conscience of the King" (II.ii.604–5).

This is followed by a cross-fade to Hamlet delivering instructions to the players (III.ii.1–45). There is no sense of urgency in his remarks. He is elegant, poised, urbane, the cultured and knowledgeable amateur at ease with professionals. Sight of the First Player practicing a gesture prompts "Nor do not saw the air." As he speaks the last lines he puts a blond wig on the boy actor, then winces in pain as he sees that he has thus transformed him into a grotesque likeness of Ophelia. But he recovers quickly and claps him reassuringly on the shoulder as he says, "Go, make you ready." To Horatio he says only, "Observe my uncle. Give him heedful note. They are coming to the play; I must be idle. Get you a place."

The court enters now, in stately procession down a long, open, curved staircase. With exaggerated gallantry Hamlet rushes up to take Gertrude's hand from Claudius and lead her down himself—much to Claudius' dislike. "So capital a calf" is said for all to hear, but it is merely good-natured raillery and the lords and ladies chuckle appreciatively. His face clouds over on "Here's metal more attractive." He takes Ophelia to her place rather roughly but masks it from the court. He seems to loathe her now but to be pretending otherwise. He sits at her feet, his head in her lap. "Country matters" is more affable naughtiness than open insult. He is loudly vicious on "look you, how cheerfully my mother looks" but "O heavens, die two months ago . . . " is done with mocking jauntiness.

The Prologue then appears and speaks. Hamlet comments ruefully on the brevity of woman's love; Ophelia, stung, immediately says, "You are keen my Lord," and is told, "It would cost you a groaning to take off mine edge" (III.ii.249–50). The camera now concentrates on the dumb-show, on Claudius' reaction to it and on the court's growing concern over his extreme discomposure. Except for one exchange of glances with Horatio, Hamlet is not seen (or heard from) until just before the exit of the court. Spectators unfamiliar with the full text of *Hamlet* are apt to have little comprehension of what is going on here. Since Hamlet has not spoken the "guilty creatures sitting at a play" passage (II.ii.588–94) or revealed to Horatio that there is to be a scene in the play which might provoke Claudius to reveal his guilt (III.ii.75–77), the only verbal indication that the performance is a trap for Claudius engineered by Hamlet lies in the single line "The play's the thing / Wherein I'll catch the conscience of the King." Evidently the audience is meant to infer Hamlet's strategem from the fact that the dumb-show very closely resembles the earlier enactment of the actual poisoning in the garden. It is not much to go on.[12]

When Claudius rises in his place and bellows for light, a torch is seen moving through the darkness and being thrust into his face, whereupon the camera pulls back to reveal Hamlet as the bearer. Hamlet then laughs diabolically, scattering the court. Gertrude pauses in her exit to stare at him disapprovingly, and he looks after her in surprise, as if realizing for the first time that she might have been an accomplice. "Why, let the stricken deer go weep" is sung out in high-pitched, hysterical triumph as Hamlet stands on the throne, waving the torch over his head; as he concludes he throws it from him. He confers excitedly with Horatio and is interrupted by Polonius, speaking Guildenstern's line "Good my lord, vouchsafe me a word with you" (III.ii.296). The dialogue continues, Polonius still "standing in" for Guildenstern, down through "but to the matter: my mother, you say,—" (III.ii.324–25). Polonius replies with Rosencrantz' line "She desires to speak with you in her closet ere you go to bed" (331) and receives Hamlet's answer: "We shall obey, were she ten times our mother." Polonius then gives his usual entrance line, "My lord, the queen would speak with you, and presently" (375), and the rest of the scene is played out as written except for the omission of "They fool me to the top of my bent" (384). Hamlet's manner through it all is one of feigned frivolity. " 'By and by' is easily said" (387), Olivier gives as an aside, making it an apprehensive reflection on the painful interview to come. The "witching time" soliloquy is whispered thoughtfully. "Now could I drink hot blood" (390) is without passion. He seems surprised to hear himself saying it; he is a man dispassionately analyzing the sudden appearance of a strange new emotion.

Coming upon Claudius, he draws a long dagger worn at his back and raises it on high with both hands, ready to stab downward through his victim's neck, then stops with it there and goes into "Now might I do it pat" (III.iii.73–96). The speech is another voice-over, its tone quietly pensive. There is no suggestion of "excuse," but no blood-thirstiness either. It is a decision rationally taken.

He meets Gertrude with the weapon still in his hand and points it at her, unconsciously, as he talks. He is harsh but not wild. When she takes fright at the sight of the dagger and says "Thou wilt not murther me?" (III.iv.21), he glances down at it, surprised to discover that he has been menacing her with it. "Dead for a ducat, dead" is full-voiced and vicious, "Nay, I know not" very quiet and "Is it the King?" a loud, wild shout of hope. He wipes his dagger on the arras after pronouncing Polonius' epitaph.

Hamlet and Gertrude each wear a locket for use in the comparison of the two brothers. As he rages at his mother for her unaccountable lust, Hamlet struggles with her on a large double bed, at the head of which hang draperies pinned open in a way that strongly suggests a *mons veneris*. But there is nothing overtly lascivious in their physical intimacy.

The Ghost is not shown this time, his presence being denoted only by the throbbing sound that accompanied his earlier appearances. Hamlet looks around wildly and falls on one side on the floor. He speaks to the Ghost reverently and remorsefully. On "How is it with you, lady?" he moves on his knees to his mother's side without taking his eyes off the Spirit.

After the Ghost's departure he speaks sternly and authoritatively to his mother and gradually grows more tender. Toward the end he kneels in front of her. She kisses him on the cheek and then lingeringly on the mouth, then draws his head to her bosom. After a time he puts his head in her lap, smiling with innocent, boyish happiness. "This man shall set me packing; / I'll lug the guts into the neighbor room" (211–12) is brisk and unfeeling. Then he gives his mother a final kiss on the mouth. All the embracing and kissing is not only passionless but styl-ized, rather like the love-making of characters in a classical ballet. Hamlet's sexual desire for his mother remains securely locked in his unconscious mind. He speaks the final words over Polonius as if filing away a moderately interesting piece of information and drags the body off with no more emotion than if it were a piece of furniture.

He is next seen arraigned before Claudius, under guard, but leaning against a pillar in an attitude of studied nonchalance. He answers

Claudius' questions about Polonius with an almost foppish flightiness which seems part pretense, part genuine indifference to his situation. He grows melancholy at mention of England. He stares intently at the King on "Farewell, dear mother" and gives the line as if deep in thought. He keeps the same tone on "My mother; father and mother is one flesh . . . " (IV.iii.51–53), treating it like a soliloquy; he seems to be working out for the first time the relationship between them; it is the dawn of a realization, a new light on things, and seems to say that Hamlet must now deal with the fact that by striking at Claudius he will be hurting his mother as well.

At the close of the scene there is a cut to Horatio receiving Hamlet's letter, from Osric. As he begins to read it in silence, Hamlet is heard speaking the words. As he describes the encounter with the pirate ship, the scene is enacted on screen and Hamlet is shown making his escape by swinging across on a rope, in the manner of innumerable cinematic swashbucklers.

Ophelia's mad scene follows, and then the graveyard scene. As Hamlet makes his entrance, the shadow of his head is seen to fall over the skull of Yorick as it lies in the dust. All the early remarks about the identity of the several skulls being knocked about by the grave-maker are cut. Hamlet goes immediately to "Whose grave's this, sir-rah?" (V.i.117). His questions and replies are not strongly marked by feelings of any sort. He is not amused nor keenly interested, but nei-ther does he seem to be in any pain. There is something almost per-functory about it, as though he wishes to occupy his mind and con-siders this conversation as good a way as any to do it. He feels a little stab of pain at being told that "This same skull, sir, was, sir, Yorick's skull, the king's jester." He reflects on his old friend's end more in wonder than in anguish. "How strange that it should come to this," he seems to say. He grows playful on "Now get you to my lady's chamber," holding the skull up along side his own head. "Make her laugh at that" is whispered in Yorick's ear, with just the trace of a smile. The skull is allowed to fall to the ground on "And smelt so? pah!"

The funeral procession follows immediately. "What, the fair Ophe-lia!" is a choked whisper, barely audible. He spreads his arms wide on "This is I, / Hamlet the Dane"; he is a brave knight throwing down a challenge and relishing the coming combat. Laertes comes out of the grave to close with him. Hamlet shouts out his protest with disciplined, hard-edged, martial ferocity until "I loved Ophelia," which is given quietly, slowly, with equal emphasis on each word; there is a suggestion of surprise in his voice, as if he has only just now been shocked into the realization by her death. Then he returns to his former bellicosity and sustains it down to "I'll rant as well as thou," on which he seems to regain his composure. "What is the reason that you use me thus? / I loved you ever" (V.i.289–90) is puzzled and hurt. "The cat will mew and dog will have his day" (292) is a firm, controlled promise of retribution to come.

The scene now shifts to the conference between Claudius and Laertes in which the plot is hatched to kill Hamlet in a duel. That scene over, Hamlet and Horatio appear, and Hamlet begins with the compliment to Horatio, "Thou art e'en as just a man . . . " (III.ii.54–55), brought over from the play scene. He says, "Nay, do not think I flatter" (57), and then jumps ten lines to "for thou hast been / As one, in suffering all . . . " and ends with "Something too much of this" (74). He speaks it as much to himself as to Horatio, as if musing aloud on the fact that men differ greatly in their relations with Fortune. At the end, he goes to "But I am very sorry, good Horatio, / That to Laertes I forgot myself . . . " (V.ii.75–79). Osric enters, as prescribed, at the end of that speech. Hamlet behaves toward him with relaxed urbanity, revealing only slight impatience and mild amusement. He corrects and mocks Osric's affectations with a good grace that is almost comradely. He paces about in silence for a great while before deciding to accept the challenge, but his reply is spirited and seemingly untroubled. The last line of the speech on providence is omitted ("Since no man of aught he leaves . . . " [V.ii.223–24]), and to fill its place he borrows a line from earlier in the scene: "There's a divinity that shapes our ends, / Rough-hew them how we will" (10–11). He smiles slightly throughout, and his tone suggests amused detachment, a willingness to accept whatever might come, without questioning either its meaning or its fairness.

He speaks the entire apology to Laertes (V.ii.226–44) in a tone of the most magnanimous courtliness. As he prepares for the duel he seems in the best of spirits, affable, charming and confident. The early bouts are protracted and exciting, and Hamlet plays them with a connoisseur's enjoyment. After Laertes pricks him in the arm, when he is turned away with his guard down, Hamlet engages him and after about three strokes sends his opponent's weapon flying aloft. When it falls to the ground, he puts his foot on it, and after throwing his own foil to Laertes, takes it up. He fights with icy calm now, bearing down relentlessly as if absolutely certain of the outcome. After forcing an opening, he contents himself with pricking Laertes in the wrist, evening the score but inflicting no harsher penalty.[13] On ''Treachery! seek it out,'' Hamlet rushes up the staircase to the gallery. When Laertes names his accomplice in the plot, Hamlet dives down on Claudius, brings him to the floor, stands over him and stabs him in the abdomen with three short, rapid, piston-like strokes. As Hamlet moves away, Claudius gets to his feet and staggers about looking for a means of escape. Hamlet blocks his way, takes up the poisoned cup and pours its contents down his throat, forcing him to the ground as he does so.

Hamlet dies sitting on the throne. He is calm and composed and seems about to smile. He speaks ''The rest is silence'' as if surprised at the discovery. Horatio delivers the funeral instructions. As the procession moves through the castle with Hamlet's body, a cannon is heard firing and its flashes illuminate first Polonius' chamber, then the chapel with the crucifix before which Claudius has tried to pray, and finally Gertrude's bed, with its symbolic hangings.

The general impression is of a thoroughly captivating man, a boy's dream of adult male perfection: handsome, good-humored, loving, intelligent, sensitive, sophisticated, brave, unfailingly masterful, a man who lived a blameless life and died a noble death. One almost expects to hear Horatio say at the end not ''Good night, sweet prince'' but ''His life was gentle, and the elements / So mixed in him that Nature might stand up / And say to all the world, 'This was a man.' ''

NOTES

1. Directed by Tyrone Guthrie, the production was mounted on a unit set (by Martin Battersby) made up of stonework galleries and levels; an apron stage was added and provided with steps allowing for movement to and from the area beneath. The costumes, by Osborne Robinson, were simplified Elizabethan. The full text was used.

2. Felix Barker, *The Oliviers* (Philadelphia: Lippincott, 1953), p. 146.

3. See *Hamlet: The Film and the Play*, ed. Alan Dent (London: World Film Publications, 1948), where the full text is given with cuts indicated by brackets. Dent was Olivier's textual adviser, and he defends his excisions in an introductory essay.

4. See, for example, John Ashworth, ''Olivier, Freud, and Hamlet,'' *At-*

lantic Monthly, May 1949, pp. 30–33; John McCarten, *New Yorker*, 2 October 1948; Robert Hatch, *New Republic*, 4 October 1948; Margaret Marshall, *Nation*, 23 October 1948.

5. Olivier seems to have been unable to make up his own mind about the reasons for Hamlet's delay. In discussing his approach to the character, he wrote, "Perhaps he was the first pacifist, perhaps Dr. Jones is sound in his diagnosis of the Oedipus complex, perhaps there is justification in many other complexes that have been foisted on to him—perhaps he just thought too much . . . ." (Olivier, "An Essay in *Hamlet*," in *The Film Hamlet: A Record of Its Production*, ed. Brenda Cross [London: Saturn Press, 1948], p. 15). One critic thought the prologue revealed that Olivier wanted to have it both ways, "to pretend to honor the traditional 'mystery' of Hamlet's hesitation while he patently accepted the quasi-scientific Oedipal interpretation" (Parker Tyler, "Hamlet and Documentary," *Kenyon Review* 11 [1949]: 529).

6. Olivier, "An Essay in *Hamlet*," p. 11.

7. James McManaway, "The Laurence Olivier *Hamlet*," *Shakespeare Association Bulletin* 24 (1949): 10. Another scholar-critic noted with pleasure that Olivier had adopted the view put forward by Kittredge and others that Hamlet was essentially an heroic activist; see R. W. Babcock, "George Lyman Kittredge, Olivier and the Historical Hamlet," *College English* 11 (1950): 256–65.

8. My account is based on a recent private screening at which, acting as my own projectionist, I was able to stop and repeat sequences. I am concerned here only with Olivier's acting of the central character; for an analysis of the strictly cinematic aspects of the film, see Jack J. Jorgens, *Shakespeare on Film* (Bloomington: Indiana University Press, 1977), pp. 207–17.

9. The main set, designed by Roger Furse, was a massive Norman castle. The costumes, also by Furse, were a fusion of styles shown in portraits by Holbein and Titian. For details, see Furse's "Designing the Film *Hamlet*," in *Hamlet: The Film and the Play*, n.p.

10. Speaking of Olivier's overall characterization, William Whitebait wrote, "He isn't Hamlet, but Henry V with a foul wind" (*New Statesman and Nation*, 8 May 1948). Olivier's celebrated screen portrayal was first seen in 1943.

11. This is one of several transpositions of speeches and scenes, none of which is indicated in the published text.

12. McManaway wrote that the drastic cutting made the performance by the players seem "a casual accident, not an essential part of the warp and woof of the story" ("The Laurence Olivier *Hamlet*," p. 8).

13. I have found no record of anyone else using this business, either before or since, but it has much to recommend it. As far as Hamlet knows at this point, Laertes is guilty of nothing more than unsportsmanlike conduct and thus deserves only to be repaid with a similar "foul."

14

RICHARD BURTON

When Richard Burton (1925–1984) appeared as Hamlet at the Old Vic in the late summer of 1953, most viewers were reminded of Laurence Olivier;[1] he had the older actor's brusque and peremptory way with the verse.[2] Passages that John Gielgud and others were wont to treat as arias he tossed off as though ashamed of them or as if in fear of being caught "quoting." Such vocal effects as he did command took the form of arbitrary shifts from shouting to whispering, or slow progressions up and down the scale which sounded artificial without quite managing to be beautiful. His delivery became somewhat more successfully musical as he settled into the role, but not so much as to invalidate J. C. Trewin's early observation that "he has not much poetry" (*Illustrated London News*, 5 September 1953).

But it was Burton's vitality and virility, his "vigorous, elastic presence," which most evoked comparisons with Olivier. Like Olivier, he was "as fiery as Hotspur" and as acrobatic as Douglas Fairbanks. To evade his would-be captors in the aftermath of the Polonius slaying, he vaulted off the stage into the audience. Still, it was not simply a carbon copy. Burton was more burly than lithe, and whereas Olivier resembled a graceful cricketer, Burton was called a "Hamlet in rugger boots" (London *Daily Express*, 15 September 1953). He was not quite an aristocrat, let alone a Prince of the blood, not so much a Renaissance courtier as a rebellious working-class youth of the fifties, an angry young man in doublet and hose. The London *Daily Sketch* described him as "the lonely, angry odd man out" (25 August 1953) and "fury" was repeatedly named as the emotion most in evidence in his portrayal. He could "set the stage ablaze with his hatred," said the London *Daily Mail*, "merely by standing still and staring blackly at nothing" (25 August 1953).

If Burton's portrayal stirred associations with contemporary class tensions, it was probably an accident of his proletarian background rather than the result of a conscious effort on his part to strike sparks of social relevance. At any rate, he did not speak in those terms when he set down his thoughts about the character in an essay written while he was playing it. Instead, he described Hamlet as "a man who could not only make up his mind, but who knew very well what he was about." No obstacle buried in the unconscious kept him from Claudius' throat. He believed in the law of "an eye for an eye" and was ready to enforce it at the first opportunity. That moment came when he found Claudius unguarded at prayer, and he held off his hand then only in order to take a more terrible and complete revenge at a more suitable moment, when his quarry was "about some act / That has no relish of salvation in't."[3]

There was a close correlation between Burton's stated view of the character and the impression he created in performance. He could be tender, ironic, melancholy and philosophic in season, but each of these moods seemed not a delaying tactic or an insurmountable roadblock but merely a temporary abatement of the righteous anger which propelled him relentlessly forward. He was a Hamlet who never lost his way, however much he might pause to examine the inner and outer landscapes he was traversing.

Most of the critics preferred to see Hamlet baffled and stalled, not the master but the victim of painful and mysterious circumstance. Burton's was a powerful performance, but not really the Hamlet that Shakespeare drew. Only Ivor Brown dissented. He considered Burton's single-minded avenger "truly Elizabethan" and was sure "it would have satisfied both the old groundlings who wanted the blood, and the gentry in the galleries, who preferred to have the blood mixed with brains" (*Observer*, 20 August 1953). Evidently Burton's contemporary audiences were equally well satisfied. He received eighteen curtain calls on opening night at the Old Vic and played to full houses throughout the season, reaching a total of 101 nonconsecutive performances on 26 May 1954. A pilgrimage to Elsinore followed in June.

Eleven years later, in connection with the Shakespeare quadricentennial observances, Burton made a second appearance in the role, in a production directed by John Gielgud. After tryouts in Toronto and Boston, it opened at New York's Lunt-Fontanne Theatre on 9 April 1964. Burton's choice of Gielgud to direct him looks odd at first glance, considering the general public perception of the great differences between the two in style and temperament. But Burton considered Gielgud's portrayal the best he had ever seen, and believed that his many revivals made him more knowledgeable about the character and the play than anyone then working in the theater. In addition, the two men had a fair foundation for a working relationship in the shared belief that it was the actor's task to play each moment for its own inherent value instead of trying to make successive speeches and scenes illustrate some all-pervasive aspect of the character or some controlling dramatic theme.[4]

To some members of the cast it thus seemed that neither Burton nor Gielgud had what they considered an interpretation, or concept, of the play, and in this they anticipated the reaction of a number of critics.[5] Robert Brustein, in the *New Republic*, called Burton "chancy and erratic, effective from moment to moment, but lacking a consistent design" (13 June 1964), and Henry Hewes wrote that "the most memorable moments in Burton's performance are unrelated" (*Saturday Review*, 25 April 1964). Others spoke not of a lack of an architectonic principle but of the absence of emotional commitment. Burton seemed distracted, apart, insufficiently connected to the passions he was called on to render. Walter Kerr felt a "defeating coolness at the heart of the venture" (New York *Herald Tribune*, 10 April 1964), and Harold Clurman could see only technique where there should have been deep personal engagement (*Nation*, 4 May 1964).

Gielgud's staging evidently contributed something to the impression that Burton and the other actors were not sufficiently immersed in their roles to carry conviction. The production was designed to give the appearance of a final run-through, prior to technical rehearsals, with the actors in street clothes, on a bare stage, employing a mixture of real, improvised and simply pantomined properties.[6] The idea was to strip the play of visual distractions in order to promote greater concentration on the text itself. Unfortunately, the rehearsal atmosphere left the cast open to the charge of being not quite up to performance pitch, of merely going through the motions.

But for every eye that spied out hollowness or lack of design, there was another that discerned and approved those qualities which had excited London in 1953. Burton was vibrantly masculine, the scourge of folly and perfidy, never "dreamy" or "milky," a champion overmatched but uncowed, hurtling along toward disaster. "Even in the moments of indecision or dismay," said Norman Nadel, "you can see his mind—not floundering or going numb, but already searching out, testing and taking aim toward a new course of action" (New York *World-Telegram*, 10 April 1964). He was not quite so ferocious as before. He had been accused of lacking charm in 1953, and he sought to remedy that by smiling more and by pausing to laugh occasionally at his own tempestuousness. But it was still a predominantly angry Hamlet, a Hamlet nettled and stung by all that was revealed to him in the glaring light of intelligence which he trained ceaselessly on the world.

Burton spoke nearly the full text and illuminated it with a combination of innovative and traditional business and line readings.[7] He came late to the presence-chamber, ignored the bows of courtiers and with his own head bowed made his way deliberately to a place apart and seated himself with his back to the King and Queen. His early replies were soft-spoken, level, without feeling. He moved away to avoid a proferred caress on "I shall in all my best obey you, madam" (I.ii.120). He began the soliloquy in listless dejection, but anger gradually bubbled to the surface. He pointed contemptuously at the King's chair on "That it should come to this!" (137) and made "Frailty, thy name is woman" (146) a furious denunciation. After building to a tumultuous climax on "incestuous sheets" he settled back into despair and ended with a hint of tears. He said "Horatio! Or I do forget MYSELF!" (161), used Gielgud's half-distracted reading on "Saw who?" and carried on the interrogation with mounting speed and intensity.

The Ghost was represented by a recorded offstage voice and a shadow on the rear wall. Gielgud himself spoke the lines, a circumstance which probably had much to do with the fact that the device wholly escaped the abuse which had greeted it when Arthur Hopkins tried it in the John Barrymore production. Burton inferred the Ghost's presence from the look of horror on Horatio's face, turned, gave a cry of anguish, crossed himself and fell to his knees. He made questions of "King? Father?" and an emphatic statement of "Royal Dane!" Having seized a sword from Marcellus on "I'll make a ghost of him that lets me" (I.iv.85), he converted it to a protective cross as he followed the shade. On "And in the porches of my ears did pour / The leprous distillment" (I.v.63–64) he covered his own ear and recoiled in pain. He took for his own "O, horrible, O, horrible, most horrible!" (80) and made each repetition a deeper descent into pain. "A couch for luxury and damned incest" (83) brought out a half-articulated cry of denial.

In the ensuing soliloquy he lowered his voice one note on each of the four words "O most pernicious woman!" (105), making them sound like "worthless coins being dropped into a canyon." It was, said Kerr, a judgment on his mother so final as to suggest that "for her Judgement Day will be an entirely superfluous occasion" (New York *Herald Tribune*, 10 April 1964). In pantomime, he took a tablet and pencil from his pocket, wrote on it, concluded with a great flourish, clapped the table shut, raised it above his head and then returned it to its place.

He varied the traditional business somewhat in the immediately following moments, waiting until "Touching this vision here" (137) to indicate that Hamlet at first starts to reveal all and then retreats because he mistrusts Marcellus. The earlier line, "There's ne'er a villain dwelling in all Denmark / But he's an errant knave" (123–24), was given without a change of tone, as a coherent piece of pure evasiveness. "Old Mole" and the other mocking epithets were given as if to suggest that Hamlet half believes the Ghost is the devil and is therefore undeserving of reverence. But he returned to reverence on "Rest, rest, perturbed spirit" (182), kissing his fingers and touching them to the ground. Kerr saw in Burton's reaction to the Ghost's message a boyish joy born of the discovery of "the wild, wicked joke of life. He has a bond now with the father he loved, and it produces something more than hate; it produces humor" (New York *Herald Tribune*, 10 April 1964).

There was plenty of mischievous humor in the lobby scene. He entered with his hair mussed, as he had illustrated he would do when he spoke of adopting an antic disposition. He had his coat half on and back to front, as Polonius discovered when he solicitously helped him into the other sleeve. Smiling moronically in reply to the old man's inquiry about his health, he turned on his heel and marched off in grotesque imitation of a wind-up toy soldier, his nose buried in his book. There were more antics: he slapped Polonius' backside on "Most weak hams" and imitated the motion of the crab by walking backward. Polonius tried twice to rephrase his question after "words" and was silenced each time by Hamlet's progressively emphatic restatement of the original answer. The first "except my life" was given casually, the second "sharply in Polonius' face" and the third "sadly and introspectively." He laid aside his "straight-jacket" as Rosencrantz and Guildenstern approached, and muttered "These tedious old fools" loudly enough for Polonius to hear it.

He was affable with the spies until he caught them conferring behind his back, on "But—in the beaten way of friendship, what make you at Elsinore?" (II.ii.269–70). Growing more and more impatient with their continuing equivocation, he slammed his fist down on a table at "If you love me, hold not off!" (291). He sometimes mounted an upholstered chair on "I have of late . . . " and bounced up and down as he spoke the remainder (295–310). Burton explained the maneuver as an attempt to "unpoeticize" the speech and make the audience listen to what was being said instead of being lulled to sleep by the sonority of the famous passage.[8] But Gary Wills saw it as one of several instances of misplaced horseplay which made Burton's Hamlet appear "not a tragic character playing a clown, but simply one too trivial to know how serious his situation is" (National Review, 2 June 1964). He paused and snapped his fingers after "my uncle is King of . . . " (363–64), pretending not to remember at first that it was Denmark. He scrutinized a miniature of Claudius worn on Rosencrantz' tie but did not manhandle it.

The "O what a rogue and peasant slave" soliloquy (550–560) had a number of distinctive touches. On "For Hecuba" the three syllables of "Hecuba" were delivered as separate and distinct epithets expressing profound disgust with the paltriness of the player's motivation. He did something similar on "Bloody, bawdy, villain . . . " playing each of the epithets for its full onomatopoetic value, growling and hissing them out and building slowly to a long "Aaaahhh" of anger and pain which faded slowly away into a sob and a whisper on "Vengeance." Glancing at his hand, poised claw-like to tear at his enemy, he dropped it and laughed at his own histrionics on "Why, what an ass am I." At the end he caught sight of Claudius approaching, pointed to him on "I'll have grounds / More relative than this," gave a "cunning little laugh" and whispered the couplet "with fiendish delight."

Burton gave the "To be or not to be" soliloquy (III.i.55–87) in the hushed, unemphatic tones of self-communing. It contrasted so strongly with his pyrotechnics elsewhere that he seemed almost to be resting on his oars, making the speech come from the outer edge of the character rather than from the depths.

He kissed Ophelia on the cheek as he greeted her, and remained "ineffably tender" with her until discovering the spies, hidden behind a clothing rack, at her "There, my lord" (101). Muttering "ah haa" to himself, he crossed to a chair and sat toying with the locket she had just returned, then spoke "Are you honest?" with studied casualness. He grew angry as he questioned her further and threw the locket on a table on "I did love you once" (114). Touched by the soft despair of her reply, he directed her to a nunnery with genuine sympathy for her plight and gave way to grief, clutching a chair for support as he cataloged his imperfections. Rejecting her offer of comfort, he urged her again to seek refuge from the world of corrupt men, among whom he numbered himself. Then, returning to the suspicion that she might be an accomplice in the present plot, he seized her wrist and made a "terrible test" of "Where's your father?" (129). Her answer convicted her, and he broke away as if wanting nothing further to do with her. But an access of rage drove him back, on the attack. He seized her and dragged her around in a circle on "You jig and amble, and you lisp . . . ," pointed to her body on "make your wantonness your ignorance" and threw her roughly down on "Go to!" (144–46). "I say we will have no more marriages" (147) was spoken close to her face as she lay huddled in fear and shame, and "all but one" was directed toward Claudius. Then deflation, exhaustion, the threat of tears and a final listless, woebegone "To a nunnery, go!"

Burton's delivery of the speech to the players (III.ii.1–45) was perhaps the most original feature of his performance, and one of the most revealing. The opening lines were not so much "advice" as a clear threat of punishment to come if his instructions were not strictly followed. One heard in his voice an adamantine determination to use the play as an assault-machine against Claudius' defenses; he was a general ordering his troops to adhere to the letter of their training during the coming battle. The middle section was more comradely, more an appeal to *esprit* than a demand for unquestioning obedience, but the final line, "Go, make you ready," was a stern command.

Burton not only spoke the suggestive lines directed to Ophelia at the start of the play scene, but spotlighted their obscenity by giving exaggerated emphasis to the first syllable of "country." After sitting by her for only a moment, he began to prowl about, like a cautious but determined hunter. Noting that Claudius was drinking and conversing with some courtiers during the dumb-show, he walked up to him, took his goblet from him, and directed his attention to the performance. "That's wormwood, wormwood" (181) was said directly to Gertrude, with a sly laugh. He pushed Guildenstern's face away on "Let the galled jade wince" (242–43) and snatched Ophelia's fan from her on "I could interpret between you and your love . . ." (246).

Having seated himself on a step just beneath Claudius' chair, he rolled over and began an attenuated version of Edmund Kean's crawl on "He poisons him in the garden . . ." (261), speaking slowly and softly at first but building the pressure as he advanced. He stood up on "The story is extant . . ." and pointed to the players with the fan on "You shall see anon. . . ." The rest of the line he parceled out in short phrases, making each one a hammer blow, until at "wife!" he whipped the fan around to point at the cornered Claudius, linking him in guilt to Lucianus. Prosecutor and defendant faced each other nose to nose on the shrieking taunt "What, frighted with false fire?" (266). Then rout and exodus as Hamlet filled the air with manic laughter. After sharing his joy with Horatio and sending him off for the recorders, he bounced in glee in Claudius' chair, as he finished "Why then belike— he likes it not, perdy" (294). He backed Guildenstern across the stage on "Make you a wholesome answer" (321) and pointed to the King's empty chair of state as he facetiously explained his distemper with "Sir, I lack advancement" (340). He pulled Polonius by the coattails down to where he could point out the clouds with the recorder (a piece of painted dowel). At the end the recorder was tossed, unbroken, to Guildenstern, and the parting word, "friends," was set off and soaked in sarcasm. In the middle of the closing soliloquy he equipped himself, Irving-like, with a candelabra to light himself to his mother's chamber.

His hands were empty, however, when he came on Claudius kneeling, defenseless, his sword put by out of reach. After stealthily removing the weapon from its scabbard, Hamlet raised it as if intending to split the King's skull with it, but stopped and moved away, distracted and prompted to second thoughts by a slight movement from his intended victim. After deciding on a "more horrid hent," he tiptoed off, leaving Claudius to gasp in cold fear at the discovery of the empty scabbard.

The clothes rack served as an arras again in the closet scene, and through it staggered Polonius, impaled on Hamlet's sword, which was extracted with effort and thrown aside in disgust. The harsh words of Hamlet's farewell were tempered somewhat by the note of sorrow in his voice. He was temperate with Gertrude also, heedful of the Ghost's

injunction to leave her punishment to a higher tribunal. The lockets
were pantomimed.

As in their earlier meeting, he knelt to the Ghost and crossed himself, looking out front while the shadow hovered on the wall behind
him. He remained transfixed, his eyes never wavering, not even when
he asked, in a distracted, automatic tone, "How is it with you, lady?"
(III.iv.115). He doubted his sanity for a moment on "ecstasy?" and
sought reassurance by feeling his pulse, but did not invite Gertrude to
put him to the same test. He was pleading and tearful as he urged her
to amend her life and submitted to her comforting embrace on "I'll
blessing beg of you" (172). But a glance offstage brought a return of
dark resolve on "worse remains behind" (179), and he now sternly
demanded the abstinence he had earlier entreated of her. Thoughts of
England filled him with mischievous joy, and he chuckled as he contemplated turning the tables on his escort. The sight of Polonius,
sprawling in ignominy, also set him chuckling, but compassion quickly
broke through to the surface, and he touched the old man's face gently
before dragging him out by the wrists.

He was lightly impudent and merry when detained at swordpoint by
Rosencrantz and Guildenstern; he illustrated "to be last swallowed"
(IV.ii.19) with a gulp, and wrung the meaning out of "sponge" by
changing pitch several times as he vocalized it. After a pretense of delivering himself into their keeping, he broke away and eluded them.

In the next scene (IV.iii) he imitated Gielgud's business of pointing
to Claudius and then to his minions on "fat king" and "lean beggar."
He sniffed the air on "nose him." Going Gielgud one better, he dashed
across the stage and planted a kiss on Claudius' cheek on "Farewell,
dear mother," and then blew him a second kiss as he said "and so—
my mother." His explanation for so addressing his stepfather (51–53)
was direct, literal and vehement, with "flesh" vocally set off and
stamped out.

"How all occasions" (IV.iv.32–66) began as calm, bemused reflection, grew steadily into self-laceration and ended as a blood-oath of
total commitment to his mission.

His mood had altered discernibly when he returned from England.
The Furies were no longer nipping at his heels. Anger seemed to have
given way to profound indifference. What did human effort, devotion
to right principle, accomplishment of goals amount to in the end? The
answer lay before him in the earth. The Clown's irreverence in the

midst of mortal decay neither surprised nor saddened him. He even joined in it, juggling with Yorick's skull before returning it. His apostrophe to the dead jester was a report of an emotion once felt but now scarcely comprehensible—simply another of life's vanities.

Ophelia's funeral roused him from his torpor, and he reacted to her death with a mixture of tears and protestation. He attacked Laertes "in" the grave—represented by a table turned on its side—and for a time something of the old fire came back into his voice. But he seemed unable to believe in it fully, unable to sustain it, as if sensing that his own emotion was worth no more than Laertes' histrionics. He shrugged it off on "It is no matter" and ended the scene in much the same mood in which he had begun it.

He carried the same deadness of spirit into the next scene. The score against Rosencrantz and Guildenstern had been settled, and Claudius remained to be dealt with, but he spoke of these things without rancor or satisfaction; they were brute facts; no great significance attached to them, or to anything else. He snapped his fingers as he said "And a man's life no more than to say . . . 'one' " (V.ii.74). His witty comments to and about Osric were automatic, the product of intellectual habit, devoid of both amusement and satiric edge. The challenge was accepted offhandedly. It was a matter of no consequence, something to fill the void. In any case, he was "ready." The final words, "Let be," articulated all that he had been feeling since his return.

The apology to Laertes (V.ii.226–44), shorn of all reference to madness, was sincere and generous and yet perfunctory; he was like a man putting his affairs in order coolly and methodically before going out to face death.

When Laertes brought death closer by treacherously stabbing him from behind, he remained steadfast in his hard-won, newfound stoicism. Calmly handing his foil to Horatio, he walked across to where Laertes cowered in shame, and examined his attacker's unbated weapon. He sought Laertes' eyes, questioningly, found them averted, took the foil from his unresisting hands and, returning to Horatio, tossed his own foil across to Laertes. Then he attacked him furiously, disarmed him, and stabbed him. Taking up the poisoned cup, he ran Claudius to ground, slashed him across the chest and forced him to drink. All the old savage hatred was back in his voice as he named the King's crimes, but "Follow my mother" ended in a sob.

After the struggle with Horatio over the cup, Hamlet pulled Claudius from his seat and took his place, breathing heavily. Rising on "O, I die, Horatio," he continued to the end in a tone of patient endurance. A glance at Claudius brought forth a little chuckle of modest satisfaction. Then, "The rest is silence" and a fall forward into Horatio's arms. After eulogies by Horatio and Fortinbras, he was raised on high and carried off.

Burton did not subsequently associate himself with Shakespearean acting to the extent that his early Old Vic successes presaged, but his place among the major Hamlets of history is nevertheless secure. The New York production set a new American record of 136 consecutive performances, exceeding by four the previous high mark reached by Gielgud. At this writing, twenty years later, the record still stands.

NOTES

1. Directed by Michael Benthall, the production was first staged without scenery, on the platform stage of the Assembly Hall in Edinburgh; it opened there on 24 August 1953, as part of the Edinburgh Festival. For the move to the Old Vic, an Italian Renaissance facade (designed by John Bailey), was installed behind the proscenium, but most of the action took place on the apron.

2. Burton was twenty-seven and was already widely viewed as the best actor of the postwar generation. For his career before and after his Hamlet debut, see John Cottrell and Fergus Cashin, *Richard Burton: A Biography* (London: Barker, 1971), and Lester David and Jhan Robbins, *Richard and Elizabeth* (New York: Funk & Wagnalls; 1977).

3. "Introduction," *The Tragedy of Hamlet, Prince of Denmark* (London: Folio Society, 1954), p. 5.

4. See the interviews with Burton and Gielgud in Richard L. Sterne, *John Gielgud Directs Richard Burton in Hamlet: A Journal of Rehearsals* (New York: Random House, 1967), pp. 286–99.

5. See William Redfield, *Letters from an Actor* (New York: Viking, 1966), pp. 73, 158, and passim.

6. What the audience saw was not actually a bare stage but a setting by Ben Edwards designed to resemble one. The "clothes" were designed by Jane Greenwood; Burton wore black trousers and a black pullover.

7. Approximately 175 lines were cut, most of them in sections of five lines or less. The larger omissions were: I.iv.19–37 (on Danish drunkenness and its consequences); III.ii.275–84 ("cry of players" and "O Damon dear"); III.iv.71–81 (on Gertrude's yielding to appetite); V.i.98–117 (on the identity

of the various skulls); V.ii.12–55 (on opening and altering the King's commission). Cuts in other characters' lines were also modest.

The acting text, heavily annotated by Sterne from notes taken during performances, is given in Sterne, *Gielgud Directs Burton*. Unless otherwise indicated, my account of Burton's business is taken from this source. Descriptions of line readings in quotation marks are also from this source; in addition, I have used the recording of the performance (Columbia, DOS 702, 1974). I saw the Electronovision film transcription of the stage performance at the time of its release (September 1964), but I have not seen it since; copies are available for study at the Folger Shakespeare Library and the Library of Congress, both in Washington, D.C.

8. Interview with Sterne, *Gielgud Directs Burton*, p. 289.

15

HAMLET IN A NEW KEY

When the newly established National Theatre took up residence in its temporary home at the Old Vic in the fall of 1963, the company's director, Laurence Olivier, chose *Hamlet* for the company's historic inaugural production and cast Peter O'Toole (1932–   ) in the title role. Olivier, who mounted the production, declared in a program note that Hamlet was to be played as a rebel, a precursor of Jimmy Porter, the vituperative protagonist of John Osborne's *Look Back in Anger*: "He abhors the world in which he lives, and is forever doubting its values, testing its honesty, deriding its pretensions. In short, he is not a good social animal but a dangerous outsider, a nuisance and a threat, often unpleasant and downright offensive."[1] But O'Toole's performance did not go far toward matching that description. Bernard Levin told his readers to "ignore all the Director's nonsense in the programme about Hamlet's resemblance to Jimmy Porter" (London *Daily Mail*, 23 October 1963), and if that was putting the case too strongly, it was nevertheless true that O'Toole's Hamlet only fleetingly recalled his director's chosen model. Olivier wrote also that this was to be a Hamlet who was "not a Romantic weakling or a paragon of charm," and to that extent O'Toole did resemble Porter, but he lacked the modern antihero's white hot fury, his capacity for heaping coals of fire on the heads of the smug and the corrupt. More a conventional hero than a raging, destructive rebel without a cause, O'Toole's Hamlet resembled Olivier's own in its revelation of straightforward, full-blooded authoritative princeliness.

Two years after the Olivier-O'Toole collaboration, another director and actor set out to present Hamlet as a man with a distinctly modern sensibility, and this time there was little or no discrepancy between conception and execution. When David Warner (1941–   ) opened in

Peter Hall's production at Stratford's Royal Shakespeare Theatre on 19 August 1965, the audience saw a Hamlet who had obviously drunk deep at the well of modern thought and feeling. It was a performance fully congruent with the view of the character that Hall outlined in a talk given to the cast at the start of rehearsals. "For our decade," said Hall, "I think the play will be about the disillusionment which produces an apathy of the will so deep that commitment to politics, to religion or to life is impossible. . . . [Hamlet] is always on the brink of action, but something inside him, this disease of disillusionment, stops the final, committed action." In this respect, Hall argued, Hamlet resembled the disaffected, apathetic young intellectuals of the present day, those for whom "there is a sense of what-the-hell anyway, over us looms the Mushroom Cloud. And politics are a game and a lie, whether in our own country or in the East-West dialogue which goes on interminably without anything very real being said." [2]

In David Warner, Hall had an actor ideally suited to show the undergraduate generation of the 1960s its own image. Warner was barely twenty-four, and so tall and ungainly that he resembled an adolescent just out of his final growth spurt and not yet quite at home in his new body. His features contained a strong promise of rugged maturity, but it was not hard to believe that there might still be down on his cheeks. His stringy, dark brown hair was worn with the studied scruffiness preferred by his offstage contemporaries. His costume also linked him to the current university scene, even though the design was basically Tudor. Warner spent much of his time in a weatherbeaten academic gown; in some scenes spectacles and an enormous woolen muffler added to the impression of a latter-day Oxfordian shuffling off to a tutorial.

The muffler was there, it was facetiously suggested, "to hide the dangerous romantic associations of a bare throat" (*Spectator*, 27 August 1965), but there was little chance of Warner's being identified with the romantic Hamlet of tradition, however attired. He obviously cared nothing about being beautiful, and though he was not obtrusively slovenly he did slouch, scratch and bite his nails from time to time. To those who complained that he did not look much like a prince, Harold Hobson replied that "few princes do." If he was indifferent to elegance, so were many real-life aristocrats, and there was "no difficulty at all in imagining his background to be an ancient castle, Eton and Oxford" (London *Sunday Times*, 22 August 1965).

His delivery, too, was innocent of refinement; cadence and beauty of tone were ignored in favor of spontaneity and conviction; instead of great speeches performed by a master of vocal effect, audiences heard a man painfully, falteringly, even clumsily, turning thought and feeling into words. The illusion of on-the-spot coinage was complete. Robert Speaight wrote, "He does these things and says these things because, as far as he is concerned, no one has ever said or done them before. The result is that even the oldest of us feel that we are seeing the play for the first time."[3]

Warner's appearance, manner and delivery established a superficial association between Hamlet and contemporary young people which acted as a signpost directing attention to the deeper, spiritual kinship Hall was seeking to elucidate. In Warner's reading, Hamlet became an outsider, an existential rebel, unable to accept the improvised, jerry-built value system hypocritically promoted by the adult world he was suddenly asked to enter, and equally unable to find his way to a credible alternative. He had relied for guidance on his father and mother and with the death of one and the desertion of the other his life had lost its center, and conviction about how to proceed seemed forever beyond his grasp. "His love for his mother, and for his father," said Hall, "his attitude towards sex, his feeling for his friends, for his country, his political responsibilities, his honour, his philosophy, his religion, whether he is man or animal, king or commoner—all these are suddenly torn apart. He is crucified by an experience so complex that it leads to a profound disillusionment and finally to a terrible fatalism."

Hall emphasized Hamlet's total dependence on his father, as guardian, mentor and model, and the devastation attendant on the loss of this repository of all his faith, through an ingenious and daring piece of staging. The Ghost was represented by a ten-foot puppet with an enormous head and movable arms, clothed in a gown ample enough to conceal both an actor to speak the lines and a stagehand to provide locomotion. Into the arms of this towering authority figure Hamlet was affectionately and protectively gathered as the Ghost told his story, and he lay cradled there as he promised, halfheartedly, to seek revenge.

The alienation triggered by the loss of this fixed point of reference, this idealized and idolized lawgiver, had already been shown in Hamlet's first scene. He was discovered seated at a council table, sandwiched in acute discomfort between Claudius and Polonius, who were represented here and elsewhere as pinstriped establishment figures, amoral and unfeeling technocrats, serene masters of a world of affairs in which Hamlet could now find neither value nor meaning. His physical inclusion in their world graphically emphasized his spiritual separateness. As the London *Times* critic said, "[He] is from the start in a condition of existential panic. He has no clear identity: all he knows is that the solid appearance of the court is a facade for shifting values and lies. No one can be trusted; and the Ghost's call for vengeance is an invitation to involve himself in the life of action from which lies originate" (20 August 1965).

It was an invitation which Warner's Hamlet was ultimately unable to accept. The soliloquies were earnest, conscientious attempts to find a ground of being, to put the cosmos and himself back together again, but each step in the enterprise marked a further descent into nihilism. He gave the speech on providence (V.ii.219–24) as an unlikely supposition, a mere hypothesis to which he could not subscribe. "There are no wings in which *he* can trust," said Hobson. "He goes to his death unreconciled, unabsolved, but also unabsolving. . . . If Hamlet is condemned, God is on trial also" (London *Sunday Times*, 22 August 1965). At the end he smiled with triumph and relief; chance had taken from his shoulders the burden of impossible decision; his duty to his father had been objectively discharged, but there was nothing of himself in the deed, no belief, no engagement. Nothing had been put right, no values embraced and defended. He was still the outsider.

No substantive textual alteration was involved in this presentation of Hamlet as a modern antihero unable to believe in the efficacy of action. The omission of Hamlet's "And is't not to be damned / To let this canker of our nature come / In further evil?" (V.ii.68–70) may have been prompted by a desire to downplay his sense of duty, but the other excisions, some 725 lines in all, seem to have been made primarily in the interest of clarity and pace.[4]

Warner's performance proved extremely popular. At the end of the Stratford season the production was moved to the Aldwych, the Royal Shakespeare Company's London home, and in the spring it was returned to Stratford for another extended run in repertory; in all, it was seen 153 times. It is not surprising that young people made up a sizable (and very vocal) portion of the audience, but it must not be supposed that this was merely a faddish, teenager's Hamlet. Hobson, reviewing the opening performance, wrote, "This *Hamlet* . . . is not only off-beat; it is better in intellect and emotion than any conventional interpretation one is likely to see for some time. There are moments when it gets to the very top of theatrical experience'' (London *Sunday Times*, 22 August 1965). And Speaight, who saw it very early in the first season, called it "the most important theatrical statement on the play which has been made for a very long time."[5] The production demonstrated that *Hamlet* could be made to speak with powerful immediacy to the disinherited, rudderless inhabitants of the age of anxiety. It was a lesson which other theater artists were quick to perceive and act upon.

Just four years later London was treated to another production of the play resonant with contemporary spiritual malaise. On 17 February 1969, Nicol Williamson, (1938–   ) under the direction of Tony Richardson, opened at the Roundhouse, a Victorian locomotive shed recently converted to an open-stage theatre. The production ran for ten weeks, as announced, closing on 26 April. Working in the daytime during the latter part of the run, Richardson directed the cast in a film version of the play, using as settings not just the stage of the Roundhouse but other parts of the building as well. Immediately following the London closing the play was restaged, with several cast changes, for a limited engagement of six weeks at New York's Lunt-Fontanne Theatre. Business and blocking were necessarily altered considerably in the moves from thrust stage to screen to the proscenium stage of the Lunt-Fontanne, but Williamson's characterization remained essentially unchanged. The account of his interpretation given here derives from my study of the film, but I have also included appropriate comments from the reviews of the London and New York stage performance.[6]

That this was to be an aggressively iconoclastic Hamlet was immediately apparent in the fact that Williamson spoke with a heavy north-country accent (incorrectly identified as "Midlands" by most of the American critics). The London cast also featured a Welsh Claudius (Anthony Hopkins) and a Scottish Horatio (Gordon Jackson), but their speech, though unmistakably regional, had been perceptibly smoothed out and standardized for stage use. Williamson's diction was wholly unreconstructed. He wore his nasal twang and flat vowels (''you'' became ''yah-ooh'') like a badge of honor. He seemed downright belligerent about it; his low accent was like a red flag repeatedly thrust into the faces of the spectators. It was impossible not to be reminded of class differences in the presence of such a Hamlet, but the production did not really emphasize social conflict. Claudius came across as only slightly more aristocratic than Hamlet. Instead, Williamson's accent betokened a dispossession of a deeper sort; it was the external sign, a counterpart in sound, of an alienation that was not social but existential.

In making Hamlet an existential outsider, Williamson followed Warner's lead. But there was an important difference. Williamson was thirty years old and with his receding hairline and straggling beard looked all that and more. He was as big as Warner, but he carried himself with the settled confidence of full maturity. If Warner was a gangling undergraduate, Williamson was a postdoctoral fellow, ambling into middle age. In keeping with his appearance, Williamson revealed a Hamlet whose outlook on life was clearly the product of years of experience, not the result of recent adolescent trauma. Warner's Hamlet, one felt, had been an innocent, an unscarred and unthreatened idealist, happily immersed in the joys of student life until the very moment when terrible news had called him home to Elsinore. The two saw the same wasteland when they looked at the world, but it was a fresh discovery to Warner; Williamson had seen it all before. His father's death and his mother's remarriage seemed only the latest entries in a list of charges against life which he had been compiling for as long as he could remember. His long acquaintance with sham, corruption and defeat had made him sour and nasty. He snarled and mocked, occasionally grew weary of it, but soon roused himself to fresh outpourings of contempt and disgust. Every reflection, every encounter, simply rehearsed or reinforced a long-held conviction about the general bleakness of the human situation. He was a man who could not be surprised, except at the failure of others to grasp the terrible knowledge which was his constant companion.

In the first scene Williamson quickly establishes the image of a man who considers life a shabby and demeaning charade and those who do not know it either fools or frauds. He wears doublet and hose, but there is a rumpled, unkempt modernity about him. Clive Barnes observed, "He is more of a peasant than a poet, and more of a clerk than either" (New York *Times*, 2 May 1969). There is a raucous party in progress, and Claudius, a vulgar sensualist, is master of the revels. Hamlet surveys the scene with palpable distaste and answers Claudius with naked

Nicol Williamson. Billy Rose Theatre Collection. The New York Public Library at Lincoln Center. Astor, Lenox and Tilden Foundations.

impudence. To Gertrude he speaks sarcastically, indirectly informing her that by her vile marriage she has forfeited the right to speak to him as a mother.

The "solid flesh" soliloquy (I.ii.129–59), like the others to follow, is given directly to the audience, in the manner of a confidential aside; it is more an obligatory report on a most unpleasant topic than active self-communing. The tone is a mixture of spiritual battle-fatigue and nausea. There is nothing to wonder at in his mother's sexual "dexterity"; it is the way of the world. He says "frailty, thy name is woman" in a light singsong as though it were "sometimes a proverb" to which the time has given proof. The sickness is general, he seems to say, just as I thought. Yet he rebels at the thought. From "most unrighteous tears" to the end he beats his forehead against his clenched fist, impotently, futilely trying to drive out of consciousness the truth which his reflections have confirmed.

After at first failing to recognize Horatio, he greets him politely but not convivially. It appears extremely doubtful that this Hamlet has ever been good company, in the usual sense. One has to believe that Horatio's friendship with him is based on a generous solicitude for a fellow human being in deep trouble; they are more like nurse and patient than boon companions. "Thrift, thrift, Horatio, the funeral baked meats . . . '' (180) is given in a way that seems to say "Here is yet another example of the general badness of things against which you have so often heard me rail." He grows tremendously excited at news of the Ghost, breathing hard and speaking at breakneck speed; it is as though he hopes the Ghost might provide if not a release at least a diversion from the absurdity of daily existence. Hamlet's penultimate speech in this scene ("If it assume my noble father's person . . . '' [243–62]) and the closing soliloquy (254–57) are both cut. Hamlet says, "I will watch tonight, / Perchance 'twill walk again," and Horatio ends the scene with "I warrant it will" (241–42).

The Ghost's entrance is represented by a flood of brilliant white light. Hamlet goes to his knees immediately and speaks in a gasping whisper, trembling in awe. He is terrified, but determined to see it through. He breaks from his friends in an instant, without recourse to a weapon. (Horatio's ten lines of expostulation [I.iv.69–79] are omitted.) The Ghost's speeches, greatly shortened, are spoken by a disembodied voice, Williamson's voice. Several key words (e.g., "blood," "murder") are made to echo and reverberate. Neither man says "O, horrible, O, horrible, most horrible.'' Williamson kneels again at the beginning of the Ghost's speech and acts throughout with wholly naturalistic terror. He does not use ''tables'' but scratches ''villain'' on the wall with a dagger as he says the word, then stabs at it on ''So, uncle, there you are'' (I.v.110).

He frowns in irritation at the calls of his returning friends. He is still deeply shaken and anxious to be alone. There is no attempt at evasion on ''but he's an arrant knave.'' It is simply the best account he can come up with in his distracted state. The ''antic disposition'' line is rushed and barely audible. Indeed, most of the lines here are sacrificed to emotional truth. Auditors unfamiliar with the text can have little comprehension of what is actually being said. The Ghost is not heard from again, except for one ''Swear'' before ''Rest, rest, perturbed spirit'' (181). That line Williamson gives leaning against a wall, eyes closed, shaking his head in pain, as if to say ''I can't bear the thought of you suffering any more.'' He seems about to faint on ''The time is out of joint'' (188).

The First Quarto sequence of scenes is used, and Hamlet is thus seen next not reading in the lobby but delivering the ''To be or not to be'' soliloquy (III.i.55–87). As with the first soliloquy, he gives the impression of having had these dark thoughts many times before. Suicide is an old temptation, to be soberly and rather wearily confronted yet again. The arguments for and against self-slaughter are as familiar to him as the multiplication table, and not much more productive of strong emotion. That a man could evince no better reason for clinging to life than his uncertainty about what might lie beyond is proof of his pusillanimity. For what is life that one should wish to preserve it? ''The oppressor's wrong, the proud man's contumely . . . ''—these are not even evils to be bravely borne; they are no more than tawdry indignities. As Irving Wardle wrote, '' 'Who *would* fardels bear?' snarls Mr. Williamson, and it is a real question, the product of a derisive, rancorous intelligence that looks at the human masquerade of crime and vanity and reduces it to a smoking heap of rubble'' (London *Times*, 18 February 1969). He gives ''Thus conscience does make cowards of us all'' in much the same tone he has used on ''frailty, thy name is woman.'' ''What pathetic and ridiculous creatures we are,'' he seems to say. He chuckles on ''lose the name of action,'' bitterly amused at the sorry spectacle of human beings manufacturing reasons for the prolongation of a meaningless existence.

On "Soft you now, / The fair Ophelia!" he sounds like the neighborhood bully who has just spotted his favorite object of torment, but he also seems to anticipate a degree of masochistic pleasure to be had from the encounter. The word "fair" is heavy with irony. Ophelia, provocatively dressed, is on her back in a hammock, ready to receive her lover. Hamlet creeps up and kneels at her head, surprising her. "Nymph, in thy orisons / Be all my sins remembered" is a mere joke; he does not for a moment suppose she was really praying, and he seems to know that she will know he is not fooled. Her greeting, "Good my lord, / How does your honor for this many a day?" (89–90), he treats as so much cant, mocking it with a sugary tone on his reply. "No, not I, / I never gave you aught" (94–95) is playful, an evasion of seriousness. Here and on the next several lines Hamlet seems to be saying: "Let us silently acknowledge what we are to each other, partners in joyless sensuality. I may have loved you once, and you me, though probably not; probably we are not capable of it. In any case, we can no longer call it love, so let us take what stale pleasure remains to us and say no more about it. And if that does not suit you, you might as well retire to a nunnery, because life offers nothing better. I don't care very much either way." All this is conveyed equivocally, however. He tells her the truth about their relationship, but in a tone which allows her to believe he might not be in earnest; if she needs self-deception to continue the affair, he is willing to play along.

The dialogue is punctuated with kisses, which have the look of accustomed foreplay. On one such kiss, right before "Where's your father?" (129), he opens his eyes just in time to catch a glimpse of someone ducking out of sight at a small aperture. He suspects it might be Polonius (the audience can see that it is), but he can't be sure. His question about the old man's whereabouts is thus not meant to implicate Ophelia but only to confirm his suspicion. She implicates herself with the nervous tone of her reply. He grows irritated and spiteful, but not enraged. He cannot be trapped into dignifying the situation with a display of powerful feeling. Treachery is universal and therefore banal. Now he directs her to a nunnery because he wants nothing further to do with her on any terms. "Those that are married . . ." (148–49) is shouted at the spy hole and is thus applied to Polonius rather than, as usual, to Claudius, whose presence remains undiscovered. The final "To a nunnery, go" is spat at her as she lies sobbing.

Williamson uses this scene to drive home a point about Hamlet's nature for which he has been preparing the audience since the beginning; it is for this reason, no doubt, that the scene is placed early. From it, Williamson's Hamlet emerges as a man with absolutely no claim to moral superiority, a man who knows himself to be as much possessed of a fallen nature as anyone in sight. His misanthropy is total; it includes himself. The point is crucial because in it lies the explanation for Hamlet's failure to act against Claudius. He cannot play the avenger because he cannot believe in his moral right to do so. When he says "I could accuse me of such things, that it were better my mother had not borne me," one believes not only that he means it but also that it is true. In this scene Williamson presents the character in as bad a light as can well be imagined. The only quality which separates him from the others and establishes a claim for admiration and sympathy is the bravery with which he surveys the devastated landscape of earthly life. "It is Williamson's excruciating honor," said the American critic Melvin Maddocks, "to give us a Hamlet blind in one eye but too honest to fake a report on more than he sees: impotence, terror and a rum end for all" (*Atlantic*, October 1969). Nothing in the following scenes goes very far toward modifying that impression.

The brief conference between Polonius and Claudius after their eavesdropping is altered near the end to prepare the way for the lobby scene. Polonius says, "I will myself go try him. Let me alone to sound the depth of him." Claudius replies with another interpolation, " 'Tis well," and then closes in the proper manner with "Madness in great ones must not unwatch'd go" (188). Hamlet appears immediately, reading. He seems to be genuinely absorbed, not putting on a show. His reply to Polonius, "Well, God-a-mercy" (II.ii.172), is cold and distant; he is irritated at being interrupted. With "Excellent well, you are a fishmonger" (174), he begins to speak eccentrically, but it is very lightly laid on; it is more an evasion of serious conversation than a ruse. He flashes his book at Polonius with absurd speed on "Words, words, words" (192), rattling off the line. He pauses and clears his throat before beginning "You cannot, sir, take from me anything that I will more willingly part withal" (215–17). The two repetitions of "except my life" are given as pseudo-earnest attempts to help a very dull-witted man understand a very simple statement. "These tedious old fools" (219) is a whispered expression of Hamlet's weariness more than a reflection on Polonius.

Williamson treats Rosencrantz and Guildenstern with dislike and suspicion from the very start. To undercut the ostensible warmth of Hamlet's words of greeting (224–26), he has Hamlet deliberately mix up their names. His tone, too, reveals what he really thinks of them. From the first moment of their acquaintance, one senses, Hamlet has put them down for a pair of lickspittles, no more to be trusted than "adders fanged." Like so much else in life, they are a stench in his nostrils, and if he now makes polite conversation with them instead of reading them off, it is only because they are not worth the trouble of a direct assault. He maintains a physical distance from them, not in fear but in revulsion. "Denmark's a prison" (243) is tossed off, a meaningless flippancy as far as they need know. The lines explaining the remark (245–46) are omitted. Hamlet has no confidence to share with these two. Further excisions take him quickly to "Were you not sent for?" (274) The usual transition from comradeship to wary antagonism is thus eliminated. Moreover, Williamson maintains an adversary relationship with them even on the "paragon of animals" speech (295–310). Instead of making it a near-soliloquy, a baring of the innermost depths of Hamlet's thought and feeling (the usual reading), Williamson turns the speech into a sort of quotation. "This," he seems to say, "is what you have been *told* about me: 'I have of late—but wherefore I know not—lost all my mirth. . . . ' Whether this is *true*, you will not learn from me." At the same time, by subtly altering his tone on key words and phrases, Williamson allows the audience, with its superior knowledge of Hamlet's condition, to conclude that it *is* true. It is perhaps the most original stroke in a highly original performance, and one which seems to make excellent dramatic sense.

There is no real joy in his reception of the players; he is conventionally polite but hardly amiable. Here, as elsewhere, Williamson sidesteps the opportunity to make Hamlet charming. Instead, he preserves and strengthens the impression of a man whose disposition has been irreversibly poisoned by the ashy taste of existence. He is all business. He wants to hear Aeneas' speech not in order to reexperience an old delight (his fond description of the speech [434–45] is cut) but because he vaguely remembers that it tells of the slaughter of a revered king. The plan to use a play to unmask Claudius is already forming in his mind. He listens with mounting excitement, his mind working feverishly. It is the nearest thing to pleasure displayed by Williamson anywhere in his performance. He cannot be put off even

by Polonius' interruption; his rebuke to him ("It shall to the barber's
. . . " [499–501]) is automatic, without feeling. It is all over very
quickly, the First Player's recitation having been greatly curtailed. He
gives his instructions for "The Murder of Gonzago" with something
like sadistic glee, like a man arranging an ingenious and devastating
practical joke.

He goes into "O what a rogue and peasant slave am I!" (550–605)
without first saying "Now I am alone." The old spiritual desiccation
is back on him now in full measure. He speaks directly to the audience, calmly and conversationally. We might be seated with him over
tea in some seedy all-night café. He analyzes the Player's performance
with wry amusement and gives a little grunt of a laugh on "that he
should weep for her?" He does not strongly condemn himself for his
own lack of passion. He seems to doubt whether he should, or could,
behave any differently. Passion, after all, might well be just another
fraud, an exercise in self-delusion and self-dramatization. He is surprised to find his fists clenched in anger on "O, vengeance!" "Why,
what an ass am I" is said as he opens them slowly, looking at them
as if they don't belong to him. He hammers things out quietly and deliberately after that. If he is to move against Claudius it must be not
with passion but with cunning. Borrowing a leaf from *Othello*, he snuffs
out several candles as he makes his plan. The seven lines beginning
"The spirit that I have seen / May be a devil" (598) are cut. He thus
neither doubts the Ghost's words nor accuses himself of "weakness"
and "melancholy"; the latter exclusion is certainly appropriate since
he has nowhere shown any sign of having either of those afflictions.
"The play's the thing / Wherein I'll catch the conscience of the King"
is whispered through clenched teeth.

There follows a quick cut to Hamlet giving his instructions to the
players (III.ii.1–45). Aided by the omission of fifteen lines, he plays
it not as a leisurely display of Hamlet's theatrical sophistication but as
a vital part of the plot against Claudius. He needs the players, and for
that reason he cordially but firmly bids them to be on their best behavior. On "Suit the action to the word, the word to the action" he seems
to be looking ahead gloatingly to the play's effect on the King.

The compliment to Horatio (54–74) is level and firm, more a sober
and objective analysis of his character than an expression of great
fondness. The last eight lines (80–88), in which the trustworthiness of

the Ghost is again put in question, are omitted. Hamlet thus seems to be using the play not to test the King's guilt but to humiliate him publicly; it is to be not a trial but a punishment.

As the court arrives, he has the air of a mischievous prankster out to enjoy himself at someone else's expense. The remarks to Ophelia are shortened, altered and rearranged. Since the nunnery scene has made it clear that they have been sexually intimate, the exchange does not have its usual import. She is no virgin being cruelly addressed as a wanton. They are lovers sharing a private joke. He speaks only briefly and without rancor about the timing of his mother's marriage, treating the event, as in the first soliloquy, as merely typical human nastiness. Similarly, "As woman's love" (154) is delivered as a commonplace and not very interesting fact. There is only slightly more edge to "O but she'll keep *her* word" (231). He nonchalantly pours wine for the King and Queen as he assures them there is no offense in the play, using a tongue-in-cheek tone designed to put them on notice that there is indeed offense. Then, as if fearing that he is too subtle for them, he says, altering the text, "This is one Lucianus, broth— . . . *nephew* to the King" (244).

The climactic confrontation is played down. Hamlet does not pummel Claudius with the words " 'A poisons him 'i the garden . . . " (261–64) but delivers them as light taps; he is out to torment, not to demolish. For his part, Claudius keeps his head; after looking Hamlet coolly and ironically in the eye, he exits with sober dignity. As Benedict Nightingale wrote, "He knows Hamlet knows and Hamlet knows he knows. One of them must go. It's a good, true moment" (*New Statesman*, 28 February 1969).

Williamson plays the next few moments more or less conventionally, dancing wildly about and speaking partly in falsetto. He retains the line "I'll take the ghost's word for a thousand pound" (286–87) rather unnecessarily, considering he has never doubted it. He says "Go away" to Guildenstern, rather than "You are welcome" (313). He takes a wig from one of the players and puts it on Guildenstern's head as he asks him to "play upon this pipe" (350–51). For the ragging of Polonius, he borrows Horatio's spectacles and, perching them far down on his nose, produces a close imitation of Polonius, who wears a similar pair in that fashion. Throughout he gives the impression of deliberately exaggerating a genuinely felt ecstasy, so as to keep it under control. Of the closing soliloquy ('' 'Tis now the very witching time of night''), he speaks only "Let me be cruel, not unnatural. / I will speak daggers to her, but use none" (395–96). He speaks with forced determination, as if greatly doubting his ability to restrain himself.

The closet scene follows immediately. Claudius later speaks about half his soliloquy ("O, my offence is rank" [III.iii.36–72]), after sending Hamlet off to England, but "Now might I do it pat . . . " (73–96) is not heard at all. With questionable logic he says, "Mother, you have *my* father much offended" (III.iv.10), in replying to Gertrude's opening rebuke. It is somewhere between a sneer and a snarl. He sinks trembling onto Gertrude's bed, clutching at the covers, after leaving his sword in Polonius. He seems to be revolted by the act, then pleased by it, then revolted anew by his pleasure in it.

He uses lockets, Gertrude's and his own, for the speech on the two brothers. As he speaks, he seems to undergo an almost magical transformation. The worldly, jaded cynic disappears, and in his place stands an emotionally battered child, sobbing and pleading with his mother to help him understand why she has hurt him so. Williamson makes it a moment of total regression, a psychotic episode. It is a *tour de force* of visceral acting, so truthful that one feels almost voyeuristic watching it. It is also a surprise. Nothing earlier has prepared for it. Yet it does not seem inconsistent or incompatible with what has gone before. It is simply a different, but credible, mode of response to the pain of life, a response that enlarges but does not fundamentally alter the basic characterization.

The Ghost is in and out in an instant; he does not speak at all, and Hamlet and Gertrude omit a further sixteen lines between them. The event does not work a change in Hamlet's condition, except to make him doubt his sanity for a fleeting moment. He continues as before, crying abjectly and begging his mother to spare him further torment. His delivery is choked and gasping, making many of the lines unintelligible. After "I must be cruel only to be kind" (178–79) he adds a tearful "Good night, mother" and then switches abruptly to a sinister tone as he says, "Good night, indeed." He departs then, closing the scene.

The "politic worms" scene comes next. Five lines are omitted from "A man may fish with the worm . . . " to "through the guts of a beggar" (IV.iii.27–31). He is his old abrasive self now, though he fires his barbs from behind the cover of pretended insouciance. He busses Claudius lightly on the cheek on ''Farewell, dear mother'' and explains himself with an absurd affectation of sweet reasonableness.

Fortinbras does not appear, but Hamlet meets his mounted troops in the street and makes his inquiries of the Captain over the din of horses' hooves clattering on the pavement. The ''How all occasions'' soliloquy (IV.iv.32–66) is another intimate chat with the audience. The opening line is treated with a banality that is almost ludicrous. He might be a Northumbrian farmer complaining about an unfortunate turn in the weather. The same tonelessness prevails throughout. There is no strenuous self-hatred or deep engagement of any sort. And yet it is not impossible to accept the reading on Williamson's terms. If the distinction may be allowed, he seems to be not an actor shunning theatricality out of a frivolous desire to be different, but an actor creating a *character* who shuns theatricality because of his unshakeable conviction that his plight is supremely unimportant. He is like the citizens in Albert Camus' *The Plague*, who after prolonged association with pestilence are no longer capable of ''exalted emotion,'' but only of ''trite, monotonous feelings.'' By the end he has managed to find in himself a desire for action, but he seems to doubt the authenticity of his response.

The graveyard scene begins with the Clown singing at his work. Hamlet does not stand apart with Horatio, observing and commenting, but goes straight to ''Whose grave's this, sirrah?'' (V.i.117–18). He speaks without inner tension; he is living for the moment, giving himself to an experience which holds some promise of pleasant diversion. He laughs heartily over ''there the men are as mad as he'' (154–55), and the subject is then dropped. The Clown follows his witticism with ''Here's a skull now . . . '' (173). Hamlet does not wax sentimental over Yorick; he makes the speech a disinterested report of yet another casualty by a veteran hardened to casualties. He wonders whether Alexander might have looked and smelled so in the grave but does not speculate on his progression from grave to beer barrel.

The death of Ophelia seems to catch him off guard, and he reacts to it with uncharacteristic shock. He advances on Laertes with tight-lipped menace, announcing himself not as a mighty warrior but as a man reluctantly taking up a degrading chore. He seems to despise himself for being provoked as much as he despises his provoker. They fight in the grave, atop the coffin. ''I loved Ophelia'' (269) is merely a peremptory and grudging explanation of his present conduct, said without abatement of his rage. On "Forty thousand brothers / Could not with all their quantity of love / Make up my sum" (269–71), he turns "brothers" into a loathsome epithet, applicable not only to Laertes but to Claudius as well. He keeps up a tone of scalding vilification until his exit.

The next scene begins with "Up from cabin / My sea-gown scarfed about me . . . " (V.ii.12). In what follows, prior to Osric's entrance, only twenty lines are retained from a total of seventy. Hamlet speaks with complete *Schadenfreude* of having delivered his erstwhile guards over to the English executioner's axe. He snaps his fingers on "Not shriving time allowed" (47).

Osric is let off with a light sentence; there is no need to break a "water-fly" on the rack. Responding to the offer of a match with Laertes, Williamson says "How if I answer no?" (170) as if defending his princely prerogatives. He might accept the challenge or he might not, as it pleases him; he is no lackey to be ordered into service for the King's entertainment. "If it please his majesty" (173) is sarcastic; he will make himself available only because he has nothing better to do. "Not a whit, we defy augury" (219) is said testily; to allow himself to be deterred by a premonition would be a contemptible indulgence in superstition. "There is a special providence in the fall of a sparrow" (219–20) is given as a quotation and made to sound like a placebo swallowed only by pious nincompoops. The rest of the speech is all tough-minded fatalism: death is as meaningless as it is ineluctable, and the moment of death is pure chance.

He takes no joy in the duel; it is merely another absurd human pastime. The whole denouement, in fact, has a Chekhovian, serio-comic, understated quality. The first bout is over in two strokes. In the second, the combatants quickly lock foils, standing side by side, whereupon Hamlet disengages, brings his weapon around behind his back and, with a snicker, "touches" Laertes on the bum. Laertes slips in the fatal wound in the usual way, and in the energetic action which follows both foils fall to the ground; Hamlet makes the exchange by putting his foot on the unbated foil and handing his own to Laertes. Then he attacks and after a few strokes it is over. He says "The point envenomed too!" (321) in that tone of tired familiarity with evil which he has so often used before. "Then, venom, to thy work" is lethargic, unheroic. He walks calmly over to where Claudius sits and runs him through with the mechanical efficiency of a professional executioner. He seems to be making the orthodox checkmating move in a chess match that barely interests him. He is fully vicious, though, on "Here, thou incestuous, murderous damned Dane . . . " (325–27).

His parting line to Laertes, "Heaven make thee free of it" (332), is merely a conventional formula, said automatically. He says "I am dead, Horatio" (333) as if reporting a fact of no great significance, and then in the same tone goes to "Thou livest; report me and my cause aright / To the unsatisfied" (339), omitting the intervening lines about "this fell sergeant, death." He does not struggle with Horatio over the cup but quietly orders him to give it up; receiving it from him, he drinks off its contents, as if wishing to linger in an ugly place no longer than necessary. He makes a nasty business of the dying, turning the words into scarcely intelligible gasps and groans. Horatio closes his eyes and ends the play with "flights of angels sing thee to thy rest!"

David Warner, it might be said, established a secure beachhead for a nihilistic Hamlet; Williamson, with superior force, swept on past him and planted the flag of modernism on the territory's highest hill. Harold Hobson declared, "Mr. Williamson's is a performance that will modify the whole tradition of *Hamlet*" (London *Sunday Times*, 23 February 1969); a number of other critics went on record with similar assessments.[7] In making Hamlet a spiritual brother to the arch-pessimists who stalk the pages of modern literature, Williamson denied the past, declared for the present and threw down a challenge to the future.

As the National Theatre had opened at the Old Vic with *Hamlet*, it also closed there with it twelve years later, on 28 February 1976.[8] Peter Hall, now the National's director, chose Albert Finney (1936–   ) for the title role and staged the production himself. It was, as many said, inevitable that Finney would one day play Hamlet. At thirty-nine he had long been recognized as one of the great actors of his generation; it was, so to speak, his duty to take on the challenge that actors of the first rank had been assuming since the play's creation.

Hall's presence in the director's chair naturally stirred memories of his Royal Shakespeare Company production with Warner a decade earlier, but it was immediately apparent that he had no intention of merely repeating himself with a different actor. The play was given in its entirety and was consequently performed at a pace that left no room for the sort of interpretive directorial flourishes for which Hall was famous. As Kenneth Hurren wrote, "Hall plays the text full and straight (and briskly, wrapping it up inside four hours including a fifteen-minute interval), keeping clear of all the wearying psychological and metaphysical theorising that have blighted the productions of our 'interpretative' directors, and for this relief much thanks—but it is after all, a negative virtue" (*Spectator*, 20 December 1975). Hobson saw the matter in a more positive light, pointing out that "Hall's great achievement, which he accomplishes by merely giving us the full text, is that *Hamlet* is a play about a country on the brink of ruin, and incapable of pulling itself together" (London *Sunday Times*, 14 December 1975). Benedict Nightingale also admired the fact that Hall's hands-off approach allowed the full text's emphasis on Danish political insecurity to emerge naturally (*New Statesman*, 19 December 1975).

But if the production as a whole bore little resemblance to Hall's earlier existential interpretation, Finney's performance nevertheless evoked strong associations with Warner as well as with Williamson. He was much more athletic than either of those actors; indeed, he was probably the burliest Hamlet since Edwin Forrest. He rampaged through the play like a maddened bear, and if Claudius escaped immediate execution at the hands of this mighty adversary it was only because Hamlet's power was undisciplined, spending itself on a myriad of targets, real and imagined. But there was a great similarity in style; like his two predecessors, Finney was markedly rough-hewn, both in speech and in deportment. He flaunted his Lancashire vowels, spent most of the play in a grubby academic gown (accented for a time with a greasy Samurai headband) and in general gave the impression of being "a disorderly drop-out from the University of Wittenberg" (*New Statesman*, 19 December 1975). Of princeliness, as commonly understood, there was no sign. He was as modern and as hard-bitten as any of the working-class protagonists of the newly prominent drama of the political left. He raced through the great speeches, scarcely bothering to make them intelligible, let alone poetically beautiful.

As usual, the naturalistic approach split the critical community, despite the earlier precedents. Irving Wardle summed up for the opposition; he had admired Warner because in that production the slovenly style had had a purpose and "the tragedy swung round and confronted us like a great dark mirror," but in the present instance he could find no redeeming features: "We have given up looking for princely Hamlets but it is no easy task to say what Albert Finney is offering instead. He cuts out pathos, reflective philosophy, and melancholy, and bases his performance on energy, bluff comradeship, and sardonic derision. The voice rasps as monotonously as a buzz saw . . . " (London *Times*, 11 December 1975).[9]

Most eloquent among Finney's admirers was Michael Coveney of *Plays and Players*. He too remembered Warner's Hamlet as "truly a performance for the mid–1960s, firing the imaginations of everyone I know of my age or thereabouts," but he saw Finney as a worthy successor, less immediately exciting perhaps, but "compulsive viewing" nevertheless. Those who attacked Finney's performance, Coveney alleged, did so for the same reason that many had given Warner a "critical bashing," because "he has dared to speak Shakespeare as he is not spoken by Gielgud, Redgrave or even Robert Eddison, an achingly mellifluous Player King on this occasion." A number of critics, nostalgic for the older lyricism, used Eddison's performance as a stick with which to beat Finney for his contrasting style. But for Coveney, Finney's lack of sonority was more than compensated for by the stunning emotional truth of the performance; in describing it, Coveney forcefully articulated the creed of the naturalistic school: "Like Nicol Williamson, the other titan of anti-heroic realism, he is able to penetrate the skin of a part and, from under it, re-define, in his own devastating terms, what we imagine to be 'grief,' 'authority,' or 'courage' or 'despair.' "[10] For such reeducation in the very grammar and syntax of sentience, word-music, even word-sense, could be sacrificed.

Marking as it did the end of an important era in the history of the British stage, this valedictory production of *Hamlet* at the Old Vic may serve as an appropriate stopping point for the present study. Finney's performance, combined with those of Warner and Williamson, put the stamp of authority on a style which is likely to remain much in evidence during the last quarter of the twentieth century and beyond. But that is a topic for some future chronicler.

NOTES

1. This was the inaugural production of the newly established National Theatre, temporarily housed at the Old Vic; it opened on 22 October 1963.

2. I quote from a condensed version of Hall's remarks, printed in *Theatre at Work: Playwrights and Productions in the Modern British Theatre*, ed. Charles Marowitz and Simon Trussler (New York: Hill & Wang, 1978), pp. 160–62. The same condensed version appeared in the program.

3. Robert Speaight, "Shakespeare in Britain," *Shakespeare Quarterly* 16 (1965): 321.

4. The promptbook is in the Shakespeare Centre Library, Stratford-upon-Avon. I have adopted the analysis of the cuts given by Stanley Wells in his extensive report on the production; see Stanley Wells, *Royal Shakespeare: Four Major Productions at Stratford-upon-Avon* (Manchester: Manchester University Press, 1977), p. 27.

5. Speaight, "Shakespeare in Britain," p. 320. Speaight wrote a second, equally laudatory review when the production returned to Stratford in 1966; see "Shakespeare in Britain," *Shakespeare Quarterly* 17 (1966): 394–96.

6. The film was released virtually without promotion and was all but ignored by film critics. No promptbook survives for either the London or the New York production.

7. See, for example, Irving Wardle, London *Times*, 18 February 1969; Clive Barnes, New York *Times*, 2 May 1969; Melvin Maddocks, *Atlantic*, October 1969. The critical reception was generally favorable in London, generally unfavorable in New York.

8. The production opened on 10 December 1975 and remained in the repertory after the company moved to its permanent home on the South Bank. The last Old Vic performance was a matinee. The official closing ceremonies were that evening and included performance of an entertainment honoring Lilian Baylis entitled *Tribute to the Lady*; *Hamlet* was thus the company's last *legitimate* production there.

9. For further commentary, see reviews by J. W. Lambert, *Drama*, Spring 1976, pp. 50–52; Robert Speaight, "Shakespeare in Britain," *Shakespeare Quarterly* 28 (1977): 185–86; J. C. Trewin, *Illustrated London News*, February 1976, p. 67; and Gordon M. Wickstrom, *Educational Theatre Journal*, October 1976, pp. 421–22.

10. *Plays and Players*, February 1976, pp. 19, 20.

AFTERWORD

There is a saying among British actors that there are only two ways to play Hamlet: fast and slow. The material examined in the preceding pages reveals that the matter is considerably more complicated than that. Still, there is a kind of rough, greenroom wisdom in the adage if "fast" and "slow" may be taken to signify great clusters of related character traits, one or the other of which the actor might choose, consciously or unconsciously, to bring into play as he goes about shaping his characterization. I would have preferred the terms "hard" and "soft" for that purpose, but the two pairs of signifiers are in any case closely related: a "fast" Hamlet is, I take it, likely to be also "hard," and a "slow" is also likely to be "soft." And once one begins to think in that way, other qualities can be seen to coalesce around one or the other of the initial terms, like metal filings drawn together by a magnet. Thus, in the "fast-hard" cluster one is apt to find also such attributes as "colloquial," "ugly," "physical," "active," "cynical," "cruel" and "angry," while in the opposed "slow-soft" grouping the opposite of those qualities find their natural habitat: "lyrical," "beautiful," "spiritual," "passive," "idealistic," "tender" and "tearful"—to name only a few of the epithets which regularly come up in descriptions of Hamlet. Such, it would seem, is the most natural and convenient way to distinguish the Hamlets of the stage, and it is not difficult to think of examples of both types: Booth could with considerable justification be called a "slow" Hamlet in the sense here proposed, and Williamson could be called a "fast" one.

But it would not do to leave it at that. There is, after all, no impenetrable barrier between the two camps; theoretically at least a truly versatile actor might elect to move back and forth between them, making common cause with each by turns. That is to say, there ought to be nothing to prevent a Hamlet from being now melancholy and now enraged, now frightened and now bloodthirsty, now withdrawn and now strenuously engaged, now lovable and now hateful, and so on. That is, in fact, the "correct" approach if one subscribes, as I do, to the view that what sets Hamlet apart from all other fictional creations is the degree to which Shakespeare dared to endow him with that radical indeterminateness which characterizes human life itself. Something approaching the full range of human possibility in thought and feeling is to be found in the character, and the conscientious actor must try to play it all. As a practical matter, however, he is not likely to be able to do so. In the nature of things the most talented actor imaginable will do some things better than others, and his portrayal of so chameleonic, so multifaceted a character as Hamlet, assuming he attempts to show all the facets, will accordingly ring true at some moments and not at others, and the audience will have seen, in effect, some parts of Hamlet and not others, even if the full text has been used. That being the case, it is probably fair to say that Hamlet has never been completely realized in the theater and never will be. Another hoary theatrical maxim has it that no actor can ever wholly fail in the role, but it would be more to the point to say that no actor can ever wholly succeed. The true Hamlet, the very man as we see him in our mind's eye when we are alone with the text in the study, must forever elude the grasp even of histrionic genius at its highest pitch of development. But there is nothing to deplore in that. Great actors have illuminated this or that aspect of the character for the pleasure and enlightenment of generations of spectators and will go on doing so. We may be sure that Hamlet will remain what J. C. Trewin called him: "The figure that down the centuries has been held at the theatre's heart of heart."

BIBLIOGRAPHICAL ESSAY

The Hamlet portrayals of nearly all the actors treated in this volume have been described, usually briefly, in their respective biographies as well as, in some cases, in theatrical histories of various types. I consulted these works (to be named in this essay), but in every case I went back to primary materials for information to be used in my own performance reconstructions. Theatrical reviews in newspapers and periodicals constituted the major source. Among eighteenth-century British newspapers, contained in the Burney Collection at the British Library, the most helpful were the *Daily Advertiser*, the *Morning Chronicle*, the *Public Advertiser* and the *St. James's Chronicle*. For the nineteenth and twentieth centuries, there were a number of British newspapers which, some for a few decades only, some for the entire period, consistently yielded lengthy reviews: the *Morning Post*, the *Observer*, the *Sunday Times*, the *Times* and the *World*. Magazines consulted (nineteenth and twentieth centuries only) were *Era*, the *Saturday Review*, the *Spectator* and the *Stage*. For performances by American actors, the newspapers most often used were the New York *Herald*, New York *Tribune*, and New York *Times*.

Apart from reviews, firsthand accounts of performances are to be found chiefly in the letters, diaries, essays and memoirs of the actors and their contemporaries. For Richard Burbage little material of that sort exists. Such observations as have been preserved are to be found in *The Shakspere Allusion-Book: A Collection of Allusions to Shakspere from 1591 to 1700*, ed. John Munro (Oxford: Clarendon Press, 1932), vol. 1. Betterton is described in Anthony Aston, *A Brief Supplement to Colley Cibber, Esq., His Lives of the Late Famous Actors and Actresses* (London: Author, 1747); Colley Cibber, *An Apology for the Life of Mr. Colley Cibber, Comedian* (1740; reprint, Ann Arbor: University of Michigan Press, 1968); John Downes, *Roscius Anglicanus* (London: H. Playford, 1708); John Evelyn, *Diary and Correspondence*, ed. William Bray (London: G. Bell & Sons, 1898), vol. 1; Charles Gildon, *The Life of Mr. Thomas Betterton* (London: R. Gosling, 1710); Samuel Pepys, *Diary*, ed. Henry B. Wheatley (London: G. Bell & Sons, 1924), vol. 2; and [James Wright], *Historia Histrionica* (1699; reprint, New York: Garland, 1974). The most important contemporary allusions to David Garrick are in James Boswell, *Boswell's Life of Johnson*, rev. ed. by L. F. Powell (Oxford: Clarendon Press, 1934), vols. 2, 3; Charles Churchill, "The Rosciad," in *The Poetical Works of Charles Churchill*, ed. Douglas Grant (Oxford: Clarendon Press, 1956); William Cooke, *Memoirs of Charles Macklin, Comedian* 2nd ed. (London: J. Asperne, 1806) and *Memoirs of Samuel Foote* (London: Richard Phillips, 1805), vol. 2; [Francis Gentleman], *The Dramatic Censor; or, Critical Companion* (London: J. Bell, 1770), vol. 1; John Alexander Kelly, *German Visitors to English Theatres in the Eighteenth Century* (Princeton, N.J.: Princeton University Press, 1936); Georg Christoph Lichtenberg, *Lichtenberg's Visits to England as Described in His Letters and Diaries*, ed. and trans. Margaret Mare and W. H. Quarrell (Oxford: Clarendon Press, 1938); *The Life of Mr. James Quin, Comedian* (1766; reprint, London: Reader, 1887); Robert Lloyd, "The Actor," in *The Poetical Works of Robert Lloyd* (1774; reprint, Farnborough, Eng.: Greggs International Publishers, 1969), vol. 1; Hannah More, *Letters*, ed. R. Brimley Johnson (London: John Lane, 1925); Arthur Murphy, *The Life of David Garrick* (Dublin: Wogan, Burnett, 1801); William Oxberry, *Oxberry's Dramatic Biography* (London: G. Virtue, 1825–27), vol. 5; [Frederick Pilon], *An Essay on the Character of Hamlet as Performed by Mr. Henderson*, 2nd ed. (London: W. Flexney, [1777]); Richard Henry Stoddard, ed., *Personal Reminiscences by O'Keeffe, Kelly and Taylor* (New York: Scribner, Armstrong, 1875); and Thomas Wilkes, *A General View of the Stage* (London: J. Coote, 1759). Garrick himself alludes occasionally to his performances in his *Letters*, ed. David M. Little and George M. Kahrl (Cambridge, Mass.: Belknap Press of Harvard University Press, 1963). For John Philip Kemble, eyewitness accounts are supplied by James Boaden, *Memoirs of the Life of John Philip Kemble* (1825; reprint, New York: B. Blom, 1969), vol. 1; John Finlay, *Miscellanies* (Dublin: n.p., 1835); John Galt, *The Lives of the Players* (London: H. Colburn & R. Bentley, 1831); William Hazlitt, "Characters of Shakespeare's Plays," in *Works*, ed. P. P. Howe (London: J. M. Dent, 1930), vol. 4; Leigh Hunt, *Dramatic Essays*, ed. William Archer and Robert W. Lowe (London: W. Scott, 1894); [H. Martin], *Remarks on John Philip Kemble's Performance of Hamlet and Richard III* (London: G & J Robinson, 1802); Theodore Martin, "An Eyewitness of John Kemble," *The Nineteenth Century* 7 (1880): 276–96; Frederic Reynolds, *The Life and Times of Frederic Reynolds* (London: H. Colburn, 1826); *A Short Criticism of the Performance of Hamlet by John Philip Kemble* (London: n.p., 1789); and Tate Wilkinson, *The Wandering Patentee* (York: Author, 1795), vol. 2. For reports on Edmund Kean's portrayal, see Samuel Taylor Coleridge, *Collected Letters*, ed. Earl Leslie Griggs (Oxford: Clarendon Press, 1971) vol. 5, and *The Table Talk and Omniana of Samuel Taylor Coleridge*, ed. T. Ashe (London: T. Bell, 1888); Barry Cornwall [Bryan Waller Procter], *The Life of Edmund Kean* (London: E. Moxon, 1835), vol. 2; James

Hackett, *Notes, Criticisms and Correspondence upon Shakespeare's Plays and Actors* (1863; reprint, New York: B. Blom, 1968); William Hazlitt, *Works* ed. P. P. Howe (London: J. M. Dent, 1930), vols. 5, 8; Frances Anne Baker [Kemble], *Journal* (1835; reprint, New York: B. Blom, 1970), and *Records of a Girlhood* (New York: H. Holt, 1879); George Henry Lewes, *On Actors and the Art of Acting* (London: Smith, Elder, 1875); Francis Phippen, *Authentic Memoirs of Edmund Kean* (London: J. Roach, 1814); and George Vandenhoff, *Leaves from an Actor's Note-Book* (New York: D. Appleton, 1860). Descriptions of William Charles Macready may be found in John Coleman, *Players and Playwrights I Have Known* (London: Chatto & Windus, 1888), vol. 1; John Forster, *Dramatic Essays*, ed. William Archer and Robert W. Lowe (London: W. Scott, 1896); Fanny Kemble, *Records of Later Life* (London: R. Bentley, 1882), vol. 3; John Foster Kirk, "Shakespeare's Tragedies on the Stage: II," *Lippincott's Magazine*, June 1884, pp. 604–16; Henry Lewes, *Dramatic Essays*, ed. William Archer and Robert W. Lowe (London: W. Scott, 1894); John Westland Marston, *Our Recent Actors* (London: S. Low, Marston, Searle & Rivington, 1888), vol. 1; James Murdoch, *The Stage; or, Recollections of Actors and Acting from an Experience of Fifty Years* (Philadelphia: J. M. Stoddart, 1880); Lady Pollock, *Macready as I Knew Him* (London: Remington, 1885); and Clement Scott, *The Drama of Yesterday and Today* (London: Macmillan, 1899), vol. 1. See also Macready's own *Diaries, 1833– 1851*, ed. William Toynbee (New York: G. Putnam's Sons, 1912), vol. 1, and *Reminiscences*, ed. Sir Frederick Pollock (London: Trübner, 1875). Edwin Forrest's portrayal is noticed in William Rounseville Alger, *Life of Edwin Forrest* (1877; reprint, New York: Arno Press, 1977); Lawrence Barrett, *Edwin Forrest* (Boston: J. R. Osgood, 1881); James Rees, *The Life of Edwin Forrest* (Philadelphia: T. B. Peterson, 1874); and William Winter, *Shakespeare on the Stage* (New York: Moffat, Yard, 1911), vol. 1. Edwin Booth's characterization is analyzed by Adam Badeau, "American Art," *The Vagabond* (New York: Rudd & Carleton, 1859); Lucia Gilbert Calhoun, "Edwin Booth," *The Galaxy*, January 1869, pp. 77–82; Edwin Milton Royle, "Edwin Booth as I Knew Him," *Harper's*, May 1916, pp. 840–49; E. C. Stedman, "Edwin Booth," *Atlantic Monthly*, May 1866, pp. 586–87; Richard Grant White, "The Clown's Real Pigling," *The Galaxy*, March 1870, pp. 397–406; and William Winter, *Life and Art of Edwin Booth* (New York: Macmillan, 1893). Accounts of Henry Irving's performances appear in William Archer, *Henry Irving, Actor and Manager: A Critical Study* (1883; reprint, St. Clair Shores, Mich.: Scholarly Press, 1970); Austin Brereton, *The Life of Henry Irving* (London: Longmans, Green, 1908), vol. 2; Henry Arthur Jones, *The Shadow of Henry Irving* (1931; reprint, New York: B. Blom, 1969); Joseph Knight, *Theatrical Notes* (London: Lawrence & Bullen, 1893); E. R. Russell, *Irving as Hamlet* (London: H. S. King, 1875); Ellen Terry, *Memoirs*, ed. Edith Craig and Christopher St.

John (1932; reprint, New York: B. Blom, 1969); and A. Templar, "The New Hamlet and His Critics," *Macmillan's Magazine* 31 (1875): 236–41. Irving comments on certain aspects of his interpretation in "An Actor's Notes on Shakespeare, No. 2: Hamlet and Ophelia, Act II, sc. 1," *The Nineteenth Century* 1 (1877): 524–30; "An Actor's Notes on Shakespeare, No. 3, 'Look Here, Upon This Picture, and on This,' " *The Nineteenth Century* 5 (1879): 260–63; and "My Four Favorite Parts," *The Forum* 16 (1893): 34–35. For Johnston Forbes-Robertson the only commentary seems to be his own brief remarks in his autobiography, *A Player Under Three Reigns* (Boston: Little, Brown, 1925). John Barrymore talks about his approach to the character in *Confessions of an Actor* (Indianapolis: Bobbs-Merrill, 1926). Rosamond Gilder gives her scene-by-scene impressions of John Gielgud's American Hamlet in *John Gielgud's Hamlet* (London: Methuen, 1937), and Gielgud adds his own recollections in an introductory essay entitled "The Hamlet Tradition: Some Notes on Costume, Scenery and Stage Business." Gielgud also comments on his various appearances in the role in *Early Stages*, rev. ed. (London: Falcon Press, 1948); *Stage Directions* (London: Heinemann, 1963); and *An Actor and His Time: John Gielgud*, in Collaboration with John Miller and John Powell (London: Sidgwick & Jackson, 1979). Various aspects of Laurence Olivier's film portrayal are examined in *The Film Hamlet: A Record of Its Production*, ed. Brenda Cross (London: Saturn Press, 1948), and *Hamlet: The Film and the Play*, ed. Alan Dent (London: World Film Publications, 1948). Olivier looks back on his performances in his autobiography, *Confessions of an Actor* (London: Weidenfeld & Nicolson, 1982). Detailed accounts of Richard Burton's American Hamlet are given in William Redfield, *Letters from an Actor* (New York: Viking Press, 1966), and Richard L. Sterne, *John Gielgud Directs Richard Burton in Hamlet: A Journal of Rehearsals* (New York: Random House, 1967).

Biographies and histories dealing with one or the other of these actors' Hamlet portrayals include the following. Arthur Colby Sprague reconstructs Thomas Betterton's characterization in *Shakespearian Players and Performances* (Cambridge, Mass.: Harvard University Press, 1953); brief mention is also made in *A Biographical Dictionary of Actors . . . 1660–1800*, comp. Philip H. Highfill, Jr., Kalman A. Burnim and Edward A. Langhans (Carbondale: Southern Illinois University Press, 1973), vol. 2. Kalman Burnim gives a detailed account not just of David Garrick's performance but also of his entire production of the play in *David Garrick, Director* (Pittsburgh: University of Pittsburgh Press, 1961); Garrick's portrayal is given full-scale treatment by George Winchester Stone, Jr., and George M. Kahrl in *David Garrick: A Critical Biography* (Carbondale: Southern Illinois University Press; London & Amsterdam: Feffer & Simons, 1979). John Philip Kemble's Hamlet is described in Herschel Baker, *John Philip Kemble: The Actor in His Theatre* (Cambridge, Mass.: Harvard University Press, 1942); *A Biographical Dictionary of Actors*

. . . *1600–1800*, comp. Philip H. Highfill, Jr., Kalman A. Burnim and Edward A. Langhans (Carbondale: Southern Illinois University Press, 1983), vol. 7; Percy Fitzgerald, *The Kembles* (1871; reprint, New York and London: B. Blom, 1969); and Linda Kelly, *The Kemble Era: John Philip Kemble, Sarah Siddons, and the London Stage* (London: Bodley Head, 1980); Sprague gives an ample description in *Shakespearian Players and Performances*. For Edmund Kean, see Raymund Fitzsimons, *Edmund Kean, Fire from Heaven* (New York: Dial Press, 1976), and Harold N. Hillebrand, *Edmund Kean* (New York: Columbia University Press, 1933). Two biographies of William Charles Macready contain a number of short references to that actor's Hamlet; see Alan S. Downer, *The Eminent Tragedian, William Charles Macready* (Cambridge, Mass.: Harvard University Press, 1966), and J. C. Trewin, *Mr. Macready, A Nineteenth-Century Tragedian and His Theatre* (London: Harrap, 1955). Edwin Forrest's Hamlet is described succinctly by Richard Moody in *Edwin Forrest: First Star of the American Stage* (New York: Knopf, 1960). Several Edwin Booth biographies summarize his treatment of the role: Stanley Kimmel, *The Mad Booths of Maryland* (Indianapolis: Bobbs-Merrill, 1940); Richard Lockridge, *Darling of Misfortune: Edwin Booth, 1833–1893* (New York: Century, 1932); and Eleanor Ruggles, *Prince of Players: Edwin Booth* (New York: W. W. Norton, 1953). Charles Shattuck's *The Hamlet of Edwin Booth* (Urbana: University of Illinois Press, 1969) deals fully with every detail of Booth's long association with the role. Daniel J. Watermeier reports on a recently discovered eyewitness account in "Edwin Booth's Performances: New Documentation," *Theatre History Studies* 2 (1982): 125–28. Henry Irving's Hamlet is touched on occasionally in Madeleine Bingham, *Henry Irving: The Greatest Victorian Actor* (New York: Stein & Day, 1978). Alan Hughes provides a full-scale reconstruction of his productions in *Henry Irving, Shakespearean* (Cambridge, Eng.: Cambridge University Press, 1981). For John Barrymore, see Gene Fowler, *Good Night, Sweet Prince* (New York: Viking Press, 1944), and John Kobler, *Damned in Paradise: The Life of John Barrymore* (New York: Atheneum, 1977). John Gielgud is dealt with in Ronald Hayman, *John Gielgud* (New York: Random House, 1971). All of the following offer information on Laurence Olivier's stage and film Hamlets: Felix Barker, *The Oliviers* (Philadelphia: Lippincott, 1953); John Cottrell, *Laurence Olivier* (Englewood Cliffs, N.J.: Prentice-Hall, 1975); Robert J. Daniels, *Laurence Olivier: Theater and Cinema* (New York: A. S. Barnes, 1980); Logan Gourlay, ed., *Olivier* (New York: Stein & Day, 1974); Foster Hirsch, *Laurence Olivier* (Boston: Twayne, 1979); Jesse Lasky, Jr., with Pat Silver, *Love Scene: The Story of Laurence Olivier and Vivien Leigh* (New York: Crowell, 1978). Three works comment on Richard Burton's Hamlet: John Cottrell and Fergus Cashin, *Richard Burton: A Biography* (London: Barker, 1971); Lester David and Jhan Robbins, *Richard and Elizabeth* (New York: Funk & Wagnalls, 1977); and

Paul Ferris, *Richard Burton* (London: Weidenfeld & Nicolson, 1981). Burton talks about his Old Vic Hamlet in his "Introduction" in *Hamlet, Prince of Denmark* (London: Folio Society, 1954). David Warner's interpretation is given considerable attention in *Theatre at Work: Playwrights and Productions in the Modern British Theatre*, ed. Charles Marowitz and Simon Trussler (New York: Hill & Wang, 1978); David Addenbrooke, *The Royal Shakespeare Company: The Peter Hall Years* (London: Kimber, 1974); and Stanley Wells, *Royal Shakespeare: Four Major Productions at Stratford-upon-Avon* (Manchester: Manchester University Press, 1977).

Several reference works, general histories and period histories also deal with a variety of topics related to the history of Hamlet on the stage. These include: Joseph W. Donahue, Jr., *Dramatic Character in the English Romantic Age* (Princeton, N.J.: Princeton University Press, 1970); John Doran, *Annals of the English Stage* (New York and London: Harper & Bros., n.d.), 3 vols.; John Genest, *Some Account of the English Stage, 1660–1830*, 10 vols. (Bath: H. E. Carrington, 1832); Claris Glick, "*Hamlet* in the English Theatre—Acting Texts from Betterton (1676) to Olivier (1963)," *Shakespeare Quarterly* 20 (1969), 17–35; Charles Beecher Hogan, *Shakespeare in the Theatre, 1701–1800*, 2 vols. (Oxford: Clarendon Press, 1952–57); Bertram Joseph, *The Tragic Actor* (New York: Theatre Arts Books, 1959); *The London Stage. Part I: 1660–1700*, ed. William Van Lennep (Carbondale: Southern Illinois University Press, 1965); *Part 4: 1747–1776*, ed. George Winchester Stone (1962), and *Part 5: 1776–1800*, ed. Charles Beecher Hogan (1968); *The London Stage, 1890–1899: A Calendar of Plays and Players*, 2 vols. comp. J. P. Wearing (Metuchen, N.J.: Scarecrow Press, 1976); George C. D. Odell, *Annals of the New York Stage*, 15 vols. (New York: Columbia University Press, 1927–1949); George C. D. Odell, *Shakespeare from Betterton to Irving* (New York: Scribner's, 1920); Charles Shattuck, *The Shakespeare Promptbooks* (Urbana: University of Illinois Press, 1965) (for descriptions of individual promptbooks consulted, see the appropriate notes, within); Arthur Colby Sprague, *Shakespeare and the Actors* (Cambridge, Mass.: Harvard University Press, 1944); and *The Stage Business in Shakespeare's Plays: A Postscript* (1954; reprint, Folcroft, Pa.: Folcroft Press, 1969).

Finally, a number of editions of *Hamlet* contain production information; in chronological order these are: the Davenant-Betterton acting edition (1676; reprint, Cornmarket Press, 1969); the Nicholas Rowe edition, in *The Works of Mr. William Shakespeare* (London: Jacob Tonson, 1709); the John Bell edition (1774; reprint, London: Cornmarket Press, 1969); John Philip Kemble's acting edition (1800; reprint, London: Cornmarket Press, 1971); William Oxberry's edition, in *The New English Drama* (New York: A. T. Goodrich, 1818), vol. 3; the New Variorum edition, 2 vols., ed. H. H. Furness (1877; reprint, New York: American Scholar Publications, 1965); and the Cambridge edition, ed. John Dover Wilson (Cambridge, Eng.: Cambridge University Press, 1934).

INDEX